SEASON

OF

UPSETS

Farm boys, city kids, Hoosier basketball and
the dawn of the 1950s

Matthew A. Werner

Made in the United States of America

Publisher's Cataloging-in-Publication data

Werner, Matthew A.
    Season of upsets : farm boys, city kids, Hoosier basketball and the dawn of the 1950s / Matthew A. Werner.
    p. cm.
    ISBN 978-0692320471

1. Indiana --High School --Basketball --History. 2. LaPorte (Ind.) --History. 3. School sports --Indiana --History. 4. LaPorte (Ind.) --Social life and customs. I. Title.

796.323/62/09772--dc23
GV885.72.I6 .W47 2014   2014917481

Cover background image provided by Bob Wellinski.

FIRST EDITION

"Basketball was all we had."

Etta Mae (Malstaff) Hannon
Union Mills High School, class of 1951

Contents

A Note to the Reader

This book is a work of non-fiction. When I started on this project, most of the events described in this book had occurred sixty-two years ago. Some went back eighty years. In research I relied on printed news reports, yearbooks, photographs, audio recordings, and video recordings. I also interviewed more than seventy people who experienced these events first-hand (please see the Acknowledgments at the end of the book). Their insights were amazing and make up a huge part of the story.

Some of the interviewees hadn't thought about that season in years. Some of them hadn't been asked about it in decades. However, the more we talked, the more things came into focus. The more information people shared, the fresher memories became. As a result, oral history plays an important role in this story. If words are quoted, they came word-for-word from a written source or from an interviewee.

Painstaking effort was taken to be accurate. Throughout the writing and editing of this story, there were two guiding principles: be truthful and be respectful. Hopefully you will find that this story accomplished both.

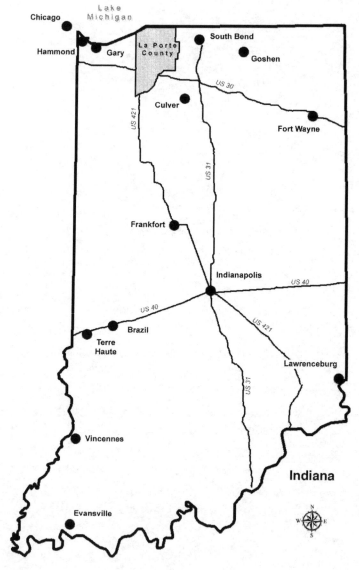

Chicago

Lake Michigan

Hammond

Gary

La Porte County

South Bend

Goshen

US 30

Culver

Fort Wayne

US 421

US 31

Frankfort

Indianapolis

US 40

US 40

Brazil

Terre Haute

US 421

Lawrenceburg

US 31

Vincennes

Indiana

Evansville

N
W   E
S

Map Produced By Melissa Mullins Mischke

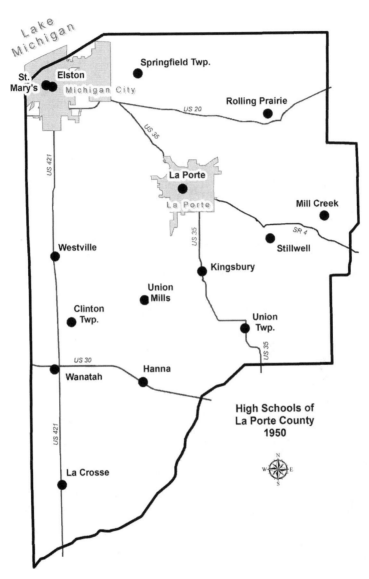

Lake Michigan

St. Mary's

Elston

Michigan City

Springfield Twp.

Rolling Prairie

US 20

US 35

La Porte

La Porte

Mill Creek

US 35

SR 4

Westville

Stillwell

Kingsbury

Union Mills

Clinton Twp.

Union Twp.

US 35

US 30

Hanna

Wanatah

**High Schools of
La Porte County
1950**

US 421

La Crosse

N
W   E
S

Map Produced By Melissa Mullins Mischke

Season of Upsets

Introduction

On my wall hangs an old black-and-white picture. Surrounded by overjoyed teammates, Dean Werner's smile peeks out between the faces of two other boys—one hand gripping a player's shoulder, the other arm draped around his beloved coach. The student manager stands front and center, a basketball in his hands. That photograph has hung on a lot of walls over the years. Bowling Green, Chicago, Milwaukee, Cincinnati. But no matter where it hung, it always took me back to Indiana.

I grew up an Indiana farm boy. One cool thing about growing up on an old farm was exploring for treasure. Well-used tools and junk shoved into rafters and abandoned rooms in barns, corn cribs, and old sheds formed the rich landscape for my explorations. I'd pull out a relic and then run to show it off. Dad, look what *I* found. His face twisted with surprise, where did you find *that*? Sometimes my dad had been looking for it for years. Yes! But, what is it? A car horn, a John Deere tachometer, spark plug gapper, chicken scale, an Allis-Chalmers PTO shaft, pulleys, a nail keg, wheat seeder, a sparrow trap. Sometimes my dad's story explained how the relic worked. Other times he reminisced about some funny story, or people long gone and a time when things were different. I listened. Sometimes I put the treasure back where I found it. Other times, I claimed it as my own.

Rummaging through the attic one day, I uncovered that black-and-white team picture in a box that also contained a toy bulldozer, a tro-

phy, and a photo album from Korea. I ran to show off my latest dis-
covery to my dad.

Look what I found.

Oh, wow. That's Dean's stuff.

Dean Werner was my uncle—my dad's older brother. The picture—an eight-by-ten glossy—had been taken after a memorable moment in 1950. A real-life David vs. Goliath story. Since I loved basketball, I claimed the picture as my own. To me, it meant anything was
possible.

Everybody knew what Dean Werner would be when he grew up: a
farmer. No doubt about it. When the army drafted Dean, they sent him
to Korea. He told all of his army buddies about his great coach and
what a great team he played on. When the other servicemen teased the
Korean locals by throwing rocks in the water buckets they carried,
Dean told them to be nice. While most of the boys goofed off, Dean
was all business and took pride in his work. He bulldozed roads, leveled fields, and helped build a school for the local community. And
Dean learned from the Korean people too. He noticed the farmers
made water run uphill to irrigate their rice fields—an idea he put into
practice when he returned home. Before Dean left, the locals gave him
a hand-made gold ring.

Dean returned to the farm in Indiana and if there was fun to be
had and a little time to spare, he was there. A few rounds of golf after
milking cows. Football games in Iowa. Chicago Bears vs. Cardinals
games. White Sox games at Comiskey Park. In the middle of a snow-
storm, Dean and a friend drove to Chicago to watch a Blackhawks
hockey game. One-hundred-forty miles round-trip. My dad watched
out the living room window as Dean's car ran into a snow drift, backed
up, powered through it, and then disappeared into the blinding snow.
On the way back home, the storm had grown worse and the boys
drove all night in starts and fits as one road after another had filled
with snow. Dean roused a snow plow driver out of bed and persuaded
him to make a path to the farm. He made it home just in time to milk
cows the next morning. It was all in good fun. Dean Werner loved life
and in every single photograph he wore a smile on his face.

In 1958, Dean and my grandfather doubled the size of the operation when they purchased a neighboring farm. It would be Dean's homestead and the two men planned to work together and grow the family business. Eventually my grandfather would retire and then the two brothers could farm together. The future looked bright.

On a wintery November day, Dean worked alone on the new farm, but when my grandfather checked on him at lunch, he found Dean unconscious on the frozen ground, bleeding badly. A turning PTO shaft—a piece of steel the size of a man's arm—had broken free from a tractor and crashed into the back of Dean's head.

That evening when Dean's aunt entered the hospital to see him, a nun greeted her at the door. "If you're here for the young man," the nun said, "pray he doesn't survive. He'll never be the same if he lives." The next morning, neighboring farmers carried buckets of steaming water to the accident scene and washed the frozen blood off the tractor. At age twenty-six, Dean Werner passed away and the boys of the 1950 Union Mills basketball team lost their first teammate.

I never met Uncle Dean—my dad was only fourteen years old when he died—but seeing him in that picture on a winning basketball team . . . I wanted to be like him. But who was he? I asked people about him, but the cloud of that tragedy overwhelmed some. For others he died too young and it had been so long ago that there just weren't many memories to recall.

I stared at the picture on my wall. Questions stirred. My curiosity took me beyond stories about my uncle. I wanted to know what made that coach, Charles Park Sanders, so special that Uncle Dean bragged about him to every man in his army unit. How did Coach Sanders inspire his boys? How did that team overcome such overwhelming odds? What led to that joyous moment the photographer captured at the perfect moment? How did it all happen? I started reading old newspapers and discovered that the Union Mills Millers were just one part of a larger story. I started asking questions and one person led me to another and then another. The stories connected like a spider's web.

The students were born in the hard times of the Great Depression and grew up in the shadows of World War II. The coaches were veterans of war and despite the fact that no Hall of Fame considered a single one of them, they left indelible marks on many lives for decades to come. Schools operated on shoestring budgets. A fire destroyed a school, but not its spirit. Sports writers took jabs at one another in the pages of rival newspapers. One cheerleader rode a tractor through a blizzard to get to the big game. An ongoing coal strike jeopardized everything. There were stories of hard times and fond memories. Smiles. Laughter. Tears.

Where else but in Indiana could a person's quest for family history end up uncovering an incredible untold story about basketball?

PART I

1

Hoosier Hysteria

Ask a Hoosier to name Indiana's current governor and he might need to think on it for a moment. Ask the same Hoosier who invented the game of basketball and he will proudly tell you that everybody knows it was James Naismith—what kind of foolish question is that? The inventor of the game of basketball may seem like the bonus question in a trivia contest to most people, but it is anything but trivial in Indiana.

In 1891 James Naismith invented a new game to manage a "class of incorrigibles." Three years later the first-known scheduled basketball game in Indiana was played in the town of Crawfordsville when its YMCA team beat the Lafayette team. From there, Indiana changed forever and the game spread to industrial cities, hay lofts, border towns, and everywhere in between. The people of Indiana didn't think of it as a *game*, but a part of *life*. And Hoosiers lived it.

In 1910 a dispute erupted. The towns of Crawfordsville and Lebanon both declared their high school team the state champion of Indiana basketball. Both teams had assembled great records—Crawfordsville finished the season 13-1 and Lebanon finished 20-2. Crawfordsville's only loss came against Lebanon and one of Lebanon's two losses occurred in Crawfordsville. To settle the dispute, Lebanon proposed a third game on a neutral court to determine the true state champion once and for all. But Crawfordsville balked and pointed to their invitation to a Midwest tournament at the University of Wisconsin-Madison as evidence of its superiority. The dispute was never settled.

The following year, the Indiana University Booster Club organized a state basketball tournament. The Club invited the high school basketball team with the best record from each U.S. Congressional district to participate. Conveniently, Crawfordsville and Lebanon were in separate Congressional districts and as fate would have it, they met in the championship game of that first state basketball tournament in 1911. When the official time keeper signaled the end of the game, the score said it all: Crawfordsville—24, Lebanon—17. For the next one-hundred years, bad blood between the rival schools raged on and it's still raging today.

Starting with that first invitational on the campus of Indiana University in 1911, the state tournament grew year after year. By the 1924-25 basketball season, the tournament had expanded to sixty-four individual Sectional tournament sites feeding a single, winner-take-all state champion. Single-room schoolhouses scattered throughout the countryside were torn down. Townships bussed students to township high schools and more students stayed in school long enough to earn high school diplomas. Still, many schools remained small but every school, no matter how small, could scrounge together enough boys to play a basketball game against a neighboring town.

Throughout the 1930s basketball continued to spread. More and more schools adopted the new game and the number of teams that entered the state tournament grew. In 1938 the Indiana High School Athletic Association (IHSAA) had 787 entrants for the high school state basketball tournament.[1] Following four successive weeks of basketball action, one team earned the right to be declared Indiana state basketball champion. The remaining 786 teams went home in defeat.

In 1925, Dr. James Naismith was invited to attend the Indiana state basketball championship held in the Indianapolis Exposition Building.

---

[1] 1938 experienced the single largest number of entrants to the state basketball tournament. In 1997, 382 teams competed in the last single-class Indiana state basketball tournament.

But when Naismith arrived at the stadium, he found himself locked out. With the stadium full and the doors locked, fans were being turned away. Naismith presented his reserved seat ticket and officials badge with no luck. He mentioned he was a special guest speaker at the event. Nope. While Naismith stood there amused by his predicament, a police captain approached and asked for his name.

James Naismith, he replied.

"Good Lord, man, why didn't you say so long ago?"

Once inside, he witnessed Indiana basketball firsthand. "As a guest of the IHSAA, I had the opportunity to watch the effects of their state tourney. The possibilities of basketball as seen there were a revelation to me. The striking features were the grade of basketball, the splendid spirit of the players and the unbound enthusiasm of the fifteen-thousand spectators who crowded the Exposition Building."

Eleven years later, Dr. Naismith returned to the State Final in Indianapolis[2] and spoke at the annual invitation dinner of the physical education department of the YMCA. Naismith said, "Basketball really had its beginning in Indiana, which remains today the center of the sport." Hoosiers puffed up with pride. Naismith recognized where basketball belonged despite the fact he invented the game in Massachusetts.

So popular was Naismith's game in Indiana that massive gymnasiums rose up throughout the state. Sometimes, a community built a larger gymnasium to spite a neighboring town as Huntingburg had done. The neighboring town of Jasper maintained a perpetual home court advantage in the Sectional tournament because it had the biggest gym in the area. To cure its frustrations, Huntingburg built a six-thousand seat capacity gymnasium in 1951, even though there were only four-thousand residents in the town. The plan succeeded as the Sectional site moved to Huntingburg.

Other communities designed gymnasiums intent on guaranteeing a seat for everyone who might possibly want to attend a game. As a result, twelve of the fourteen largest high school gyms in the United

---

[2] Talk about a good luck charm: Naismith attended the 1925 and 1936 state basketball tournaments and Frankfort High School won both times.

States are located inside Indiana's boundaries. The nation's largest high school gymnasium in New Castle, Indiana, can seat 9,325 fans. Coincidentally, the home of the Duke University Blue Devils, Cameron Indoor Stadium, seats 9,314 fans.

Yes, Hoosiers built their temples big. And they needed all those seats. By 1960, nearly 1.5 million spectators attended the four levels of the Indiana high school basketball tournament—the Sectional, Regional, Semi-state, and State Final. That is a staggering number, considering Indiana had 4.7 million residents at the time.

Call it *Hoosier Hysteria*. That phrase is synonymous with Indiana's crazy love affair with basketball. For some people, it harkens back to the final four teams that met in Indianapolis as the result of the single-class basketball tournament, but very few teams ever reached that point. Between the implementation of the Semi-State format in 1936[3] and the last single-class tournament in 1997, *ninety percent* of Indiana high schools never advanced to the coveted State Final in Indianapolis.

Undeterred by their overwhelming lack of success, towns across Indiana cheered raucously for their boys who played their hearts out nonetheless. The basketball team remained the focal point of community pride and provided the most popular entertainment. Attendance swelled at games in nearly every corner of the state. Miracles occurred on occasion as David beat long odds and toppled Goliath. Telephones rang off their hooks and newspaper reports buzzed as a state of euphoria swept through a small town, only to be crushed in another Sectional, Regional, or Semi-state matchup. No matter—it was just as memorable and in 1950, LaPorte County was the epicenter for such Hoosier miracles.

One season. One county. Fifteen schools. The smallest high school had fifteen boys to field a basketball team; the largest had more than five-hundred boys. Industrial cities. Small towns. Rural farms. Long odds and surprising upsets so big they never happened before and never happened again. This isn't a story about the team that won it all or a

---

[3] The Semi-State whittled the State Final field down to four teams. Before that sixteen teams advanced to the State Final.

talented star who became a household name. This story belongs to the other teams—the ninety percent that played a critical role in establishing the mystique known as *Hoosier Hysteria*. And one key figure—the coach at the center of that wild season—was born in the cradle of Indiana basketball.

2

Charles Park Sanders

Most people credit Reverend Nicholas McCay, general secretary of the Crawfordsville YMCA, with introducing the game of basketball to Indiana in 1892, and two years later the first-known scheduled basketball game between two teams from different towns occurred in Crawfordsville on March 16, 1894. After Crawfordsville High School won the first state basketball championship in 1911, it was followed by Lebanon (1912, 1917, 1918), Wingate (1913, 1914), Thorntown (1915), and Lafayette Jefferson (1916). The furthest distance between any two of these schools: thirty-eight miles. As a result, the area became known as the "Cradle of Basketball" and Crawfordsville was its capital.

In the nearby town of Kingman, just one year after Crawfordsville won the first Indiana state basketball title, Charles P. Sanders was born on November 3, 1912. Few people called him by his first name, though. Instead, most of his friends knew him by his middle name: Park. He was a lanky six-footer with dark, recessed eyes and a clean part down the right side of his hair. The relatively new game of basketball made a big impression on young Park Sanders. He grew up playing the game with his older brother Carl, who played for Kingman High School's Black Aces. Park followed in his big brother's footsteps and was a key part of the school's teams in his junior and senior years of high school, 1929 and 1930. With 502 residents in Kingman, the school had a limited pool of boys to field a basketball team. Park and his teammates were lucky to have the Ewbanks and Merrymans, as the two families contributed five of the team's twelve boys. Park's senior year, many people considered Kingman to be the favorite to win the Fountain County basketball tournament; however, his team fell three points short in a disappointing loss to Veedersburg.

When he graduated high school, Park again followed his brother's lead and matriculated to Central Normal College outside Indianapolis. Just one year removed from the stock market crash of 1929, the Great Depression raged on, and like many ambitious young men and women, Park Sanders found it impossible to stay in college. After one year of classes, he went on hiatus before resuming his studies four years later. In 1936 he finally accumulated enough credits to finish at Central Normal and earned his teaching credentials. He returned home to Kingman, where the Black Aces had just won the school's first and only Sectional basketball championship, and that fall Park Sanders taught school alongside his uncle, Virgil Sanders, who was a history teacher.

But he didn't stay in Kingman for long. Three years later, he followed his older brother Carl, who had moved 130 miles north to LaPorte County where he coached and taught at Union Mills High School. Park found a job teaching fifth and sixth grade at Springfield Township School on the north end of the county. Whether the job provided more money, or Park wanted to be closer to his older brother, or as one relative quipped, "the women were prettier up north," nobody knew. But one thing was certain: Park Sanders' move was not a popular decision with his mother. She ran a restaurant in Kingman and wanted her boys closer to home. So desperate was she to keep Park close by that she offered to buy him a car if he stayed, but it was no use. Park had made up his mind. And as he would prove time and again, once he made up his mind, he could be quite stubborn and didn't care what other people thought.

As unpopular as his decision to leave Kingman was with his mother, it soon became very popular with the kids of Springfield Township School. That name—Park Sanders—elicited strong feelings. When people spoke his name they always emphasized the *Park* and punctuated the *Sanders* with a smile.

On the first day of class in 1939, Dick Buell and his fellow class-mates found a young, handsome, outspoken man with a wry smile, a cool look in his eyes, and a calm demeanor standing at the front of the room. He was immediately popular with the girls in the school, but Park Sanders didn't give special treatment to anyone.

"Park didn't take no crap," said Dick. "If you were right, then you were right. No problem. If you were wrong, then you were wrong. He had two paddles—one with holes in it—and if you were late coming back from recess, you might as well put your hands on the blackboard. He was a disciplinarian. Kids knew it and loved him for it. Everybody loved him."

Indeed, the rules applied equally to everyone. Not a soul could be found who accused Park Sanders of playing favorites. He was liberal with his praise and consistent with his punishment, but he was also known for his compassion. Every student was special to him, including Shirley Shippee, who was another of Sanders' first students at Spring-field Township School.

Shirley grew up on a ninety acre farm with her two sisters. The girls' father suffered from debilitating rheumatoid arthritis, making farm labor especially hard, but he got by the best he could and Shirley's mother spent most of her days working alongside her husband in the barn, fields, and pastures. "We were poor, but we didn't know it at the time," Shirley's sister Jane recalled. "We didn't realize how hard it was." One year, Shirley's mother had saved up enough money from picking blueberries to buy a new bull. She and her husband were repairing a fence one day when something agitated the animal and it gored Shirley's mother, forcing her father to fight off the enraged beast with a hammer. Back in the house, the family assessed her injuries, which in-cluded broken ribs. Her rough condition laid her up all summer and since Shirley was the oldest of the three girls, responsibility to run the house fell on her shoulders. Shirley was ten years old.

While most students focused their efforts on becoming a farmer, laborer, or factory worker, oftentimes before finishing high school, Shirley had a strong desire to learn. Shirley was studious and smart. She had a genuine thirst for knowledge, so Park Sanders encouraged her.

He told her to follow her heart and to study hard. He believed Latin would have been good for her education and convinced Shirley to sign up for a correspondence course because Springfield Township School didn't offer the subject. "Shirley thought so much of Park Sanders. He inspired her to go to college—she was the only one of us three girls to go to college. He impressed her to get a good education," said Shirley's sister Fran.

Springfield High School already had a basketball coach, but Park loved the game so much that he volunteered to organize games between the younger classes during the day. The games provided quality recreation and school-wide bragging rights as one class beat the next.

Officiating one midday scrimmage, he tossed up a jump ball between Dick Buell and another student. The two boys leapt into the air, the ball was tipped in one direction, and ten boys quickly chased after it before they all got into their positions—offense and defense. Sanders couldn't have been prouder, if he hadn't been in so much pain.

STOP, STOP, STOP! Another teacher yelled and grabbed Dick Buell by the shoulders. Are you alright?

Of course, I'm alright. Why?

When Dick jumped for the ball, Park's thumb ended up in his mouth. Not too hard to imagine that happening. But the thumbnail somehow had lodged between two of Dick's teeth, leading to a terrific freak incident. When Dick ran after the basketball with the other boys, Park pulled his hand in the opposite direction. There was only one problem—the thumbnail stayed in Dick's mouth instead of on the thumb where it belonged. While Park Sanders grabbed his thumb and howled in pain, the boys continued playing as if nothing had happened.

The teacher plucked the thumbnail from Dick's teeth and the game resumed. As for Park, a trip to the doctor was in order, but that incident never upset him. Those things happened from time to time and the boys were playing basketball after all. Instead, he probably remarked on the part that really mattered in Indiana. *Did you see how Dick stayed focused on the game? He's gonna be a good ball player one day.*

Park Sanders' positive influence on the people of Springfield Township extended beyond the young boys and girls in his classroom to include the man responsible for overseeing the school's operations. In the rural communities of Indiana an elected official—the township trustee—made all of the business decisions for the township-run school. However, most trustees were farmers or small businessmen rather than professional educators. In Springfield the trustee was Kenneth Buell, Dick's father. "Park would stop out to the farm and they'd talk about who should be teachers and whatnot over a bottle of Drewrys," Dick said. "My dad didn't talk to everybody like that, but he trusted Park. They'd sit there on the porch over a couple of beers and talk."

Park Sanders had a good relationship with the community, the parents, and the kids. He respected his students and they in turn respected and adored him. Life was good and it only got better for him. The students adored one teacher even more than Park Sanders: the attractive young teacher next door, Miss Florence Drazer, whom everyone agreed was a genuine sweetheart of a person. Smitten with her handsome new colleague, Miss Drazer told him he had such beautiful teeth. Park tripped over his words as he muttered his simple reply, "Oh, uh, yeah. Um, thanks." He couldn't bear to tell the beautiful young teacher the truth—they were false teeth.

"We could see something was going on as kids—they were getting pretty tight," said Dick Buell, and all of the students thought the two would make a beautiful couple.

On Sunday, December 7, 1941, Park and Florence were together when they heard the news on the radio: Pearl Harbor had been attacked. Park knew what would come next. He turned to Florence and said, "Well, I guess I'll be going soon." Five months later he shipped out to basic training in the Army Air Corp at the age of twenty-nine, but before he could leave, his class threw him a going-away party. Two weeks later, the school year ended without him.

In Union Mills, Park's older brother Carl had experienced his fair share of success as a teacher and basketball coach. His Union Mills Millers had won the coveted county tourney in 1935 and the County Conference championship in 1939. Success on the basketball court meant the small town embraced Carl as one of its own and the townspeople hated to see him go. But the nation was at war and duty called every able-bodied man to fight on the country's behalf, including successful basketball coaches.

For three years, unbeknownst to everyone, Carl Sanders had written a regular newspaper column, "Off County Backboards," under the pseudonym Professor B.B. One issue had always frustrated him and in his last entry before heading off to war, Carl revealed his secret identity and pressed local communities to build bigger, safer gymnasiums for

Carl and Park Sanders
Courtesy of Brenda Sanders-Warnke

student-athletes to play basketball in: "A few will be so selfish as to say, 'If they don't want to play they don't have to.' O.K. keep your nickels—but brother, times a-wastin' and you can't take it with you. St. Peter is waiting for you and your loud singing in the front row on Sundays won't get you through those pearly gates."

Communities largely ignored Carl's appeal, including the very school where he had experienced so much coaching success: Union Mills.

The following school year, Miss Florence Drazer left Springfield School. She had moved into her father's house and was teaching third grade at her alma mater, Clinton Township. September 8, 1942, was the day after Labor Day and the first day of classes all across the county. One of Miss Drazer's students, Jim Hagenow, vividly remembered that first week and his new teacher. Something was different. Wrong even. "She was real sad and all upset and none of us knew why. And then he [Park Sanders] showed up at the school and he was dressed in his military uniform. The two of them stood in the hallway talking and, of course, all the kids were buzzing in the classroom. He kissed her good-bye and we all went, 'Oh looky there! He kissed her!' She came back in the room crying." What Jim and the rest of the children didn't know was that Miss Drazer had just become Mrs. Florence Sanders. The couple had married over Labor Day weekend while Park Sanders was on leave, but he had to return to the Army Air Corp camp at Scotts Field in Illinois.

A short time later, The Army Air Corp deployed him to England where he served as a calisthenics instructor. While overseas, he received letters from his former Springfield student Shirley Shippee, who kept him up to date on her academic progress as well as the goings-on at Springfield Township School. Sanders wrote back and encouraged her to keep working hard and to pursue her dream of a college education. Shirley Shippee followed his advice. She earned her college degree and went on to spend thirty-five years in New Guinea teaching people to read and write.

3

The Door! Laporte County, Indiana

LaPorte County exists at the point where Indiana and Michigan meet along the Lake Michigan shoreline, which has provided Hoosiers with access to the Great Lakes—a significant port for trade and travel. But it was another geographic feature that gave the county its namesake. Legend has it that when French explorers passed through the area in the 1670s, the thick forest gave way to an expansive prairie. Relieved to uncover the new landscape, the explorers declared, *La porté!* The door. And the name stuck.

As far as human history is concerned, the Potawatomi Nation, Ottawa, and Blackhawks were the first inhabitants of this land. At first they shared the area with the newly arriving Americans; however, that relationship quickly deteriorated. Incoming white settlers and the Battle of Tippecanoe forced the Native American tribes out of the area for good. The state that owed its name to the indigenous people of its land—Indiana—suddenly had no Indians inside its borders.

By the twentieth century, people had changed the land's geography to accommodate their demands. The prairie and forest had been carved up into farm fields, fence rows, barns, siloes, houses, and roads. In the name of progress, people filled in lakes and ponds to make room for expansion or to dispose of their waste and they drained marsh lands so farmers could grow more crops. Highways and railroads crisscrossed the county and the industrial cities of LaPorte and Michigan City paved streets and built factories.

One early manufacturer that moved to LaPorte in 1915, the U.S. Slicing Machine Company, gave the local high school its mascot: the LaPorte *Slicers*. Allis-Chalmers, a tractor manufacturer, owned the biggest factory in town and virtually everyone was connected to the company one way or another. Not only was it the largest employer in the city, but it also benefitted area farms where it tested the functionality and durability of newly designed equipment.

Allis-Chalmers delivered tractors, silage and forage choppers, and blowers to Ben Werner's farm in Union Mills. The company provided the machinery, the labor, and the mechanics. Always mechanics. The machines were still in the design phase and needed to be tested. When something broke—and something always broke—the mechanics stopped and examined the failed part and tried to figure out *why* it had failed. My grandfather Ben rolled his eyes and shook his head. He had work to do before the afternoon milking and didn't want to be there all afternoon figuring out *why* it had broken. He wanted to get work done. But the equipment was free. The labor was free too. My grandfather only needed to provide lunch, cigars, and all the wine the workers could drink. So he tolerated the mechanics and let them figure things out, only to complain about it later.

Conveniently located near the center of the county, LaPorte served as the county seat. Many of Indiana's ninety-two counties took great pride in the architectural design and construction of their courthouses and LaPorte was no exception. Rising four stories from the ground with a clock tower climbing another three stories out of the center of the building, it was constructed of Lake Superior red sandstone. Featuring more than forty-five unique faces carved into its façade and numerous gigantic stained-glass windows, the building truly was, and still is, a sight to see.

Of course, the red sandstone used to construct the courthouse never would have arrived if it weren't for the port in Michigan City through which the heavy stones shipped. Located right on the Lake Michigan shoreline, nobody accused Michigan City's early settlers of being impractical when it came to naming its city. Known for its beach, sand dunes, and lighthouse, the lakefront lured vacationers from Chicago and South Bend, but the town was better known for its industry and blue-collar sensibilities. The port provided area residents with jobs in shipping, manufacturing, and steel. Thousands of area residents manufactured railroad cars at the Pullman-Standard Car Manufacturing Company—the largest manufacturer of freight and passenger cars in the country.

October 1929. Black Thursday. Black Monday. Black Tuesday. The runaway success of the stock market had seesawed to chaos and panic. The stock market tanked as frightened investors sold their shares. Prior to the crash, my grandfather was confident corn prices would rise, so he chose to wait before selling his grain. When he finally sold his crop, the price had fallen more than fifty percent from its high mark just a few months earlier. The Great Depression was under way and by 1932, the Dow Jones Industrial Average bottomed out: eighty-nine percent off its high mark three years earlier. The year 1932 also marked the year that the high school graduating class of 1950 was born.

At the turn of the century, the number of residents in LaPorte County had increased ten to twenty percent decade after decade, but in the 1930s population growth stalled as everyone wallowed in the Great Depression. Jobs were scarce and pay was low when workers found employment. As a whole, the people of LaPorte County worked hard, had strong values, and made the most of the incomes they scraped together. For many, it was a hard life, but a life well-lived. Rather than whine and complain, they carved out an existence.

Gene Gielow grew up in Michigan City. He and the neighborhood kids played baseball together, but there wasn't money to buy equipment. Black tape held the boys' tattered baseball together and when their bat cracked, they had no choice but to cobble it back together with a screw and play on. "My dad, during the Depression, made seven bucks a week and we got by. My mother would buy my brother and me ice cream cones and not get herself one because she just didn't have the money."

President Roosevelt's New Deal and the Works Progress Administration provided millions of jobs for displaced workers and gave many Americans hope. But it wasn't enough to lift the country out of its worst economic slump. Then, Pearl Harbor changed everything.

When the United States entered World War II, Americans had a newfound objective. Something to rally around. Something to work for, fight for, and believe in collectively. Everything was dedicated to the war effort. Bob Spencer grew up in Westville and was nine years old when the United States entered the war.

> During World War II we would go out and collect junk, tin cans and things. In the old days people threw all of their junk out in the ravines and we would take a big wagon full and might get a nickel for them.
>
> The other thing we did was picked milkweed pods. They were using that in life preservers because cork came from all the islands where the Japanese had taken over, so they didn't have any cork anymore so that is what they used to put in the life preservers. We would get those milkweed pods and pick them. You would have a basket about half the size of this room which was about ten pounds because there was no weight to them. But it was something to do for the war effort.

Everyone pitched in. Households recycled tin cans, newspapers, and glass bottles. Uncle Sam drafted millions of men into military service. Others voluntarily enlisted. Manufacturers converted their production to equip the military and these new contracts increased the demand for workers. Women entered factories in droves to feed the military's overwhelming need for goods, supplies, and equipment.

In Michigan City, Pullman-Standard produced troop sleeper cars to transport soldiers. After struggling for so many years, Americans were eager to fill these opportunities and many people worked two jobs to keep things rolling. This newfound prosperity turned out to be a mixed blessing. Everybody who wanted a job had one, yes, but there were fewer goods available to purchase—American production was dedicated to the war effort. Gene Gielow's father had opened a radio and television business, but during World War II radio manufacturers converted their production to fill lucrative contracts for military supplies and there were no new radios to sell. So, Gielow's store turned its attention to repairing old radios and Gene worked in his dad's shop. "During the summertime, I would go down there and spend six days with him. It was a dollar a day [he paid me], so I made as much as he did back in the Depression."

Automobile manufacturers produced no cars from 1942 to 1945 and spare parts were in short supply as well. Jim Strakowski's family moved to Springfield Township, which was located halfway between Michigan City and LaPorte. His parents worked second shift—4 p.m. to midnight—at Michiana Products during the war. It was tough to keep cars running without parts, so it was a good thing Jim's dad was a machinist and he used his ingenuity to improvise. "You couldn't buy anything without a ticket or a [ration] coupon," Jim said. "You couldn't buy tires or inner tubes. My dad put a boot in one of the tires, removed the air valve from the inner tube, and filled the tube with sand. It was what he had to do to keep the car going." Now that's gumption.

Farm equipment makers stopped making tractors as well. Allis-Chalmers reached peak employment at 3,200 workers during the war as it converted its operations to producing 90 mm guns and M6 track vehicles. On the Werner farm where my uncle Dean grew up, the Case DC tractor they used for everything wouldn't stay in gear. The hand lever that engaged the clutch kept popping out of gear and the tractor would roll to a slow stop. Of course, with no parts available to fix the problem, Dean and my grandfather improvised. They selected the gear, engaged the hand clutch, and then wrapped baling wire around the handle to *keep* it in gear. One major challenge—in the event of an emergency stop, you had to act extra fast and remember to remove that wire before releasing the clutch; otherwise, it wouldn't stop and there likely would be a serious accident. A little dangerous? Sure. Then again, what do you make of someone driving a car on tires filled with sand?

Building supplies were difficult to acquire as well, which posed a particular problem in the tiny town of Stillwell. In the summer of 1941, glowing orange embers from a passing steam locomotive set a barn on fire. The flames spread and leveled the town's school. No problem, the townspeople thought. Temporary Quonset huts were moved to the school grounds while construction of the new building got underway. A minor inconvenience. A brief setback, that was all. When the Japanese bombed Pearl Harbor and America entered the war, construction supplies were earmarked for projects that contributed to building the massive war machine and construction on Stillwell School halted. The Quonset huts were no longer temporary and it would be three long, cold winters before the new school could be finished and classes finally moved into a proper school building. Meanwhile, the Quonset huts served as lousy classrooms. Chicken coops. That's what Everett "Goog" Dunfee, called them anyway. He was in fourth grade when classes began in the makeshift school buildings. Each hut was divided into two classrooms and each classroom had a small oil heater to keep it warm during the winter months.

Despite the lack of a school, basketball went on unimpeded. A local farmer plowed a field on the school grounds, then rolled it into a hard surface. Backboards and goals were fastened onto poles and the boys practiced outside on the dirt in the cold. Bill Singleton also was in fourth grade that first year after the school burned. "We played outside all winter. We dribbled a ball on the frozen snow. We had no inside facilities and when the new school was built, they only built a half of a gym. There wasn't enough money to build the whole thing, so we practiced on that half and all of our games had to be played away."

Lila Ames entered Stillwell School in 1943 after her father, Tom, began renting a farm there. He, his wife, and the four children moved in January. Lila was the oldest child and she remembered her mother was not happy when they arrived at their *new* home. When they walked in the door, light shone through the walls of the tired old farmhouse. "We went and got newspapers and we stuffed the walls with newspapers," she said. "Then we got wallpaper and covered it over. No electric. No running water."

Lila was in the fifth grade when she started classes at Stillwell School. Eager to escape the cold of that drafty old farmhouse, she found no respite in the Quonset huts. In the winter months the huts failed to fend off the imposing cold air. The walls were too thin and the oil heaters were no match for a northern Indiana winter.

Tom Ames struggled to get by and his family struggled with him. Money couldn't be spared for store-bought clothes or material, so Lila improvised. "My dresses—my dad bought me a treadle sewing machine and he would get feed from Bortz Feed Store. They were feed sacks with print and we'd shake them out, cut them, wash them, and I made my skirts and things from those feed sacks for school." And when Lila outgrew her shoes, her dad cut a hole to make room for her big toe to make them last a few more months.

Lila Ames with her siblings
Courtesy of Lila (Ames) Hagenow

When Lila Ames arrived at her new school, she noticed something strange about her fifth grade class. Yes, there was a kid named Goog and classes were held in strange round sheds called Quonset huts, but there was something else that shocked her even more. She was the only girl. As the odd girl out, she was the primary target of her classmates' teasing and had nowhere to turn for support. In the fall of 1944, the start of sixth grade, relief arrived and Lila no longer was alone. A new girl joined the class. Myrtle Allmon.

Myrtle's father worked as a hired hand on a farm in southern Illinois. The family lived in a one bedroom house and Myrtle remembered that old house and the Depression well. "We lived near a railroad track and the people who rode the rails in the Depression days—they would get off and they would come to the house and they would beg for envelopes and pencils and stamps so they could write to their families." The Allmon family didn't have much, but they got by much the same way everybody else did at the time: hard work and gumption. "It was hand to mouth. It was difficult. Very, very difficult. Mom always had chickens and froze fruit and homemade bread."

Myrtle's uncle had moved to LaPorte County where he found work in the new Kingsbury Ordnance Plant (KOP) making ammunition for the war. Completed in February 1942, the KOP was built near the small town of Kingsbury and encompassed more than thirteen-thousand acres. During its peak war-time production, the KOP employed 20,785 people. Her uncle wrote a letter to his brother and told him about the wages the ordnance plant paid. Myrtle's father did the math: in one day at the ordnance plant he could earn as much money as he had made in an entire week on that farm. Myrtle's parents were no fools. They packed up their few belongings, piled the three children in the car, and traveled north to LaPorte County to work in the ammunition factories.

When the Allmons first arrived, they had to share a house with a couple other families. There simply wasn't enough housing to accommodate the rapid influx of people filling the jobs that suddenly were available in the KOP and the factories of LaPorte and Michigan City. In time, the Allmon family did find a small house of their own. "Things were a lot better," Myrtle said. "We started having things we never had before. A few more clothes and more food and a better car." She and her sister also got their own bedroom. "Boy, I thought that was nice to have." Despite the booming wartime economy, sacrifices still had to be made, though. Like many rural families in the forties, the Allmons went without indoor plumbing, relying on an outhouse instead.

Considering the housing shortage and the massive ordnance plant, the United States planned 3,150 new houses in a newly built government city. Initially called Victory City, the town soon was renamed Kingsford Heights, but locals simply referred to it as *the Heights*. The planned community never reached three-thousand homes, but it still drew people from around the country to work in the nearby ordnance plant. Factories drove economic growth in LaPorte County and provided thousands of much-needed jobs that drew people from far and wide. These newcomers needed goods and services, including medical care. In Union Mills, Dr. Louis Moosey established a medical practice. No doctor was closer to the KOP than Doc Moosey. After shift changes and on weekends, patients lined up on the sidewalk outside Moosey's tiny office waiting to be seen.

The tavern business thrived during the war as well and provided unintended entertainment for local children. Stillwell was nothing more than an intersection of two railroads with a tavern, a small grocery store, a church, and a school. Friday was payday and in the afternoon, kids climbed the nearby railroad signal tower, which provided the best vantage point of the town's tavern. As the parking lot filled up, the kids watched the circus unfold. The parking lot filled with cars and men and women headed into the tavern to enjoy the fruits of their labor. They cashed their checks, drank, danced, and flirted. They fell in love and the loving sometimes flowed out into the parking lot. Fights occasionally spilled out the door and into the road. If someone got a deep gash from a fist, Doc Moosey would stitch them back up. It was a remarkable economic cycle.

While Americans reveled in this newfound prosperity, nobody forgot that their young men had been deployed overseas fighting for their country. Bill Hannon's older brother James flew fifty-five missions over France, Italy, and Corsica in a P-47 Thunderbolt fighter plane. Bill was thirteen years old when his family got a visit from a man from the Army Air Corps who informed them James would not be returning to Westville. He was returning from a mission when something went wrong. Although he managed to parachute successfully from the airplane, his chute caught on the tail and he was killed in action. James had been a star on the Westville basketball team, got good grades, and matriculated to Purdue University. Bill aspired to do everything his older brother had done, so when he wasn't working on the family farm or at the Texaco station in town, he studied hard and shot hoops every minute he could.

As the war drew to a close, millions of veterans came home. Some resumed their old lives and were eager to return to a normal routine. Park Sanders was in one of the first waves of returning veterans and he was ready to get back into the classroom and to start a life with his wife who'd been waiting for him for three years. Other returning veterans used the G.I. Bill of Rights to attend college and many of them studied education to become teachers. They hoped to find jobs when they graduated, but their future was largely uncertain. In LaPorte County there were fifteen high schools eager to hire qualified teachers with energy and passion.

4

From the Front Line to the Sideline

Most American towns came to be as a result of a transportation route such as a waterway, railroad, or highway. Union Mills was no exception. Sitting in the south-central part of the county, the creek that ran through town once fueled the wheel of a three-story grist mill. That mill provided the inspiration for the town's namesake as well as the school mascot, the Millers. Soon afterward, three railroads intersected the town, but highways all stayed clear and there never was so much as a single flashing traffic light in Union Mills.

To be fair, Union Mills actually consisted of two separate towns—the other being Wellsboro. A single railroad track running north-south separated the two towns and each one had its own post office: a whole three-quarters of a mile apart. How two post offices existed so close together, nobody really knew. It had been that way more than seventy years and nobody had heard of such a thing anywhere else in the country. Other than its prevalent postal service, the greater Union Mills-Wellsboro area was your typical small town. It had one grocery store, two general stores (one with a dance hall on the second floor), an animal feed store and grain elevator, one bank, a hardware store, two taverns, two garages/gas stations, a drug store/soda shop, a dairy, a tomato cannery, one doctor's office, one dentist, one barber shop, two depot train stations (one for each town, believe it or not), and a Ford dealership. Not too shabby for a town populated by 505 people.

As World War II slowly wound down and classes started in the fall of 1945, Dick Howell began his junior year at Union Mills High School. But he didn't stay long. One week after school started, Dick decided he had better things to do than sit in class, so he quit. "Wellsboro had a [railroad] tower and they threw signals and had to run the switches manually. So, they would telegraph from one tower to the next at different stations to tell them what trains were coming. The guy who ran the tower got sick and he wasn't strong enough to pull the switches anymore, so I was doing that and I wanted to learn the telegraphing thing as well." Besides, who needed a high school education anyway?

Three weeks into the new school year, fifth-grader Gene Goad was playing at recess when he noticed the township trustee walking around the school grounds. Goad stopped to watch him and noticed the trustee's guest: a man dressed in an Army Air Corp uniform. The two men walked around the building, took note of the baseball diamond, and carried on their conversation.

The soldier was Charles Park Sanders and he needed a job. Being the younger brother of Carl Sanders—Union's successful basketball coach before the war—certainly didn't hurt his chances of landing the job either. Neither did his military service. Patriotic Americans eagerly hired the fresh war veterans. Besides, the trustee had grown desperate. The school year was well under way and he didn't have a qualified teacher to head his fifth and sixth grade class, nor a person to coach the school's athletic teams. The next morning, Gene Goad sat in silence alongside his classmates as Park Sanders stood at the front of the class, and the new teacher quickly got his undivided attention. "One day I had a fingernail file and I was filing on my desk like a stupid idiot. Evidently he heard that and he came by with that pointer and he broke that sucker over my head. I had a welt from here to here, but I never told Dad. I quit filing after that!"

Park Sanders soon learned about a high school junior who recently had quit school. He had heard stories like this before. He understood the motivation to quit school, but he didn't think it was sound reasoning. He also knew kids enjoyed playing sports and being a part of a team. He wanted every student to be involved, one way or another, and he felt that being a part of something bigger than oneself was meaningful. It kept students in school and it kept them working on their studies. If a student-athlete couldn't keep up his grades, he couldn't play and Sanders believed a high school diploma led to a greater life.

One Saturday afternoon in downtown Union Mills, Dick Howell heard a stranger call out his name. "I don't know a lot about you," the stranger said, "but I understand you played a little baseball and basketball." The stranger—Park Sanders—warned Dick that he was only seventeen and didn't know what he was doing. Not yet anyway. Sanders didn't apply any pressure and patiently listened to Dick's reasoning. Then Sanders asked him if he'd thought about returning to school—a question nobody else had ever bothered to ask.

Sanders was the new coach at Union Mills, he explained, and because Dick had quit, he would have to sit out until January 1—missing all of baseball and part of the basketball season. But Dick could practice with the boys and would be a part of the team in the meantime.

"He talked me into coming back to school. I practiced with the baseball team and then the basketball team until I was eligible. I played for him ever since."

Baseball was played in the fall in the rural county schools and at an early practice that first season, Coach Sanders taught the boys a lesson about respect and discipline. The boys lined up on the baseball field while he spoke to the team. Two of the boys started laughing and giggling about something. As smooth as if it had been part of his practiced speech, Sanders walked "right up to them, slapped each one of them in the face, and went right back to talking without skipping a beat. That's the way he was and that set the tone right there," Dick recalled with a laugh.

But nobody ever held a grudge against Park Sanders, including those two boys. They knew they should have been listening instead of goofing off. And Sanders never held a grudge against either one of them. It was just like the kids in Springfield Township School had learned about him. If you were right, you were right. If you were wrong, you were wrong. It was as simple as that.

Like many teachers of that era, Park Sanders had a paddle that hung prominently near his desk. Every year Sanders asked the shop class to make him a new one. Every year the shop class proudly obliged. One year, the shop drilled one-inch holes into Sanders' paddle, theoretically to increase the velocity with which the board could reach a student's backside.

Every student who met "the board of education," as Sanders called his paddles, then signed his or her name to it. One of his old paddles read like a rap sheet: Ronnie, Glen, Dennie, Shirley, Ann, Dennie (a second time). And on it went. When you broke a rule, you were called up to the front of the room. Mr. Sanders calmly explained the broken rule and the consequence. The student put his or her hands on the desk and received the swats on the backside.

Nobody could accuse Park Sanders of being unfair or showing unreasonable favoritism. Every student knew the rules and every student received equal treatment. "I got to meet it," Laverne "Pinki" (Haspel) Bowman said of Sanders' paddle. "I was talking too much in the back of the classroom. So, I heard, 'Pinki, get up here at the front of the class right now.' He made you feel it! Oh yeah. He didn't tap you—it was a good swat. You went back to your seat and your rear end was stinging."

One thing Park Sanders couldn't stand was lying. It was the ultimate betrayal and sign of disrespect. Dennie Thomas was a student in Park Sanders' class when a visitor beckoned the teacher into the hallway. "No talking while I'm gone," Sanders told his young charges. Of course, he knew better. No sooner had he left the classroom than all of the kids started talking. So, when Sanders' meeting finished, he crawled out onto the fire escape and peeked into his own classroom window. He watched the adolescents chattering away, oblivious that they were being watched. After taking inventory of everyone breaking the rule—and everyone had broken the rule—Sanders walked back into the classroom.

"Alright, who was talking?"

The students looked nervously around at each other and then every one of them slowly raised a hand. That is, everybody but one student: Suzie. Sanders' eyes locked on the girl without her hand up.

"Suzie, you weren't talking?"

"No, sir," she replied.

His ire rose and he tried to give her a way out. "Are you sure?" he asked again.

"Nope. I wasn't talking."

Sanders frowned. "Yes, Suzie, you were talking. I stepped out on the fire escape and I saw you talking just like everybody else." Suzie was summoned up front and had to put her hands on the desk where she promptly received two swats. One for breaking a rule, and the second swat was for lying.

"If there's one thing I won't stand, it's lying," he told the class.

Sanders wasn't mad at Suzie. Oh, no. He was disappointed. Disappointed that she couldn't, or wouldn't, tell him the truth. Disappointed that she didn't respect him and the class enough to be truthful. Sanders let his disappointment be known on Suzie's backside and it stung. The rest of the class got off the hook. After all, kids were kids and they were going to talk. Sanders knew that and little things could be overlooked. Understood, even. But lying? He just couldn't bear it.

Although corporal punishment was the norm of classroom management through the 1940s and 1950s, its heavy-handedness didn't always sit well with Sanders. When an upset student returned to his or her seat, the look of hurt on their face oftentimes pulled on his emotions and he couldn't stand it. He'd slowly made his way to your desk. He'd nudge you. Mess up your hair. He'd smile or make a wisecrack. Soon, you were smiling again and there were no hard feelings. The lesson was simple. Rules were rules and the consequences were well known. You had misbehaved and that was the price to pay. Everybody—everybody—was treated equally. No exceptions. Although Sanders played the role of enforcer, he didn't like it any more than you did. Above everything else, he wanted every student to learn and to succeed.

You knew who was in charge when it came to Charles Park Sanders—*he* was. Yet, he never raised his voice. He was soft-spoken and his connection with people captivated their attention and their focus. It was that connection that led you to believe in him. To listen to him. To follow him. He let you know you'd made a mistake with just a look. The look of stern disappointment said it all. You knew better, the look said. Your lapse in judgment not only let him down, but yourself and, worse yet, your classmates or your teammates. But Sanders believed in all of his students. A lapse in judgment was temporary and students could learn. They would learn.

Students liked him. Players liked him. Everybody liked him. He was genuine. He was even-tempered. He was fair—always fair—and he loved a good laugh as much as the next person. Step out of line, though, and you got the paddle.

"He wasn't like a teacher. He was more like a friend who was talking to you all the time. But if you got out of line though, he would give you a swat to let you know that he was still in charge," Pinki (Haspel) Bowman said. "I mean he could come back at you and still be that authority, but I think because of his friendly attitude, you didn't want to make him mad at you. You didn't want to do anything that would cause him to be angry." And nobody wanted to disappoint him.

On the basketball floor there was only one thing Park Sanders wanted—no, *demanded* —from his players: always try your absolute best. If you gave everything you had and lost, nobody could disrespect you and you could walk away knowing you were beaten by a superior opponent. There was nothing wrong with that. Lying, cheating, disrespecting an opponent, and not giving full effort were cardinal sins as far as he was concerned.

But one thing stood out about Park Sanders the moment you met him. "The man always wore a hat," recalled Dick Buell. He rarely could be seen without a fedora on his head. It became his trademark. Some people simply referred to him as "The Hat." Some teachers, administrators, and people in the community didn't approve of him wearing a hat so often, especially indoors, which he often did. But "he didn't give a damn," said Dick Tillinghast, who played for Sanders at Union Mills.

Principled, yes, but the man had his limits and he had made up his mind: he would wear his hat where and when he wanted, whether people liked it or not.

In the years that immediately followed World War II, Park Sanders found himself surrounded by other newcomers to the coaching profession. From 1943 to 1949, all fifteen high schools in LaPorte County had hired at least one new head coach, and sometimes two, in that span of time. Each man had his own story that led him there. Most stories included military service during the war and some were more unusual than others.

We're not midgets

Legend held that the town of Wanatah got its unique name from a Potawatomi word: *wah-taw-taw*. Knee deep in mud. Although that interpretation has never been proved, it made sense. Wanatah sat on a marsh, a swamp, a cesspool. Before the town built a water tower, tap water in many homes was barely drinkable. Before it had a sewage system, strange puddles occasionally bubbled up in lawns, much to the frustration of town residents. But, marshy soil often meant fertile farmland, so farmers settled in and called it home. The town overcame many of the challenges nature threw its way and why shouldn't it? Even Chicago was once a swamp.

As the game of basketball spread throughout Indiana in the early twentieth century, schools were slow to adopt official mascots. Nobody cared all that much. As a result, mascots often came from some dull reference to a town's name. The Mill Creek team once was called the Mill Creekers. The LaCrosse team—the Crossers. A sports reporter with no better reference for the team from Union Mills High School called the boys the Union Millers. The townspeople and students of Mill Creek and LaCrosse eventually selected proper mascots—the Wildcats and Tigers. The Union Mills community wasn't quite as ambitious and its team remained the Millers. In other instances, mascots came about from a compliment, an insult, or some other casual observation of a team's character or physical attributes.

On December 9, 1929, the sports section included the following headline: "Westville victim of Wanatah Midget Five." The story started out, "Wanatah's quintet of small but fast hardwood men whizzed their way to a 24 to 10 victory." It was nothing new to refer to a team of basketball players lacking height as midgets. In fact, there was an independent basketball team in LaPorte known by the same name. Probably as a joke. But the description apparently amused Wanatah townspeople and students. They certainly weren't offended anyway because the school took the name as its own and its teams became the Wanatah Midgets.

As the United States conscripted men into military service in droves to fight in World War II, a shortage of athletic coaches soon followed. During the war, Wanatah's high school principal filled in as the head basketball coach. When the war ended, he managed to hire a well-qualified coach from one of the first waves of returning veterans at the start of the 1946-47 school year: Mr. Johnny Petrick.

Petrick was a slick-talking wheeler-dealer who had graduated from Hammond High School. There, he played on a state championship football team and a basketball team that played in the state finals in Indianapolis. To hire a coach with his credentials, Wanatah landed a major catch. The new coach had assembled a fine baseball team and a reasonable basketball team from the get-go, but he made one seemingly innocent mistake and all the victories in the world couldn't save him or his job.

Hammond High School. The Wildcats. It was one of the biggest schools in the state and it had experienced quite a bit of success on the athletic field, attested by John Petrick's résumé. And there he was coaching a team called the *Midgets*. "We're not midgets," he complained to the boys.

Perhaps he was ahead of his time and found it insensitive to call his team Midgets. Or, since the starting center was six-feet-two-inches tall, he could have felt that Midgets wasn't a suitable name for the boys. Then again, maybe he just thought the name was dumb, as one student recalled. Whatever his motivation, the new coach applied his powers of persuasion and moved to change the school's mascot. The student body assembled and took a vote. The ballots were counted and it became official. The Midgets were no more. Wanatah High School began a new era and the basketball warm-up jackets had ROCKETS prominently embroidered across the chest.

In the waning months of World War II, Germany launched a powerful new weapon: the V-2 rocket. Its speed exceeded three-thousand miles per hour and it was nearly impossible to shoot down before it reached its target. It was the world's first long range ballistic missile capable of crossing vast stretches of land and water. Fortunately for the Allies, the weapon was developed too late to have a significant impact on the war's outcome. Nevertheless, the V-2 rocket ushered in a new era of human history and Wanatah was on the cutting edge with its new mascot name. As for *accepting* the name—not so much. The townspeople hated the name change and, in turn, they hated Johnny Petrick. After one year, the school dismissed him as teacher and coach.

The following school year, the student body met again, took another vote, and the mascot name reverted to the Midgets once and for all. Rather than buy new warm-up jackets, the embroidered letters R-O-C-K were removed and M-I-D-G were stitched in their place. Also, Wanatah hired another war veteran fresh out of college to be its new teacher and coach. A man who turned out to be the nicest person any of them had ever met: Mr. John Dunk.

"John Dunk was the most wonderful man I ever met," said a former cheerleader. "He was so kind. If you made a mistake, it was no big deal. He'd just talk to you about trying. He was great to have as a teacher." Dunk was an average guy who tended to have a relaxed look about him at all times. "He was one of the most easygoing guys you ever saw in your life," a former reporter said. "He just never, ever got ruffled."

A former player, Arnie Rosenbaum said, "He didn't crack the whip. He didn't yell and holler. He just told you what he had to tell ya and that was it."

John Dunk maintained the same calm demeanor on the sidelines of a basketball game as he did in practice. In fact, he once leaned over to one of his players during a game and asked what the score was. "It's right there," the player said. "Well, I can't see it," Dunk replied. His vision was poor and he couldn't afford to update the prescription in his glasses.

Born in Lafayette, Indiana, Dunk grew up in the tiny nearby town of Dayton. During the war, he was a solder in the First Infantry Division, otherwise known as the Big Red One. He took part in the first amphibious invasion of northern Africa and as soon as night fell in the battle of the Kasserine Pass, German tanks overwhelmed the Big Red One and it was quickly surrounded—enemy infantry in front and paratroopers in back. Dunk ran out of ammunition and he could hear German soldiers yelling in the distance. Then, his team's half-track caught on fire and he scrambled to get out. Amidst the confusion, he and a fellow soldier became separated from the group and wandered around, ducking and hiding from the enemy for five days before they found their way back to the unit. Back with his unit, he fought in Algeria, Tunisia, and Sicily before being wounded in battle. He earned two Purple Hearts and the Bronze Star Medal, but Dunk's service didn't end there. When he recovered from his injuries, he worked in the Adjutant General's Office in the United States until his official discharge.

When Dunk arrived in Wanatah, he thought that the Midgets was an odd name for a team, but he never said anything about it. Apparently, he had no interest in fighting that battle.

Do one thing: win

Harlan Clark grew up in southern Indiana. Plainville, to be exact, and his wife Betty grew up seven miles away in Elnora. Harlan and Betty were basketball people through and through.

"The thing that really impressed me with Elnora—besides her," Harlan said, pointing to Betty, "was their gymnasium. It was a little bigger than this room—maybe not as wide—and if you wanted to substitute into the game, you had to climb up a ladder about ten feet high and the scorer and official sat up there." The floor was crooked and with a little motivation, the ball would roll downhill from one end of the gym to the other.

"Your gym wasn't much better," Betty laughed.

There were few paved roads in Plainville or Elnora, but the highway between the two towns was paved, which turned out to be a blessing. Betty roller-skated seven miles from Elnora to Plainville and that's how she and Harlan met. For their first date, she roller-skated those seven miles and then roller-skated seven miles back home afterward.

"We decided that there weren't any decent boys in Elnora and there weren't any decent girls in Plainville, so we had no choice," Harlan said with a smile. Harlan enrolled at Indiana State University and in his second year, Japan attacked Pearl Harbor. And the draft soon followed. "Word was out that when you were twenty, there was a stack so big for every county that everyone in that stack was inducted into the army. Well, I knew when mine was going to go out, so I thought I wasn't about to go to the service and leave her running around by herself—*unattached*. I mean, I am smarter than that! So, I thought, why not just get married? That will solve that."

Harlan and Betty Clark married one day before Harlan's twentieth birthday and the word that had gotten out was correct. Uncle Sam sent Harlan a letter right after his birthday and he shipped out for basic training. While Harlan served in the Army Air Corps, Betty worked at an ammunition depot in Bedford, Indiana. While Betty saved her money, Harlan unwittingly discovered a way to keep from getting shot.

Stationed in Casablanca, Harlan's camp held tryouts for a baseball team and he became the camp's pitcher. The team then travelled around the Mediterranean to play games against other camps. During one trip the team boarded a B-17 plane and flew to Cairo, Egypt, to play a seven-game series. During the flight the men played cards to pass the time. "We had a card game going and it hadn't dawned on anybody yet and I said, 'Wait a minute—you're the pilot and you're the co-pilot—right?' They said, 'Yeah,' so I asked who was flying this thing?" Good question. It turned out two other guys were flying. And neither one was a pilot.

The Americans had almost run Rommel out of Africa and the plane was flying over the scarred battlefields where tanks and equipment smoldered in the desert. One of the team members got curious and asked, "What's down there? Can we get a little closer?" Back at the controls, the pilots obliged and swooped down toward the ground, nearly skimming the earth. "Oh my God, you could have reached out and touched the ground!" Harlan said. Even when he was trying to stay out of harm's way by playing baseball, some lunatic behind the controls of an airplane led him right back into it. "We won that war too! We won hands down!" he added with a laugh.

When tryouts for a camp basketball team were posted, Harlan figured he was a shoe-in. He had played on a Regional champion basketball team and freshman basketball at Indiana State under Coach John Wooden. "Playing basketball and baseball wasn't all that bad. Seriously, that was the only entertainment that they had in Casablanca. There was an amazing amount of people who wanted to watch the baseball game because they didn't have anything else to do." Cairo, Tel Aviv, Jerusalem, Bethlehem—the teams flew all over the Mediterranean. When he wasn't entertaining the troops, Harlan operated a radio for the Air Corps.

When servicemen returned home, it took some time to adapt to civilian life, but Betty was waiting for Harlan when he returned. "It took some of us wives, after they came back, a little while to settle them down." Harlan returned to Indiana State University to finish his degree and Betty's help paid off. "She knew more about anatomy and kinesiology than I did. She went all through this with me. I knew most of it—she had all of it." With Betty's tutelage, Harlan finished his degree in 1948 and then it was time to get a job.

A friend named Percy had two jobs lined up—one near Lafayette and the other at Rolling Prairie in LaPorte County. Percy asked Harlan what teaching licenses he held. Everything but math, Harlan answered. Percy said, okay then—I'll take the job by Lafayette and you can take the Rolling Prairie job since you've got what they need. Harlan thanked his friend and made an appointment with the people at Rolling Prairie High School. Harlan and Betty Clark had no idea the journey that was in store for them to land that first job. Just before reaching town, they stopped by the side of the road. "Got out on the edge of Rolling about a half mile and pulled off under a tree—it was summertime—she had a clean white shirt, all dressed and pressed in the back. So, we put my clean shirt on and my tie and went for an interview."

When Harlan walked into the school, nobody there had the authority to hire him, or even to interview him. The receptionist told him he needed to see the township trustee. Great. "But, where is he?" Harlan asked. Out plowing a field, was the response. The receptionist gave him directions and off he and Betty drove.

"So, we headed out and lo and behold, went down this road, there was a house and there was this guy out on a tractor plowing away in his overalls. Here we were dressed all up, in my clean white shirt and tie, had my hair combed and everything. He knew I was coming. He got off his tractor, comes over to the fence. We introduced—I introduced him to Betty in the car and we discussed Percy, he was going to take the other job, and he sent me up to try and get this one." The township trustee said he was all for him and only asked one thing of Harlan: WIN.

"I think we can handle that," Harlan replied.

"Okay, the principal lives down in Burns City," the trustee told him, "so you have to go and see him."

Burns City, Indiana. Just down the road from the Bedford ammunition depot in southern Indiana—where Harlan and Betty had just come from.

So, Harlan and Betty headed back to southern Indiana. "Dumb enough, she got me all dressed up again. We find the principal's house and here was a guy in paint clothes on a twenty foot ladder, painting away."

"Hi, you Mr. Osborn, the principal?" Harlan asked.

"'Yes I am," the guy on the ladder said. He told Harlan he'd talked with the township trustee who said the job was his.

"Well, thank you."

"I think the trustee only cared about one thing," the principal said.

"Yeah, he told me, he didn't care what I did as long as I win."

And that is how Harlan Clark ended up teaching and coaching in Rolling Prairie.

We didn't turn the boat around

I'll never forget the moment I met former Stillwell coach Hobart Martin. We first talked on the phone and he had a voice you don't forget. Deep and loud, it hammered through the telephone. I expected to see a giant when we met at his house and there he stood: all five-feet-four-inches of him. But when he talked, the coffee rippled in my mug. His laugh caught me off guard before pulling me into a bear hug. "He certainly wasn't tall," Bill Singleton said of his old coach. "We were all much taller than he was—but there was no question about who was in charge. He could holler loudly." But he rarely had to. That voice commanded attention. When he spoke, his words resonated with purpose.

Hobart grew up in the small town of Young America, Indiana. Nestled in the southwest corner of Cass County, the town had neither a railroad track nor a creek running through it. Its population peaked at three-hundred people. The high school didn't even bother putting together a baseball team, which required nine boys to play on the field. But basketball only permitted five boys on the floor at a time. Like every other small school in Indiana, the Young America Yanks had a basketball team and from 1939 to 1941, Hobart played guard for the team.

When Hobart graduated from Young America High School in 1941, he considered his career options. He grew up on a farm, but since his older brother already was working with their dad, that wasn't a viable option. He thought maybe he'd like to be a coach and a teacher, so he moved to Muncie and studied education at Ball State University.

During Hobart's first semester of college, the United States declared war. The following semester, the military drafted his older brother and he knew it was only a matter of time before he'd be drafted too. Instead of returning to Ball State the next fall, Hobart stayed on the family farm and harvested the fall crop with his dad. Sure enough, the U.S. Army sent a letter to the Martin family farm that winter. One son wasn't enough, they had decided. Uncle Sam wanted Hobart too. Infantry. Eighty-sixth Blackhawk Division.

While in basic training, Hobart saw an opportunity to leave the infantry in favor of the Army Air Corps. He jumped at the opportunity, was accepted, and sent off to flight training where he passed the certification to become an air pilot and bombardier. Things were looking up for Hobart until a new order suddenly appeared: anybody originally established in a ground unit had to return to it. No more flight training. He was sent back to the 86th Infantry Division and his heart sank. "I felt worse that day than the day I got my draft notice. I *knew* what that meant." A big push on the ground was coming.

France. Koln, Germany. The Rhine River. The Ruhr. The Danube. Austria. Munich. Although the Blackhawk Division experienced 1,233 casualties, Hobart survived the European theater on foot. When Germany surrendered, the war wasn't over. The Blackhawk Division was shipped across the Atlantic, railroaded across the United States, and loaded onto ships off the California coast.

Although Hobart felt he had seen enough war, the Army sent him and the rest of the Blackhawk Division across the Pacific Ocean to invade the island of Japan. Everyone had heard the stories of *Bushido*, or "honor unto death," which had been distorted during World War II to lead Japanese soldiers to prefer death over surrender. Hobart wasn't looking forward to the God-awful terror his unit would meet when their boots hit the sand on the Japanese shore.

The ship carrying these men was in the middle of the Pacific Ocean when a voice announced the news over the loud speaker: Japan had surrendered. The war was over. There would be no need to scramble headlong into a Japanese onslaught. On board the ship, there was a collective sigh of relief and then the boys screamed and hollered with joy. "Everybody was glad," Hobart said, "but we didn't turn the boat around!" Instead, the Blackhawk Division sailed onto the Philippines where Hobart eventually finished his tour of duty.

When asked about Truman's controversial decision to bomb Japan, Martin didn't waiver. "Let me put it this way: if our unit had to invade Japan—I probably wouldn't be talking to you today."

When the Army released him from active duty, Hobart returned to Ball State University. This time around, the U.S. government footed the bill courtesy of the GI Bill of Rights. When he earned his degree, Hobart laughed, "It only took me seven years."

He still wanted to try coaching and Stillwell High School in LaPorte County needed someone with his credentials, so he checked it out. When Hobart visited the school, the second half of the gym had been finished and he discovered a new school building with a small but good gymnasium. Stillwell had a familiar feel to it—the classes were about the same size as he had experienced back at Young America High School. The town was small, the people were friendly, and the school needed a coach. Hobart accepted the job as business teacher and coach in the fall of 1948.

Despite the interesting lives each man had experienced during that period, none was more unique than that of Union Township coach George Bock. When Japan invaded Pearl Harbor, he was studying biology at Manchester College and he wanted nothing to do with any war. The Civilian Public Service had been established to provide conscientious objectors an outlet to perform "work of national importance" in lieu of military service and George signed up. At first, his assignments involved working in national forests in Michigan and Oregon where he planted trees, felled dead trees, and prevented forest fires. When volunteers were needed to serve as guinea pigs to study a disease, George saw an opportunity to apply his biology education and signed up. He boarded a train and rode to Connecticut.

After the initial meeting and being inoculated with he knew not what—a placebo or an infectious disease—George went to work in the Connecticut Forest Preserve. A month later while working in the forest, something suddenly struck him. "My eyes burned. My eyes turned yellow. My stomach did flip-flops on me. Headaches. You just feel rotten all over." He didn't receive a placebo. He had been injected with infectious hepatitis. The illness was a major problem during World War II, but doctors didn't know what caused it or how to treat it. George and four other men were sent to the New Haven hospital to be observed by a medical team. There, he was put on a strict diet and fed lots of cottage cheese. He never liked cottage cheese, but that's what he

signed up to do, so he ate it anyway. One month in the hospital was
followed by another month while doctors regularly tested his blood. It
was a long road to recovery, but George was never bitter. Far from it.
He had served his country and would have done it again if asked. Doctors had developed a better understanding of the disease and how to
treat it. "I was glad I participated in it," he said.

One man after another found his way to the teaching and coaching
profession in LaPorte County. Fifteen in all. Charles McComas of
Westville and Norm Hubner of LaPorte were beyond the draft age at
the start of the war and taught and coached during that time. The rest
of them trickled into the area after they completed their military service
and in many cases their college degrees. Noel King returned home to
Clinton Township, Harlan Siegesmund arrived in Hanna, Lenny Black
landed in LaCrosse, Waldo Sauter in Kingsbury, and Steve Pavela at St.
Mary's High School in Michigan City. In 1949 schools added three new
coaches: Dee Kohlmeier at Michigan City Elston, Bob Gray at Mill
Creek, and Bill Yates in Springfield Township. With that, the field of
fifteen coaches at the fifteen high schools was set for the start of the
1949-50 school year.

High School	Mascot	Head coach	War Service
Clinton Twp.	Trojans	Noel King	US Navy
Hanna	Panthers	Harland Siegesmund	Marine Corps
Kingsbury	Kings	Waldo Sauter	US Army
LaCrosse	Tigers	Lenny Black	Marine Corps
LaPorte	Slicers	Norm Hubner	---
M.C. Elston	Red Devils	Dorrance Kohlmeier	US Navy
M.C. St. Mary's	Blazers	Steve Pavela	US Navy
Mill Creek	Wildcats	Bob Gray	US Navy
Rolling Prairie	Bulldogs	Harlan Clark	Army Air Corps
Springfield Twp.	Indians	Bill Yates	Marine Corps
Stillwell	Vikings	Hobart Martin	US Army
Union Mills	Millers	Charles Park Sanders	Army Air Corps
Union Twp.	Tigers	George Bock	Civilian Public Service
Wanatah	Midgets	John Dunk	US Army
Westville	Blackhawks	Charles McComas	---

5

A Post-War World

While LaPorte County schools changed up their basketball coaching staffs, the world experienced tremendous change as well—but it was no game. In 1945 President Franklin D. Roosevelt suddenly died three months after his fourth inaugural address and Vice President Truman was thrust unexpectedly into the position of commander in chief. When he consoled Eleanor Roosevelt, he asked, "Is there anything I can do for you?" To which Mrs. Roosevelt replied, "Is there anything we can do for you? For you are the one in trouble now." No doubt, she knew what she was talking about and she meant it.

The war in Europe did end, but the war against Japan dragged on. The United States demanded unconditional and total surrender, but the Empire refused. The invasion of Japan would have been a blood bath and President Truman didn't look forward to the increased waste of human life. Eager to put an end to the war once and for all, he ordered the world's first atomic bomb dropped on Hiroshima on August 6. When Japan failed to respond, Truman ordered a second bomb dropped on Nagasaki three days later. In a four-minute speech addressing his people, Emperor Hirohito said that, "the enemy has begun to employ a new and most cruel bomb, the power of which to do damage is, indeed, incalculable, taking the toll of many innocent lives." With those words, Japan finally surrendered.

THE BUCK STOPS HERE read the sign on President Truman's desk and he quickly established himself as a tough and decisive leader.

Casualty estimates from those two bombs ranged from 100,000 to 200,000 people. Eighteen years after that fateful decision, Truman wrote, "I knew what I was doing when I stopped the war that would have killed a half million youngsters on both sides if those bombs had not been dropped. I have no regrets and, under the same circumstances, I would do it again." Hobart Martin attributed Truman's decision to saving his life. He knew he wouldn't have survived an infantry invasion of Japan. He also fully understood the destruction the "new and most cruel bomb" had inflicted because he witnessed it first-hand. In a strange twist of fate, he accompanied a small group of VIPs, including the Secretary of War Robert Patterson, on a flight to Hiroshima. The plane touched down, but the door never opened and nobody got off. For fifteen minutes the men onboard peered out the windows.

"You want to talk about destruction. It was one devastated piece of land, I tell ya."

Then, someone gave the word—Okay, let's go—and the plane flew away.

The years immediately following World War II challenged the United States. As war production powered along, everyone who wanted a job had one. As soon as the war ended, defense contracts were cancelled. Factories laid off thousands upon thousands of workers within days of Japan's surrender. Fear increased. Where would all these people work and what exactly would they do? To add to these concerns, twelve million GIs returned home eager to attend college or to start a new job. The women who had proved their worth in offices, factories, and on construction sites suddenly found themselves out of work, displaced by men. Exacerbating everyone's fear was an economic concept new to most Americans: inflation.

The Great Depression preceded the war and before that people had experienced decades of flat-line prices and wages. During the war, the U.S. government installed price controls on most consumer goods, and prices remained steady. Inflation had been zero. Of course, there weren't many items to buy since nearly everything had been dedicated to the war effort. With the war over, Americans were flush with cash and eager to buy things they couldn't get before: cars, radios, televisions, houses, alarm clocks, refrigerators, ovens—you name it. Companies scrambled to revert to their pre-war operations while trying to come up with new, redesigned products. Pent up consumerism spilled over and supply couldn't keep up with demand.

The price of meat served as one classic example. During the war, food had been rationed and when the war ended, people demanded meat on their dinner plates. The packing industry told consumers if there were no price controls, they could produce more. Americans took their beef to Congress and legislators relented. Price controls were removed and just like that the price of beef doubled to one dollar per pound. Now families could get meat, but fewer could afford it.

In response to rising prices and decreased buying power, union workers demanded higher wages. When they didn't get them, they walked off the job. In the twelve months following the Victory over Japan, more than five million workers had gone on strike at one point or another, thwarting manufacturers' efforts to ramp up production of consumer goods, and the troubling spiral continued.

Across the globe the world didn't become a land of peace just because the war had ended, either. Quite the opposite. Joseph Stalin declared Eastern Europe under Soviet communist influence and blocked it from the rest of the continent. Winston Churchill declared an "iron curtain" separated the two parts of the world and the name stuck. In 1947 Truman declared the United States would support Greece and Turkey to prevent Soviet influence from infiltrating their countries and to stymie the spread of communism, and thus the Cold War began.

All of these developments frustrated Americans who were not happy with the direction of the nation and they blamed President Truman. Republicans took control of Congress in the midterm elections in 1946, and in 1948 the Republican party nominated Thomas Dewey to run against Truman for president. Leading up to the election, Dewey led in every poll.

The underdog and sitting president, Harry Truman, was never completely happy in the White House. He once said, "Nobody but a damn fool would have the job in the first place, but I've got it damn fool or no and I have to do it as best as I can." And he believed he was the best man for the job, so he did what he did best: he took his message straight to the people on a whistle-stop tour of the country.

Harry S. Truman could relate to the struggles of many Americans. He wanted to attend West Point Academy, but he was rejected. He wanted to attend college, but his family couldn't afford it. He tried running a men's clothing store, but the venture failed after a couple years. When Truman tried his hand at politics, his career slowly ascended as he fought corruption and advocated for the men and women he felt were being ignored, and his efforts paid off. Americans re-elected him president and he beamed as he left his naysayers speechless.

The people of LaPorte County had a lot in common with Truman. Perennial underdogs. Hard-scrabbling. Tough. Everyman and everywoman types who fought the good fight. Their limitations and their luck shaped their lives, yet they refused to give up. They overcame long odds and pressed on. Strange, though. Despite all their similarities, fifty-three percent of LaPorte County voted for Thomas Dewey instead.

The year 1949 opened with the first presidential inauguration broadcast on television and ten million people tuned in to watch Truman's address. It was a considerable number at the time. Whereas every household had a radio, there were roughly one million televisions in the United States and most of those belonged to tavern owners. Furthermore, nearly half of all televisions were owned by people living in New York City, but that soon changed as television sales jumped six-hundred percent in 1949, which was good news for Gielow's Sales and Service in Michigan City. The family business was in a prime position to capitalize on the new must-have consumer product. But televisions weren't cheap—Gielow's advertised a brand new twelve-and-a-half inch black and white TV for $280.[4]

Things continued to ease. Companies started cutting prices—automobiles, rug makers, battery makers, radios, refrigerators, kerosene, milk, and steel producers all announced price cuts. Households

---

[4] $280 in 1949 was $2,798 in 2014 dollars.

stayed ahead of inflation. In LaPorte, Allis-Chalmers' assembly lines hummed along as the company reverted to manufacturing farm machinery and even kept a line dedicated to military equipment. Standard-Pullman continued to make rail cars in Michigan City. Even the Kingsbury Ordnance Plant stayed open, albeit on a smaller scale. Fears of runaway inflation, bread lines, and rampant unemployment never materialized. Times could still be tough, yes, but people continued to get by and things were much better than they had been before the war. Despite the good news, Truman continued to face challenges on the home front where an ongoing battle re-emerged that captured the attention of millions of Americans and frustrated the nation.

One of the most powerful men in the United States was John L. Lewis, president of the United Mine Workers of America (UMWA). Already sixty-nine years of age, Lewis had run the miner's union for twenty-nine years and had no intention of stepping down. A powerful speaker, Lewis' face begged for a caricature artist to sketch his features: foreboding look, heavy jowls, a thick mop of hair combed straight away from his face. His skin was as pale as a ghost, and his eyebrows—Lord, those eyebrows!—were a pair of bushy albatrosses perched above each eye ready to take flight.

Trains still dominated transportation and the movement of goods as coal-powered steam locomotives crisscrossed the American landscape, belching plumes of black smoke as they went. Electricity was generated by coal-fired power plants. Factories relied on coal to power their machines and heat their buildings. In Indiana, sixty-two percent of Hoosiers relied on coal to heat their homes and over 100,000 households still used coal-fired cook stoves in their kitchens to prepare meals.

To provide all of this fuel, coal miners toiled in tunnels dug hundreds of feet below the surface of the Earth. In some mines the ceilings were so low a man couldn't stand upright. Falling debris, tunnel collapses, and a lack of oxygen were hazards of the job. Ever-present coal dust coated men's lungs. Many workers died or suffered career-ending injuries and there was no safety net to care for them or their surviving families. Then, as mine operators transitioned to machines that could drill, bore, extract, and move coal at lower cost, miners lost jobs. But John Lewis fought back. Under his leadership, working conditions improved. Pensions had been created and healthcare provided. Welfare funds helped to care for injured men, widows, and children. But not everyone appreciated his efforts. Lewis frequently found himself one of the most loathed men in America. He frustrated the President of the United States and Congress repeatedly called for his head. Labor was the ultimate bargaining chip miners held, so what could they do? They struck.

After the war, strikes became an annual event. Dependent on coal for work, electricity, and heat, Americans grew weary of the miners' tactics. Unfair, un-American, self-centered, and a threat to national security were popular reactions. When a strike dragged on, Americans and the press accused coal operators and miners of being in cahoots to pump up coal prices. In response, Congress passed a new law: the Taft-Hartley Act. One provision of the law limited strike activity and gave the president authority to order employees back to work if he deemed the situation a national emergency. Many believed this provision was directed at John L. Lewis.

In 1949 negotiations for a new labor contract between the mine operators and the UMWA had stalled. Mine operators wanted to keep wages the same and to install one of its own men on the board that oversaw the union's welfare fund, which had run dry.

On behalf of the coal miners, Lewis demanded a wage increase to keep up with inflation and an increase in payments to the welfare fund, but Lewis had no interest in having anybody but his loyal cronies on the welfare fund board. The two sides couldn't reach an agreement. But when the labor contract expired at the end of June 1949, miners continued to work in the pits without a contract. For the time being, anyway.

As summer slipped away and the days grew shorter, Americans grew keenly aware of the drama surrounding John Lewis and the coal miners. As the saga dragged on, Indiana basketball fans eventually had great cause for concern too.

6

Autumn Meant Baseball

The day after Labor Day 1949, Dean Werner and thirteen of his classmates walked through the front doors of Union Mills High School for the first day of their senior year. A week earlier, the Soviet Union had surprised the world by detonating its first atomic bomb. Nobody expected the country to have a nuclear weapon so quickly and now both the United States and its bitter rival, the Soviets, were capable of nuclear annihilation. But the students of LaPorte County had more pressing concerns on their minds: the abrupt end of summer and readapting to the demands of a full day of classes.

That first week was a hard one for many students, but it tortured farm kids especially. Many farm boys and farm girls went barefoot all summer long, running through fields and chasing cows and chickens around barnyards. Now they were stuck indoors wearing brand-new leather shoes and wool socks, sitting quietly at a hard wooden desk. The socks started to itch. Feet sweat. The shoes cramped heels and arches. Kids wiggled their toes. Blisters formed. Some students untied their shoes and secretly slipped them off their feet. When the teacher caught them, the shoes went back on for good.

Stuck indoors with no air conditioning, the warm air pressed against a student's skin and sweat trickled slowly—ever so slowly—down their neck, their arms, their back, and legs. Windows were thrown wide open, but rather than helping, it only teased students. A slow breeze passed through the room and kids smelled that sweet summer air wafting into the classroom. Their eyes followed the scent. They looked outside to see leaves on the trees, sunshine, and green grass. They would have given anything to climb that tree, or sit in the shade under the branches, relaxing their legs on the cool grass.

Instead, students scratched pencils on paper and quietly worked on their lessons, waiting for three o'clock to arrive so they could be released from school and run free again. A clock marked off the seconds.

Tick. Tock.

Tick. Tock.

Tick. Tock.

Come on, three o'clock . . . don't do this to me. Not today. Please!

In Union Mills the school bordered a pair of busy railroad tracks. In the distance a train whistle blared and students listened for the CHUG-CHUG-CHUG of an oncoming steam locomotive. When the train got close enough, a student yelled, "Train!" while another rushed to the windows and pulled them shut. If the windows had been left open, the locomotive's smoke stack would have scattered coal ash across all of the desks in the classroom. When the train passed, the windows reopened and attention drifted back to the lesson at hand while students tried not to look at the clock.

When the final bell rang, baseball or football practice provided a welcome respite from the long class day stuck indoors. And where you went to school determined whether you played football or baseball.

The governing body for all high school sports was the Indiana High School Athletic Association (IHSAA). Of the 767 member schools, 490 schools played baseball, but only 149 fielded eleven-man football teams. While city schools such as LaPorte, Michigan City, and Saint Mary's played football in the fall, autumn meant baseball season for everyone else.

There was good reason many schools didn't field baseball or football teams in Indiana, and evidence was found right there in LaPorte County. So small was Clinton High School that one year every member of the senior class was an officer: president, vice president, secretary, and treasurer. Clinton graduated only four students that spring. If the pitcher ran out of gas, Clinton head coach Noel King called timeout and sauntered out to the mound like any other coach. But he didn't motion to the bullpen. Nobody was warming up in the bullpen because the bullpen was empty. The entire team—all nine boys—were out there on the field. It was a lonely bench when the team played defense. When Coach King reached the pitcher's mound, he hollered into the outfield for his relief pitcher and the boys traded positions. If a player got sick, the coach had to think—who was the best athlete in the junior high grades? That boy was effectively drafted. Brought up from the farm team—literally! He had to skip or delay his afternoon chores on the farm to spend the afternoon in right field.

Football helmets, pads, uniforms—who had money for that? Many county schools didn't spare money for jerseys. The Union Mills Millers baseball team might have been mistaken for a ragtag gang playing stickball, or knocking off a beer truck for that matter. The boys wore sweatshirts and t-shirts of every conceivable color. Baseball caps advertised the Chicago White Sox (an Old English-style "C" on the cap), or the Milwaukee Braves (at least it was an "M" for Millers), or no team at all. Among the various county school teams, some boys didn't have enough money for cleats, so they wore high-top Chuck Taylor All Star sneakers. Try rounding second base in a pair of those! So common was this dilemma throughout the state of Indiana that 276 IHSAA-member schools didn't even bother with a baseball team. A *football* team? Yeah, right.

In the county schools, nobody got cut from the baseball team. If you had a mitt and wanted to play baseball, you were on the team. If you didn't have a mitt and wanted to play baseball, you were on the team and a mitt would be found somewhere. If you were an able-bodied boy and didn't have to go home to do chores, you were on the baseball team. Athletic bodies were a precious commodity.

Anybody who spent much time living or traveling around the area knew there were two distinct parts of LaPorte County: south county and everywhere else. South county is rural with a few small towns. It was once part of Starke County to the south across the Kankakee River, but early residents had difficulty crossing the pesky river to get to the courthouse and asked to be annexed by its northern neighbor. The change was made and LaPorte became the second largest county by area in the state.

For baseball purposes, the county remained split into north and south divisions. Clinton, Wanatah, LaCrosse, Hanna, Union Mills, and Westville made up the South Division. Kingsbury, Stillwell, Mill Creek, Rolling Prairie, Springfield Township, and Union Township made up the North Division. The teams competed head-to-head in their respective leagues along with occasional interdivision play, much like the American and National Leagues do today, and then the two top teams played for the LaPorte County Baseball Championship.

But they did not play that championship game on one of the county school fields. Lord, no! They were treacherous sand lots of terror. At Union Mills, the backstop was fashioned out of used lumber, old railroad ties, and actual chicken wire from the local farm supply outfit. Home plate was accented with crab grass. The third base line ran along the nearby railroad tracks and when a locomotive rumbled by, the home plate umpire stood up and called time out. The boys turned their faces away from the tracks as the passing train belched coal ash into the air. After it had passed, players brushed the soot from the steam engine's coal furnace off their shoulders and the game resumed.

At Springfield, the home plate umpire stared at the school building in deep centerfield and the outfield was overrun with sand burrs—nature's cruel Velcro. Shoelaces bound together and burrs clung to players' socks, causing pain as the prickly weed seeds poked ankles. Removing the nuisance was no easy task. The burrs stuck fingers as if testing your blood-glucose level. Nobody wanted to play outfield at Springfield High School. Stillwell head coach Hobart Martin told his players, "Just don't think about it. Get it out of your head and it won't bother you." But how could they? Every time a player moved, the tiny needles reminded the boys of their presence.

Hey, I'm right here—stuck in your shoe, the burrs announced.

Martin advised his boys to wear silk stockings to keep the prickly pods from sticking to their socks. Yeah, right. There wasn't a single player who'd be caught dead wearing silk stockings. Hell, none of them could even afford silk.

Nonetheless, the Stillwell Vikings went 4-1 in the Northern Division and the Union Mills Millers won all five of its games in the Southern Division. The two teams would face off in the championship game.

New York City dominated major league baseball that year. The New York Yankees won the American League pennant and the Brooklyn Dodgers won the National League pennant. Both teams won ninety-seven games and lost fifty-seven. The Yankees were led by Yogi Berra, Phil Rizzuto, and Joe DiMaggio. The Dodgers had Pee Wee Reese, Duke Snider, and Jackie Robinson. All of the county school boys dreamed about being Joe DiMaggio.

On October 9 the Yankees won the World Series, four games to one, at Ebbets Field in Brooklyn. A week later, Stillwell and Union Mills faced off at Ames Field in Michigan City. And some small controversy surrounded the game's location.

Michigan City and LaPorte competed for everything. Athletically the two schools played in the same conference and they fought for bragging rights for the best team. Their businesses fought for attention, train lines fought for passengers, hotels fought for guests, the factories fought for employees, merchants fought for customers, and the two newspapers fought for readers. The county baseball championship always had been held in the county seat: LaPorte. But that changed in 1949. That year the game was played in Michigan City. Most LaPorteans didn't notice the change. It was a small event held on a single Saturday afternoon. Who cared?

Michigan City seized on LaPorte's apathy and offered up Ames Field, a minor league baseball diamond that doubled as the football field for the high school team. Some bleachers had to be dismantled and reassembled for the Stillwell-Union Mills baseball game to take place, but rather than pass along the expense to the county schools, local merchants and the Michigan City board of education footed the bill. The game drew four-hundred fans, a small crowd for such expense, but the city envisioned bigger things. Joe Eyler, the sports editor in LaPorte, recognized Michigan City's coup and wrote, "It made us feel just a little ashamed of LaPorte. The county basketball tourney is going to Michigan City this season. We have now lost the baseball final—probably for good just because nobody around here seemed to care one way or the other. LaPorteans may not miss the baseball games but we'll bet there are some sad merchants around here when the town is 'dead' during the county basketball meet."

Two teams and four-hundred fans for a baseball game was one thing, but the twelve teams, three days, and thousands of fans that the county basketball tournament drew—that was a different story. Michigan City wanted to woo the small-town rural residents to visit its businesses and the change of venue represented a big win for the city.

Before the big game, both coaches remained modest. Coach Martin told the press, "If Ev Dunfee is pitching good ball, we'll be in the game. Otherwise we'll be lucky to do much." Coach Sanders said, "If Rosey (Ray Rosenbaum) is right, we'll beat them." The two men were talking about their starting pitchers, and neither one could have been more right.

In Union Mills the boys took batting practice against their ace pitcher, Ray Rosenbaum. "That's how we learned to hit," Eben Fisher said. "If we could hit him, we could hit anybody! And I hit him one time. He used to throw that left-handed curve. Horrible! I played right field when Ray was pitching. I caught one ball all season. We used to talk in the outfield because nobody could hit him. If they did hit it, it would be a ground ball in the infield."

Indiana Baseball Hall of Famer Ken Schreiber won 1,010 baseball games and seven state titles as a head coach, but before that he played for Michigan City Elston High School. One summer, he faced Ray in an American Legion game and he quickly learned who Ray Rosenbaum was. Ray threw a one-hit shutout that afternoon. "I don't think any of us even got a smell," Schreiber said. "[He] certainly woke up a few city slickers. One of the greatest athletes I ever went against. A hellacious pitcher. Outstanding. I never faced any better. He could run. He could hit. He could pitch."

Charming and devilishly handsome, Ray Rosenbaum excelled at anything he set his mind to. The six-feet-one-inch left-hander worked

hard on his family's farm, kept up his grades in school, and delivered a
wicked curve from the pitcher's mound. After he struck out thirty-
three batters in back to back no-hitters, the Associated Press (AP)
picked up the story, but it failed to mention Ray also had hit a home
run and a triple in one of those games. Yes, if a player could hit Ray
Rosenbaum in practice, he could hit anybody. Anybody but Everett
"Goog" Dunfee, that is, who proved that he was no slouch on the
pitching mound either.

It was a beautiful Indian summer afternoon when the Stillwell Vikings and Union Mills Millers met at Ames Field to play for the
LaPorte County baseball championship. Partly cloudy. Temperatures in
the low seventies. Perfect baseball weather. Perfect day for a pitcher's
duel.

The Union Mills Millers showed up in their mismatched hand-me-
downs that included gray and white sweatshirts and red and gray t-
shirts. A couple of the boys had baseball jerseys, but none of them
matched. All of the boys brought their own hats. The Stillwell Vikings
got lucky that year. The local businessmen had gotten together and
bought uniforms. Bright white wool flannel tops with VIKINGS embroidered across the chest. One of the boys wore argyle socks. Another
boy sported Chuck Taylor All Star sneakers. Upon first glance nobody
would have believed this game was any sort of championship matchup.
Then they started to play.

In the first inning Union Mills got a hit, but stranded the runner. In
the second inning, Ray Rosenbaum struck out the side—one, two,
three. A walk, a stolen base, and a hit led to the Millers' first run. No
runs, no hits in the third inning. Dunfee got the first hit off Rosenbaum in the fourth, but couldn't get home. In the bottom half of the
inning, three errors loaded the bases against Stillwell, but Dunfee
pitched out of the jam and the Millers didn't score. No runs, no hits in
the fifth inning. Stillwell got two hits in the sixth, but couldn't get a
runner across home plate and Dunfee struck out three Millers in a row
just like that. In the decisive seventh inning, Stillwell couldn't get on
base and Ray Rosenbaum retired the side.

When the dust settled, Dunfee struck out nine batters and Rosen-baum struck out thirteen more. The Stillwell Vikings were aggressive—laying down bunts to force the left-handed Rosenbaum to turn and throw to first. Three Stillwell base runners were gunned down trying to steal second base. The second inning produced the game's only run. Final score: Union Mills – 1, Stillwell – 0.

In sports, somebody has to win and somebody has to lose. It was a bitter pill for the Stillwell Vikings to swallow, but they still had hopes of capturing glory in 1950. With baseball officially over, the boys focused their attention on the game that mattered most in Indiana: basketball. Whereas many teams couldn't assemble a football or even a baseball team, all 767 IHSAA member schools fielded a basketball team.

7

The Sports Writers

LaPorte County had two major newspapers: the *Michigan City News-Dispatch* and the *LaPorte Herald-Argus*. Keeping with the spirit of the intra-city competition, the sports pages of the two papers fought for readers.

Both newspapers hired new sports editors in 1948—Bill Redfield covered sports for the *News-Dispatch* and Joe Eyler for the *Herald-Argus*. Both men were twenty-eight years old when the basketball season started in 1949. Other than that, the two men shared few similarities and had many differences.

The *News-Dispatch* wanted to expand its circulation in the small towns around LaPorte County and with Redfield's demeanor and his experience working at so many small town newspapers, he was the right man for the job.

Born in Stevens Point, Wisconsin, Redfield grew up the youngest of seven boys and his older brothers punished and teased him. He probably didn't catch much of a break at high school either. Pictures of Redfield in his senior yearbook showed a portly young man whose face seemed oversized even for his large frame, and the buttons on his sweater strained around his body, as if it were two sizes too small. Nonetheless, Redfield found his place at PJ Jacobs High School. He was the editor of the high school newspaper and under his leadership the paper expanded its circulation to 28,050 copies in seventeen issues his senior year. That's a lot of copies for a high school newspaper.

Joe Eyler
Courtesy of Susan Eyler-Engweiler

Bill Redfield
Courtesy of Jill Redfield

Growing up, Redfield's daughters jokingly called their dad a hobo based on stories he'd told them of riding the rails and traveling from town to town. Redfield was a traveler, alright. His experiences earned him a degree from the school of hard knocks and he had covered a lot of geography in his young life. He started at a weekly newspaper in Morrison, Illinois, and then went on a barnstorming tour working in Hailey, Idaho; West Allis, Wisconsin; Stoughton, Wisconsin; Clinton, Iowa; Litchfield, Minnesota; Owatonna, Minnesota; McAlester, Oklahoma; and Wichita, Kansas. He was the sports editor at the *Daily Republican* in Mitchell, South Dakota, before working as the director of sports publicity at Virginia Tech. When the Michigan City job came up, Redfield was working as a general reporter in Port Arthur, Texas. For those keeping score, that was twelve towns in ten different states and he did all of that before his twenty-seventh birthday.

When World War II broke out, Redfield tried to enlist in the Army, but Uncle Sam wouldn't take him. Flat feet, they said. His vision didn't help his cause either. Redfield wore thick glasses and within a few years he would be fitted with tri-focal lenses. Covering a sporting event in another city, Redfield always drove to the game, but at the end of the night he asked his colleague, photographer Bill Swedenberg, to drive back. The reason? Redfield could barely see in the dark.

Sharp dressing wasn't Redfield's priority. He wore disheveled clothes and his work desk resembled an overflowing volcano of paper. Some colleagues marveled at his ability to get so much work done from that cluttered mess. His handwriting was so sloppy he was the only person who could interpret his notes. When he spoke, the words tumbled out of his mouth so quickly that many people found him difficult to understand.

On the exterior Bill Redfield was gruff. No-nonsense. Phone conversations often were short.

"What's new?" he'd ask.

"Nothing."

"Okay, bye." And he'd hang up.

If you didn't have anything to say, Redfield moved on. He had work to do. He wrote the entire sports page himself with a little help from a high school student who helped out during the basketball season. But he always got the job done without sacrificing the quality on the page. And he did this six days a week!

Despite that gruff, no-nonsense nature, Bill Redfield had a heart of gold. One time, he and a fellow employee got into a heated argument over the radiator temperature setting. Both men were sick with the same symptoms and Redfield went to see his doctor. When he got back to the office, he emptied half of his prescription pills onto his colleague's desk.

"Here. You need them too. Here are half of my pills," Redfield said.

It wasn't a peace offering—that was the way Bill Redfield operated. He'd give a person in need the shirt off his back or the tablets in his prescription bottle.

Another time, Redfield attended a youth baseball game and saw a kid who couldn't afford good equipment. Being sports editor of the Michigan City newspaper didn't make him rich by any means, but he went out and bought a baseball glove and gave it to the coach. He didn't dare give it to the kid himself. The boy deserved his pride. Better it be anonymous, he felt, as if somebody just happened to find a brand new baseball glove somewhere.

Hobart Martin remembered the two sports writers well and summed up their differences this way: "Eyler was more businesslike and Redfield was more off-the-cuff. Eyler—he'd been to Stillwell, but not very often, whereas Redfield ended up out at Stillwell two or three times during basketball season. He'd always hit us around noon and I'd say, 'Bill, we might as well go down to the cafeteria and have some food,' and we'd eat."

Bill Redfield loved to eat and he made a point to attend as many athletic banquets as he could. He felt it was important to be there in person and to see the athletes, their parents, and the coaches out in the community. He'd say a few words, try to make everyone laugh, and shake hands. And he loved the food. The two sports writers shared the love of sports and the love of potluck dinners. Joe Eyler long believed that a man could travel around the world and not find a better meal than the annual potluck dinners served by the families at the LaPorte County school banquets.

Joe Eyler was six-feet-two with a broad athletic build and his hair styled into a crew-cut. When he spoke, he leaned in a little bit and talked out of the corner of his mouth like one athlete conferring with the other during a game. He grew up the son of an advertising copy salesman and earned varsity letters in football and track at Highland Park High School in Illinois. During the summers of his teenage years, he ushered at Ravinia Park where the Chicago Symphony played. There, he developed a fondness for classical music.

At age seventeen, he got a job as a bull cook[5] for a lumber company in Hudson Bay, Ontario, and eventually enrolled at the University of Minnesota where he played football and baseball as a freshman. During World War II, Eyler served four years in the army—including twenty-eight months stationed in the China-Burma-India campaign—and

---

[5] A bull cook is part errand boy, part gopher. They ran every conceivable odd job in a lumber camp.

earned the rank of second lieutenant. He saw Gandhi in person and the chance encounter had a lasting effect on his thoughts about war, life, and politics. He felt people should *always* treat each other with respect, dignity, and fairness.

By the time he arrived in LaPorte, Eyler had developed a love of early jazz and often drove to the Jazz Record Store in Chicago to seek out obscure albums. He loved to cook and experiment in the kitchen as well. Although he donned professional work attire every day, he hated to dress up and didn't care for suits and ties. As a form of silent protest against the dress code, he would accent his dark suit and white shirt with red socks or a red sweater vest.

Eyler proofread his work relentlessly. On his desk was a large spike with yellow copies run through it that he'd worked over. He didn't take much interest in clutter—if something didn't work, he preferred to get rid of it rather than keep it lying around.

While he didn't criticize referees or umpires, and high school athletes generally got favorable treatment, he scolded fans, community members, and coaches on several occasions when he felt their attitude or behavior ran afoul of good sportsmanship. He could take a good ribbing when his writing missed the mark, or his predictions fell short, but he was quick to correct people who put words in his mouth.

Nothing demonstrated the difference between the two writers better than the first editorial each man wrote in his respective newspaper in 1948. In the first installment of "Joe's Jottings," Eyler took exception to a fan from Wanatah who felt the paper's use of the term "underdog" had a negative effect on his team's morale. The fan wrote, "Maybe you have never given a thought to the feeling a so-called underdog gets when he reads the sport page about the game his team played."[6] Eyler's response set the tone for how the sports page would be written under his watch.

---

[6] Talk about irony—the Wanatah townspeople insisted on calling their basketball team "Midgets," but referring to them as "underdogs" was completely unacceptable.

As we see it, someone has to be the favorite and someone has to be the underdog unless the teams are evenly matched. The term "underdog" carries no stigma with it. It is merely a handy term.

We realize that these boys are doing their best to win. Nobody likes to lose. One of our newspaper policies is scrupulous honesty and fairness. We try in every way possible to live up to this rule.[7]

It is very difficult for us to write an objective story from a box score. For that reason we ask, nay, plead with you fans and coaches to give us as much news as possible. We want to print the sports news. The size of this page depends on you. Write, wire, phone, walk, or run to this office with your local sports news—we'll get it in. Letters are greatly appreciated. Particularly those with "beef" and criticism.

Bill Redfield's first installment of "Followin' Thru" showed off his sense of humor and that "off the cuff" style Hobart Martin mentioned.

HOWDY! Maybe you noticed the new byline on this column. Maybe not. Whether or not you did, I want to make one thing clear right off. I'm not the reason the paper costs a nickel more this week. Not the whole nickel anyway. The boss says I'm only three of it.

So don't let the three mills stop you from answering, "Howdy!"

And if you've got ideas, or want to say what you'd like to see on this page, by all means pass 'em along—by mail, phone, in person, or carrier pigeon. They'll be welcome.

The two men's writing styles reflected their different personalities and one was no better than the other. In fact, they complemented each other quite well, even though the two men competed for readers week in and week out. Few realized it at the time, but the people of LaPorte County were incredibly lucky. Bill Redfield and Joe Eyler treated their readers to some great, entertaining writing in the sports pages—writing

---

[7] Joe Eyler always wrote editorials in the third person: we. He later wrote, "If there is anything we hate it is 'I this' and 'I that' liberally sprinkled throughout a column. Also there is a kind of safety in numbers."

that became as much a flavor of the day's news as the newsmakers themselves.

8

Predictions and Final Preparations

Orange and black were the colors of the previous season's most dominant basketball teams. The Westville High School Blackhawks won both the County Conference championship and the county tourney while the LaPorte High School Slicers beat Michigan City Elston three times and breezed through the Sectional to win its sixteenth Sectional championship. That gave the Slicers six more Sectional titles than Michigan City and fifteen more titles than the twelve county schools *combined*.

As a standing tradition, the *LaPorte Herald-Argus* provided in-depth, pre-season basketball coverage of area teams and everyone looked forward to seeing it. The newspaper featured all twelve county basketball teams complete with rosters, team schedules, interviews with the coaches, a write-up, and a team photograph. Of course, this coverage wasn't rolled out in one special issue, or even in one week. Oh, no. The newspaper teased readers and the features trickled out over a three-week period. But even though the county schools started playing basketball games a full two weeks before LaPorte High School opened its season, readers had to wait for the Slicers' feature to be published first before any other team appeared.

Westville was the odds-on favorite among the county schools to repeat its success from the previous year. Joe Eyler wrote that "Only injuries to key players, a serious morale problem or strength not heretofore displayed by the other clubs could dislodge the champs." Nine seniors—seven who had significant playing experience—rounded out the team that expected to build on its success. Not only did Westville return seventy-five percent of its high-scoring offense, but the team returned its first (Don Layton), second (Bill Hannon), and fourth (Ron Wozniak) highest scorers. Many people believed Don Layton was one of the best athletes in the county and six-feet-four-inch Bill Hannon could play the post as well as anybody. And the team gelled well. "We spent all of our high school and really grade school time together, so we came to know each other. We had a lot of confidence that things were going to go well our senior year," Bill Hannon said.

The Westville townspeople supported their team all the way too. "We never had big crowds come to watch baseball or track meets," Bill added. "It was always basketball. We did have a wonderful community in which to play basketball. There were a lot of fans around. They would come to the games. They would have dinners after the season was over to honor the team. They sponsored trips to Chicago to watch the Minneapolis Lakers play the Harlem Globetrotters. It was a basketball community, no doubt about that." On top of all that, the Westville boys believed in themselves. "We had a lot of confidence that things were going to go well our senior year," Hannon said. "We always wanted to have a good basketball team."

"We expected to win again," said senior Bob Spencer. He referred to the County Conference and the county tourney, but Coach Charles McComas had his eye on a bigger prize: the Sectional tournament. First, one issue needed to be addressed. Although the farm boys on McComas' team were tough and strong and experienced hard physical labor, they had a different persona on the basketball court. "We played too easy. We didn't knock somebody down if they scored a couple of times to get their attention—to make them think," Bob said. To toughen up his team, McComas scheduled games against bigger schools with strong basketball programs. Westville picked up games against North Judson, South Bend Catholic, and Gary Roosevelt. Anyone who doubted McComas' thinking only needed to ask the fans in Culver. When the Culver Indians hosted the LaPorte Slicers, a fan took offense to the rough play of one LaPorte player and attacked him with her purse after the game. Of the incident Joe Eyler wrote:

> Dick Hostetler, who loves it best when the going is rough, was finally stopped in his tracks at Culver Saturday night and it took a woman Culver fan to do it.
>
> When the victorious Slicers left the floor for their dressing room at the end of the game, a stocky female bore down on Hostetler with cries of "you dirty so and so" and aimed a swift kick at Dick's pants. The Slicer star, who has faced 200-pound linemen without flinching on the football field, made it safely to the dressing room.
>
> The "Horse" who can be a little spirited at times on the floor, left a few Indians on the floor with his "off-tackle" plays. The "lady" who was not a typical Culver fan, thought Dick was a little rough on the home boys. Such are the conditions which prevail in this "Hoosier hoopla."

Coach Park Sanders expected his Union Mills boys to have a good season too. The previous year, his team finished the season with eleven wins against nine losses. They suffered a two-point overtime loss to County Conference champion Westville, and split two games against the County Conference runner-up, Stillwell. The Millers also had a trio of experienced seniors including the first (Tony Hadella), second (Ray Rosenbaum), and fourth (Loren Uridel) highest scorers. The team was missing one piece of the puzzle to have a great team, and Sanders found it in a transfer student from Chicago.

Eben Fisher's dad was an engineer for the federal government and moved where his job took him. The family moved to the corner of Buckingham and Clark in Chicago: two blocks from Wrigley Field. "I used to shag fly balls at Wrigley Field. One of my friends—his dad was a professional baseball player for [the Cubs]."

Prior to Eben's junior year, the family decided his grandparents needed help. Eben would move with his mother and siblings to his grandparent's house in Union Mills, while his father would stay in Chicago during the week and take the train to Wellsboro on the weekends to be with the family.

One spring afternoon before the move, Eben visited his grandparents and ventured down the street to Union Mills High School to check things out. "The guys were running back and forth in the yard to the building in the back where they kept equipment. I thought, what the heck are these guys doing?" So, Eben asked a student standing nearby.

"Well, they're practicing track," the student said.

"Well, God, I could beat those guys with my street clothes on."

Coach Park Sanders was standing within earshot. "Who are you?" he asked.

"I'm Eb Fisher and I am going to go to school here in Union Mills."

"Well, I heard your comment. I'd like to see you run."

Eben's confidence shrank and he swallowed his tongue. "Okay, I'll try it."

The boys lined up and Sanders called them to start. Down the boys ran to the equipment shed and while the Union Mills track team was still coming back, Eben finished with ease. The race wasn't even close. As usual, Sanders kept his cool.

"Would you like to run track?"

"Not really."

"Well, you're going to run track," Sanders informed him. And that's how Eben Fisher met the man who would be his coach in baseball, basketball, and, yes, track too.

In the fall of 1949 Eben enrolled at Union Mills High School, but it was a difficult transition at first. Far fewer courses were offered than he'd experienced in Chicago and the secretary enrolled him in algebra.

"I already had that as a freshman!" Eben protested.

His class at Lakeview High School had been bigger than all of Union Mills' grades one through twelve. After surveying his new situation, he wondered, "What am I getting myself into?"

Soon Eben made friends and the boys snuck into a neighbor's yard and opened a gate that held goats in a pen. Why would anybody do that? Entertainment. Eben and his newfound friend got a kick out of watching people chase goats all over town. Small-town life turned out to be better than he had expected.

With Park Sanders' missing piece in place, his team was poised to give the other county schools a run for their money. "We knew we were going to have a good ball club," Eben said. "Park Sanders knew that because, of course, we had Rosenbaum, Hadella, and Uridel. It was just whether we were gonna play together." Time would tell, but Sanders didn't worry about that.

Stillwell had another senior-laden team: six boys with significant varsity playing experience. The boys grew up playing basketball together on the dirt field after the school burned and they played on into high school. There were twelve students in the senior class and six of them had been in school together since first grade. "We were pretty close-knit, our class," Bill Singleton said. "We were close because we were small. Every year we were back in school again together so we were more like a family than we were a class."

Stillwell's boys had reason to be optimistic with their new head coach, Hobart Martin. The previous coach knew his basketball, but he blew smoke in the players' faces after he'd taken a drag off a cigarette and the boys felt that if you weren't one of his favorites, you wouldn't get a chance to play. Martin delivered newfound hope. "When Martin came, everybody had a chance. It was a different environment entirely," Bill said.

With the new coach, some of the boys, including Everett "Goog" Dunfee, started their mornings by running four miles before school to get in shape. "Our junior year we started to run and do all of our stuff. He didn't let up on a few of us. He kept tooling [teaching] all the time. He really inspired us."

Coach Martin and the boys got well-acquainted. When you signed on to teach and coach in the county schools, you were THE coach. Baseball, basketball, track, junior high basketball. Everything. They played baseball, basketball, and ran track for Martin as juniors. As seniors they played baseball for him and were embarking on their second basketball season together. Martin knew a small school's success pivoted on having the right players at the right time. "I was fortunate having a bunch of good guys," he said. "I remember Lou Holtz making the remark that if you get a real good quarterback on your football team that makes a good coach [laughing]. I think that is the same old thing. You have to have players."

And he had the players. The previous season, Martin's first year as coach, Stillwell finished second in the County Conference. People had grown accustomed to hearing the mantra: Swing and Wing win again! Teammates Bill Wing and Gael Swing led the team in scoring the previous two seasons as the team won twenty-nine games and lost twelve, but the team failed to take home any of the big prizes: the County Conference championship, the county tourney, or the Sectional tournament. Losing Bill Wing to graduation meant somebody on the Stillwell team would have to step up to the plate and fill his void. There was only one question: Who would it be?

In Michigan City the two coaches at St. Mary's High School came as a package deal from the University of Notre Dame. There, Steve Pavela played baseball and basketball and Joe Yonto played football. Joe had played on the 1946 Notre Dame football team that went undefeated and finished the season ranked first in the country. As for Steve, the St. Louis Browns offered him a contract to play baseball at the age of fifteen, but he passed it up so he could eventually play at the college level. After his sophomore year, he joined the navy and when he returned to Notre Dame after the war, he resumed his spot on the baseball team, but his basketball days were over—apparently there were many talented new boys taller than five-feet-eight-inches to fill the basketball roster.

The two men were in their second year as teachers and coaches and under Yonto's leadership as head football coach (and Pavela's assistance), the St. Mary's Blazers recorded its best football season ever: seven wins and two losses. Now the two coaches switched positions— Pavela headed up the varsity basketball team while Yonto assisted with the B-team. The team worked out at the Naval Armory, just a short walk from the Lake Michigan beach, and the boys quickly learned what was expected of them. Coach Pavela had to dismiss a couple of players from the team. "Oh yeah, they broke training rules," he said. Those rules included a no smoking policy that three of the boys violated and got caught. "It was not a very easy thing for me to do. Look at it another way today and oftentimes you put them temporarily on the sideline and let them come back after they paid the price." But Pavela and Yonto were young coaches fresh out of Notre Dame and did not yet have the benefit of hindsight.

A few blocks away, Elston High School completed a fine football season of its own in one of the toughest athletic conferences in the state. The Northern Indiana High School Conference (NIHSC) counted twenty-one schools as members that stretched across northern Indiana. Eleven members of the Western Division played in Lake County and included Hammond and Hammond Tech. Both schools were within walking distance of the Illinois state line. The Eastern Division included Michigan City and LaPorte as well as teams in South Bend, Elkhart, Goshen, and as far away as Fort Wayne, just a short drive from the Ohio border. East Chicago Roosevelt went undefeated to capture the NIHSC championship, earning the school the distinction of being declared the number one football team in Indiana.

Elston shut out four opponents on its way to seven wins against only two losses. In the final United Press (UP) state football poll, Elston ranked seventh.

Like many industrial Midwestern towns, Michigan City was crazy about sports. During the summer months, fans tuned their radios into the Chicago stations to listen to White Sox and Cubs baseball games. In the fall they listened to Bears and Cardinals football broadcasts. In the winter months though, sports fans focused their attention on the local basketball team and young men aspired to be a part of that scene.

Lawrence Witek grew up in Michigan City, the son of a barber, and his neighborhood had a big influence on his life. "In a three-square block, there had to be twenty, twenty-five boys and most of them were older. So, you learned a lot more from the older guys." Lawrence learned to play football, baseball, and basketball from pick-up games on the block. The older boys played for Elston's high school teams and ingrained in his mind that he too would attend Elston and participate in varsity sports. But while he was in elementary and junior high, he attended Saint Stanislaus Catholic School.

Nuns staffed the faculty at Saint Stanislaus, and many expressed little interest in sports or the boys who played them. But one was different. Sister Georgine, the principal, took a keen interest in the boys who participated in athletics. "She was interested in basketball and on Mondays, she would ask me how I did Saturday. That kind of made you feel good as a young person growing up, that you were accomplishing something, and that she was interested in it."

Encouraged by Sister Georgine and the boys in the neighborhood, Lawrence practiced and played hard. He was a proud member of that successful Elston football team, and now it was time for basketball. Making the team was "a very satisfying personal feeling and it was an accomplishment," Lawrence said. "I'm barely five-foot-seven or maybe five-foot-eight if I stretch a little bit. I grew up in a neighborhood where there were a lot of athletes. I was ten years old and I was playing with guys who played for Elston and they were eighteen or nineteen. So, you know, the whole subject of basketball and going to Elston, I grew up in that atmosphere. There were a lot of guys that were four, five years ahead of me in school. They were all interested in the game and if they saw you down the street, they would stop in and ask, "How's it going? Hey, how did you do last week?"

As basketball tryouts got underway at Michigan City Elston, competition was tough. Far more boys went out for the team than were available spots on the varsity and B-team. Gene Gielow remembered the first time he tried out. "I thought it was a big deal to make the team. I think it is something that a lot of kids look forward to and a lot of kids went out for the team. I can remember going out on the floor the first night coming up from the dressing room going onto the floor and couldn't dig up any saliva I was so nervous." And running the boys through drills Gene's senior season was a new head basketball coach, Dorance "Dee" Kohlmeier.

Before its 1954 miracle, Milan, Indiana, had Dee Kohlmeier. A lifelong Milan resident and sports fan repeatedly told Kohlmeier's son that his dad "was the best athlete to ever come out of Ripley County." That was no exaggeration to make a child feel good about his father. After he entered Hanover College, Kohlmeier learned the game of football and became an integral part of the team as a halfback. He excelled in basketball and track and lettered eleven times. In 1942 he enlisted in the navy and served as a lieutenant on a tanker ship in the South Pacific theater. "Hanover and the navy pulled me out of an ordinary life," he used to tell his sons, and that was more than just a tired cliché. Dee was just a boy when his mother died. His father worked for the railroad and couldn't take care of him and his older brother, so they were split up and raised by separate grandparents. Dee's grandparents didn't speak a lick of English—only German. A college scholarship and military experience opened a lot of doors to a kid who once seemed to have few opportunities in life.

When the war ended, Kohlmeier continued his military career at the Naval Armory in Michigan City. He was a great golfer too and worked part-time as an assistant golf pro at the Pottawattamie Country Club. Not yet thirty years old, Dee Kohlmeier was a tall, athletic man with thick black hair combed back from a handsome face and a strong jaw. He'd experienced a lot in his young life and brimmed with confidence. More than one girl had a crush on the new teacher and as the new head coach at Michigan City Elston High School, he drew the admiration of the boys on the team as well. Kohlmeier knew basketball; he could talk the game, he could coach the game, and he could play the game as well as anybody. When he wasn't coaching and teaching, Kohlmeier captained the Michigan City Moose independent basketball team that had won three state titles in a row.

The new coach forged a strong bond with his senior guard, Lawrence Witek. "I liked him a lot. He was a very personable guy. He was a good coach. He knew his stuff. He was not a screamer or a yeller, or any of that stuff. He was cool but he had a lot of experience. You knew that when he said something, he wasn't just reading out of a book and telling you to do this or do that. He was experienced and a good guy."

As tryouts carried on, Coach Kohlmeier was glad to see a new student in the gym. Bernie Hoogenboom had transferred from Coldwater,

Michigan, where the six-feet-two-inch center had helped his team win the state basketball championship the previous year. The Coldwater team had high hopes for Bernie's senior season, but his dad worked for Railway Express and his job took him to Michigan City. Back in Coldwater, "Coach Eby tried hard to encourage me to stay with friends in Coldwater for my senior year," Hoogenboom said, but he decided to move with his family instead. Being the new kid in school could be difficult, but playing an important role in the most important sport in town helped Bernie fit into his new environment.

While Coach Kohlmeier had whittled his roster down to thirty boys with more cuts yet to come, Stillwell head coach Hobart Martin lucked out. Twenty-two boys went out for the basketball team and, lo and behold, twenty-two boys *made* the basketball teams. It worked out perfectly.[8]

Fifty-two. That's the number of students who won a trip to Washington D.C. While the battle for spots on the basketball team carried on, so did the battle for newspaper subscriptions and the LaPorte Herald-Argus had devised a scheme that penetrated the small rural towns in the county: a contest! The county school seniors who sold the most newspaper subscriptions won a free four-day trip to the nation's capital. Considering some of the kids hadn't left the county and most of them had never left the state of Indiana, the trip presented a major opportunity. When the contest results were announced, thirty-two boys and twenty girls had won the coveted prize.

On October 26 representatives of the newspaper and the Baltimore and Ohio Railroad boarded a train with fifty-two high school seniors at the Wellsboro train station that neighbored Union Mills and rode to the nation's capital. When they arrived, a photographer assembled all the kids in front of the Capitol building for a picture and every one of them was given a wide-angle copy to take home. Seeing all the sights in

---

[8] Stillwell had only twenty-nine boys in the whole high school. If Michigan City Elston had that same percentage of boys try out for the basketball team, four-hundred boys would have turned out.

Washington D.C. was a tremendous opportunity, but keeping tabs on fifty-two teenagers was no small chore for the chaperones. At the conclusion of the trip, no doubt more than one representative said, *I'm never doing this again*, but the very next year the newspaper ran another contest and subscriptions remained steady.

In the newspaper section, "County High School News," Clinton High School reported the following entry: "Speaking of fun, the seniors report a marvelous time on the Washington trip. They are not telling about all the things that they did but we can imagine. Another day or two and they will be back down to earth again."

The number fifty-two had significance to the rest of the nation as well. Coal miners had grown tired of working without a contract and walked out of the pits. The strike had gone on for fifty-two days. When it began, coal supplies were at record highs, but supplies had dwindled and Americans started to take notice.

The Interstate Commerce Commission considered a three-week supply of coal an emergency situation and ordered railroads to cut schedules when supplies dwindled to that point. When the Chicago and North Western Railroad reached that reserve level, it cancelled forty-eight trains that passed through Chicago and its suburbs. Across the country at least thirty-thousand railroad workers had been laid off. The Chicago Public Works, which used coal to pump water to more than four million people, fell "critically short" of reserve supplies. This prompted the public works commissioner to say, "I'm not shouting calamity, but I'm sweating out a terribly critical situation."

UMWA representatives and mine operators were no closer to reaching an agreement than when the contract expired five months earlier. Despite the impasse, John L. Lewis surprised everyone and ordered miners back into the pits. The union said it was "an act of good faith to contribute to public convenience," and John Lewis himself acknowledged "the public inconvenience" Americans had to absorb as a result of the strike. But Lewis' order had a catch: if an agreement wasn't reached by November 30—just twenty-one days away—Lewis' men would strike again and he believed the likelihood of reaching an agreement before that deadline was "remote." The UMWA issued the following warning to Americans: "It is urged that private households and public institutions provide themselves ad interim with necessary coal supplies to tide them over a further suspension period in event that the contemptuous arrogance of the coal operators remains undiminished." It was going to be a long winter.

As the county school seniors returned from their trip to Washington D.C. and the ongoing coal mining drama continued, basketball practice carried on unimpeded and the upcoming season swept everyone into a fevered pitch as cheerleaders, principals, coaches, and community members all prepared for the games to begin.

Stillwell held tryouts for cheerleaders, or *yell leaders* as they were often referred to. Seniors Myrtle (Allmon) Skinner and Lila (Ames) Hagenow were there.

"Back then we didn't wear any pants, slacks, or jeans to school—Daddy didn't let us do that anyway," Myrtle said. "But I remember Lila and I got some slacks so we could wear them to try-outs and not have our dresses slip up when we jumped. Talk about modesty! [Laughing] Now they practically wear bikinis!" Best friends and the only girls in the senior class, Myrtle and Lila made the cheerleading team.

Springfield High School held cheerleading tryouts and five girls made the squad. In Union Mills and Westville, the student bodies elected their yell leaders. Wanatah High School handled things a little differently. The principal simply asked a couple of girls if they would be cheerleaders and they politely obliged.

Union Township's yell leaders picked new outfits. The two girls wore blue skirts and gold sweaters while the one boy on the squad wore blue trousers and a gold sweater.

The LaPorte Athletic Association held a basketball rules clinic at the Civic Auditorium. Two officials and members of the LaPorte Slicers team demonstrated some old confusing rules as well as explained new rules instituted that season.

At Rolling Prairie boys worked in shifts to prepare the basketball floor for action. When the cleaning machine broke, Coach Harlan

Clark and one of the boys drove to Mill Creek High School to borrow their machine. Running out of time before the first game, the janitor eventually finished the task.

Before lending out their machine, the Mill Creek janitor finished cleaning the basketball floor and painted the goals orange to comply with the new rules for the 1949-50 season.

At Clinton, the second team "was resplendent in new trunks." They were "the boxer style with elastic waistband" and were "royal blue in color." There was no mention of new uniform tank tops. Sorry, boys—maybe next year.

The North Liberty Lumber and Coal Company donated lumber to Stillwell High School while letters and numbers came from a local businessman. Everett "Goog" Dunfee's dad volunteered his time and turned that pile of wood into a board that identified the names and numbers of both the visiting team and the home team players. It hung prominently next to the scoreboard. Stillwell also took delivery of new bleachers just in time for the first home game. This doubled the gym's capacity to five-hundred seats.

Wanatah's entire student body gathered in the assembly hall to watch a film of the previous year's state basketball championship between Jasper and Madison. And with that, everybody was ready for the new season to begin.

PART II

9

Cage Season Commences

While the city schools continued to finalize their basketball rosters, all twelve county schools were ready to play, and so they did. Opening night witnessed no surprises. The Saturday headline read: FAVORITES POST WINS AS COUNTY QUINTETS OPEN. "Westville, defending champ, powered to a 60 to 28 win over Union Township on the latter's floor. Union Mills beat Hanna, 44 to 33, at Union Mills. Stillwell crushed Kingsbury, 42 to 16, at Stillwell; Rolling Prairie rolled over LaCrosse, 52 to 28, at Rolling; Mill Creek nudged Springfield 36 to 32, at Mill Creek and Clinton topped Wanatah, 46 to 29, at Clinton." And just in case anyone accused Stillwell of running up the score on Kingsbury, Joe Eyler pointed out that Coach Hobart Martin played all eleven boys on his team in that game.

Two weeks later, LaPorte High School opened its season at home in the magnificent Civic Auditorium. Industrial magnate Maurice Fox, whose family established the Fox Woolen Mill in LaPorte, purchased a full city block to construct the Civic—a palace built for the people of the city. Dedicated in 1930, the structure included bowling lanes, meeting rooms, and even public showers, which were a big hit when the building first opened. But the main feature was the auditorium. A theatre stage stood on the far end and the main floor fit a full-length basketball court. Elevated above the floor, 2,200 stadium seats surrounded the court on three sides. Beyond the seats the walls swept up to a gently arched ceiling high above the floor. Concerts, dances, conventions, wedding receptions, proms, and civic events had been held there. It also was the home of the LaPorte Slicers basketball team.

LaPorte hosted the Horsemen of Gary Mann High School on opening night and senior Ralph Jones lined up with his teammates inside the locker room. The boys ascended the staircase to the main foyer, passed fans buying tickets and concessions, and ran through the entry into the massive auditorium where cheering fans showered the team with applause. "It was a big thing to be a Slicer basketball player because you got to go to the Civic," Ralph said. "I always liked coming out because the locker rooms at the Civic were in the basement and I always liked coming up those for the varsity. You came up in a line and went on out."

The crowd was a sea of people dressed in orange and black. The high school student body, nearly one-thousand strong, attended the game and sat together in one section. Junior high students sat in bleachers between the stage and the baseline. Adult fans filled in the rest of the seats and the auditorium was filled to capacity. Everybody was ready to raise their voices in support of the home team.

In the southern tip of the county, LaCrosse High School played its first home game in a brand new gymnasium. Guests of honor included Bill Ferrier, the man credited with introducing basketball to the town, as well as IHSAA board president R.B. Miller. At a cost of $130,000, the building not only housed the gymnasium, but a stage and cafeteria as well. [9] Nearly one-thousand fans turned out for the dedication and the gym was filled to capacity. That also made it the largest county school gymnasium by a wide margin.

The new gym was long overdue. LaCrosse's old playing floor was more like a big room in which they happened to play basketball. The ceiling was so low that, local legend held, its arch rival Wanatah once tossed a game-winning last-second shot there. When it went in, Wanatah fans cheered, but officials ruled the ball had touched the ceiling and waved off the basket. Ugly jeers and bitter arguments ensued to no

---

[9] Meanwhile in Kokomo, Indiana, Memorial Gymnasium was completed at a cost of $800,000 and sat 7,000 fans.

avail. Wanatah still lost and somehow the officials escaped without in-
jury. The far wall served as the sideline and it even had a cut-out—the
wall went along for some length and then jutted out two feet into the
playing area before continuing on its path to the baseline. The
hometown boys used this to their advantage. A player would hide in
that little two-foot alcove and when a teammate collected a rebound he
would jump out on a fast break all alone, leaving opposing teams to
wonder where he'd come from. More than one visiting player streaked
down the sideline with his eyes focused on the dribbler at mid-court
and ran into that hard corner as well.

The new gymnasium was a huge improvement. It had permanent
tiered seating that provided ample leg room—fans rested their feet on
the same platform the person in front of them sat their behind. The
ceiling didn't interfere with any shots. The stage provided space for
extra seats. But being a county school, expenses were spared wherever
possible. The playing floor was only seventy-four feet long—the bare
minimum length considered acceptable by the National Basketball
Committee and a full ten feet short of the recommended dimension.

Stadium seats, 2,200 fans, walkways, foyers, a stage, a cafeteria, and
high ceiling—most county schools *dreamed* of these features and after
the grand opening at LaCrosse, Joe Eyler took a hard look at all twelve
county school gymnasiums.

> There are only four county schools with adequate playing
> floors right now. They are Hanna, Mill Creek and Stillwell in
> addition to LaCrosse. Four others come under the category
> of barely passable. They are Clinton, Westville, Rolling Prai-
> rie, and Union Township. Kingsbury and Springfield might
> be rated as poor. Wanatah and Union Mills might just as
> well be playing outdoors.
>
> Some great teams have come out of the county. Great,
> that is, on county floors. But the vast expanses of the Civic
> auditorium or the Michigan City High school gym ruin most
> county teams before they have a chance during tourney
> time.
>
> You can't expect a county powerhouse like Westville
> (or any other), which spends the whole season scraping el-

bows in a 'cigar box' to step on a large floor and run with
the Slicers, Red Devils or St. Mary's Blazers in the sectional.

Basketball players have been called *cagers* for decades. The term referred to playing in gymnasiums like the one at Union Mills High
School. Constructed in 1915 while basketball was still in its infancy, the
game outgrew the gym almost immediately and despite Carl Sanders'
pre-war plea as Professor B.B. to build a better, safer gym, townspeople pinched their pennies and refused to pay up. When asked about
Union Mills' gymnasium, Rolling Prairie head coach Harlan Clark
summed it up best: "It. Was. *The.* Worst."

"You couldn't even shoot a darn free throw!" one opponent complained, and that was true. The top of the backboard butted up against
the ceiling. When a player arced the ball for a simple shot—it hit the
ceiling. Players were forced to shoot line drives and try to bank it in.

There were no boundary lines painted on the floor—instead, the
walls *were* the out-of-bounds lines. When the basketball hit a wall, it was
a turnover. Dead ball. And possession went to the other team. To in-
bound the basketball, a player stood on one foot while pressing the
sole of the other sneaker against the wall behind him. Across the far
sideline and the right baseline, walls ran floor to ceiling. In front of the
spectator seats on the remaining two sides, a short concrete wall
topped with a horizontal steel rail marked out-of-bounds. When a player wanted to check into the game, he had to crawl under the railing and
immediately found himself on the playing floor. One backboard was
mounted two feet from the wall while the other hung near that steel
railing and the short concrete wall. It was an accident waiting to happen and accidents did happen.

Everett "Goog" Dunfee played basketball outside after Stillwell's
school burned down, but that was preferable to his experience in Union Mills' gym. "When you saw that back wall, it was pretty tough. I got
hauled off there during one game. They got me right above the knee. I
didn't want to drive all the way through. So, I drove up and then
somebody nailed me. It wasn't on purpose—because it was really tight
quarters. Even just running down the sides."

Union Mills always played a zone defense, and why wouldn't they? When three boys spread their wingspans and stood side by side, fingertip to fingertip, the first boy nearly touched the far wall and the third boy almost grabbed the railing in front of the bleachers. Painted on the floor, the free throw circles overlapped the center circle. The barn at the Werner farm where seniors Loren Uridel, Ray Rosenbaum, and Dean Werner played during the summer months had bigger dimensions in every direction—nineteen feet high at its peak and thirty feet wide.

Cracker box. Shoe box. Cigar box, Crayon box. Whatever you called it—it was small. Coach Park Sanders always said, "You only have to take three steps and you are down at the other end of the gym."

Thanksgiving eve 1949, the LaPorte County Conference witnessed an early season matchup expected to have huge implications for the conference championship. The Westville Blackhawks—defending champions and pre-season favorites—visited Union Mills in its sorry excuse for a gymnasium.

When Westville arrived, the team hauled Herman into the gymnasium with them. Standing three feet tall, Herman had a tall wooden base with a pillar at each corner. Between the pillars stood a shiny basketball player that reached up toward a wooden top plate. An eagle adorned each corner of the plate and positioned prominently between the four eagles sat a full-sized gold basketball. Donated by the LaPorte Lumber and Coal Company, Herman was the County Conference traveling trophy.

Herman started life as a prize to the 1948 LaPorte County Basketball Tournament champion: Mill Creek High School. Herman's rules dictated that Mill Creek would keep the massive trophy until they were beaten by another county school team, whereupon it would be relinquished to the victor. The following season Herman passed through the hands of boys from Wanatah and Stillwell before Union Mills carried it into the 1949 county tourney. There, it became the possession of the Westville Blackhawks who kept it all spring and summer and now carried it into Union Mills gym.

As exciting as the traveling trophy was, the two teams battled for a greater honor. "Our greatest rival—certainly that year—[was] Union Mills," said Westville senior Bill Hannon. The winner of this game would claim the early honor of being top dog in the county. Furthermore, it was a matchup of some of the best players among the small county schools. Even though LaPorte never played the small county schools except in the Sectional, Ralph Jones knew the matchup was a great one. "[Ray] was a hell of a baseball player. Probably the best athlete in the county in 1950. Bill Hannon was probably the best basketball player, but Ray was the best athlete. He could do everything."

Bill Hannon of Westville and Ray Rosenbaum and Tony Hadella of Union Mills were the leading scorers in the county. Rosenbaum and Hannon both played center and they had battled it out for years—sixth grade, seventh grade, eighth grade, B-team, and the varsity squads. They knew each other well. "Ray was a good player and I know you had to be on your toes to compete with him," Bill said.

Smart fans didn't wait for game time to draw near—they showed up early. The game probably could have filled the Civic Auditorium, but the Union Mills gym sat no more than four-hundred people, but the school *sold* more tickets than that. When the seats had filled, people squeezed into a small lobby near the corner of the gym that overlooked the seats and playing floor. But that space didn't even extend half the length of the gym. Standing-room fans three or four people deep couldn't see the game when the action moved to the far end of the court. Still more fans packed into a hallway beyond the lobby. For these late arrivers, the noise of the crowd marked the game's progress. A cheer went up, followed by an even wilder cheer. A whistle blew and then jeers poured from the fans who witnessed the action.

He travelled!

Get that bum out of the game!

Hey, why don't you put on my *glasses—you sure could use 'em!*

Get your head out of your ass, ref!

What happened? someone would ask. A quick recap was sent back with various interpretations of the action that unfolded, mostly biased toward the home team. And imagine, everybody paid the same fifty cents to be there.

With fans squeezed into every possible square inch of that shoe-box, Bill Hannon and Ray Rosenbaum stepped into the center circle for the opening tip-off. The referee stepped between them, looked up, took careful note of the short ceiling, and tossed the ball into the air to start the game.

Westville senior Bob Spencer dribbled the ball up the floor and witnessed an impossible scene. On defense, Tony Hadella, Ray Rosenbaum, and Loren Uridel stood with arms spread wide, fingertip to fingertip, in front of the basket. Their wingspan covered the width of the diminutive court. Crowded between them, Bill Hannon futilely fought for position. Stuck in the far corner, one Westville teammate tried to carve out a little space of his own while another boy found himself pressed against the steel railing in front of the fans. Between all of the players, two referees jockeyed for their own position to officiate the game.

Union Mills packed its zone defense in tight. On the corners of the free throw line stood the Miller guards, Dick Tillinghast and Eben Fisher. Their smirks suggested, *go ahead—shoot it*. Many unsuspecting players had been lured into taking that wide-open shot. When they did, the ball invariably bounced off the ceiling as the shot arced in the air. The referee blew his whistle. *Out of bounds! Possession: Union Mills.*

But Bob Spencer was too smart for that—he'd played in Union Mills' gym many times before. But what could a player do in such a confined space?

"There wasn't much you could do," Bob said. "You had to just put your head down and try to drive and hope they didn't call a foul on you." So, that's what he and his teammates did. They buried their heads and into the fray they drove!

"Playing at Union Mills, you had to change your way of playing because the floor was small and the ceiling was low," Bill Hannon said. "They had the same difficulties that the visiting team did, except they were a little more used to it than the visiting team was." This was true. When the Millers were on offense the situation was the same and they looked at big Bill Hannon—all six-feet-four inches of him—standing in the center of the Westville defense.

Dick Tillinghast remembered one of Coach Sanders' lessons. "He was a big proponent of tipping [the basketball]. If you're on offense and you're down there and the ball comes off, tip it. In practice we did that all the time. It doesn't take much. You don't have to jump too high to tip the ball." So, Union Mills launched a shot and relied on the ball being tipped, tipped, and tipped again, hoping one of them would eventually fall in the basket.

On the game went. Drive, shot, tip, tip, foul, shot, rebound, foul, drive.

It took five whole minutes before Hannon tossed in the game's first field goal. A minute later, Hadella scored one for Union Mills. In the first quarter the two teams shot eleven free-throws and made ten. The score was tied, 7 – 7.

Drive, foul, shot, tip, tip, rebound, foul, shot, turnover, foul, shot, tip, drive, foul.

At halftime everyone was exhausted and frustrated by the wild game that had unfolded and Westville held the edge, 20 – 19. The players climbed over the railing off the floor and up the five narrow steps to get to the locker rooms. As they reached the top of the stairs, sweaty boys rubbed against the men and women crowded into the lobby and hallway leading to the dressing rooms. When halftime ended, the boys chasséd back through the crowd and down to the basketball court.

Union Mills sparkplug forward Tony Hadella had mastered an unusual shot. He'd streak across the lane just inside the free-throw line and then launch a low, hard line-drive off the backboard. SMACK – BONG! It ricocheted off the backboard, caught the front of the iron hoop, then slid down through the net. Fifteen seconds into the third quarter, Hadella's shot regained the lead and the team never looked back.

Shot, drive, tip, drive, foul, shot, foul, tip, tip, rebound, foul, drive, foul.

Turnover, foul, shot, foul, tip, drive, foul, foul, foul, foul.

The game slogged on through the second half—the referees called fifty personal fouls during the game. Hadella led all scorers with twenty-nine points on eight field goals and thirteen free-throws. In the battle of the athletic centers, Hannon and Rosenbaum finished with fifteen and eight points respectively.

Union Mills won the contest, 48 – 43, and the Millers hoisted Herman the traveling trophy into the air in triumph while Westville wrestled its way back to the locker room. Union Mills sat on top of the County Conference standings alongside Stillwell and Rolling Prairie.

"The thing I remember from that game is we got beat," Hannon said. All other memories of that game disappeared almost immediately. He was as competitive as any player in the county and he wanted to win every game. The loss was a big disappointment, but he made no excuses concerning the lousy gymnasium. Both teams played in the same conditions and the home team always had a slight advantage. That's the way it was.

The season was still young and the Westville Blackhawks weren't about to give up yet. The coveted county tourney was more than two months away and the boys would try to win every game before then. That didn't happen, but "we were close," Hannon said with a smile.

In his column, Bill Redfield revealed a silver lining from the Blackhawks' loss: "Westville Coach Charles McComas has some consolation. He won't have to lug the trophy around to every game as has been his job since last January's conference tourney."

After the game, the junior class shooed everyone out of the tiny gymnasium. The Jolly Vets were escorted inside and quickly set up their instruments—prepared to play for both round and square dancing. Students gathered outside in the cold and streamed in as soon as the ticket table was set up in the stairwell. Admission: fifty cents.

Nearly every Friday night one of the county schools sponsored a dance and invited students from the other schools to attend. The arrangement was as necessary as it was convenient—not only were many of the kids from the various towns friends and distant relatives, but with sixty kids in the whole high school, admission fees would barely cover the cost of the band. And make for a very small dance party.

The dances were a great way to forget about the cold weather, hard times, and the next morning's chores, but they also served as a valuable source of information. Gene Goad was a sophomore at Union Mills. "You couldn't wait until the games were over to head to Hanna, Union Mills, Mill Creek, Stillwell, or Wanatah to a dance and they were always coordinated. No two schools had dances the same night, so that's how you found out who won [the basketball games], because all of the players and cheerleaders all showed up."

On occasion other games ended early and students showed up at the neighboring school ready to attend the dance, only to find out that *this* basketball game hadn't finished yet. So, they watched the end of the game, if they could get inside, and waited.

Everybody looked forward to the dances. "On Friday nights, there'd always be a dance at one of the schools after the games and we'd all go," said one Kingsbury student. "It was a great time. They were just sock hops, but we didn't mind. Union Mills always had the best dances."

"It seems to me we were more interested in the dances Friday after the games than in the game itself," said Wanatah senior Gene Rice, "at least I was!"

When the dance finally got underway in Union Mills gym that night, a familiar scene unfolded—boys from the different county schools leaned against a wall together, or slouched over the railing of the bleachers and talked about basketball, cars, girls, and farming. On the playing floor the boys were competitive—they always wanted to beat each other—but once the game was over they were friends. "People would ride together, go there, [catch] up on the scores and stuff like that. There wasn't a lot of dancing going on. The girls were out there dancing with each other and we were talking about basketball," Bob Spencer said.

Finding a ride was a critical part of getting to the dances. Most families had only one car and few students could afford one. According to Bob, "Nobody had cars or even when we graduated two or three guys had cars—old jalopies that they fixed up. In fact, I never drove a

car until after I graduated from high school and bought my first car."
At Union Mills only three students in the entire high school had a car.

As a result, fathers dropped off their kids at the dance and then went to the local tavern to play cards, have a few beers, and do the same thing the boys at the dance were doing: talk about basketball, women, and farming. Other parents just sat in the parking lot and whiled away the time listening to the radio—and why not? Less than twenty percent of county households had a television and there weren't many channels to watch anyway.

The following week, Union Mills High School submitted a report to the "County High School News" section: "The junior class held a dance following the Westville-Union Mills game. The round and square dancing was evidently a great success with half the county schools being represented. The class was glad to see several of the parents and friends of the school at the dance."[10] Just like every other Friday night, the dance turned out to be a big hit for everyone.

While LaPorte started its season at home and the county schools played each other, Michigan City Elston started its season on the road and they traveled all the way to Frankfort the day after Thanksgiving to do so. As it did for all away games, the team chartered a bus to make the trip. And not just any old bus, but a swanky South Shore,[11] outfitted with fully functioning heaters in the back—an important feature during northern Indiana winters. The road trip intended to treat the boys to something special, perhaps even make them a bit more worldly—at least as worldly as a trip across Indiana could make teenage boys—but there were challenges. "It was kind of tough because you weren't home," Lawrence Witek said. "You had a hotel you had to go and sleep in, you know, and then you've got a crazy buddy there, so we lost a lot of sleep."

---

[10] In other "County High School News," Clinton Twp. reported, "Another casualty has occurred. This time it is Lawrence Staller, who was the victim of a hand saw. We hope his left hand will heal soon."

[11] The South Shore was a transportation company primarily known for its electric rail cars that connected commuters between South Bend, Indiana, and Chicago.

Frankfort had one of Indiana's most storied basketball programs. The Hot Dogs, as the team was known, already had won four state championships in the tournament's first thirty-nine years of existence, and on Friday night, Frankfort pounded Michigan City, 60 – 28.

The next morning, the boys groggily boarded the bus and rode on to Lawrenceburg to play another game on Saturday night. Although Michigan City held the lead at the start of the fourth quarter, the boys ran out of gas and Lawrenceburg poured in twenty-one points in the last quarter to win the game. It was a tough loss to a familiar foe for Coach Dee Kohlmeier who grew up in nearby Milan.

After the game, the boys retired to an upscale hotel in downtown Cincinnati while Coach Kohlmeier caught up with old friends and family who came to see him. The following morning, the boys dragged themselves onto the charter bus and left the banks of the Ohio River to make the 280 mile journey north along twisted two-lane highways back to the Lake Michigan shoreline. Tired and defeated, the road trip turned out to be a brutal start to the season and the boys knew things wouldn't get any easier when they started playing in the NIHSC. "Believe me, we felt on shaky ground when we ventured into southern Chicago area and northern Indiana. Elkhart, South Bend Central, and Gary were the powerhouse teams of the time," Bernie Hoogenboom said. Powerhouses indeed. The high schools of Hammond, Gary Froebel, South Bend Central, and Gary Mann consistently ranked among the top teams in the Associated Press state basketball polls.

In its third game, Elston hit the road again, but this time traveled only twenty-two miles to Valparaiso. There, the boys avenged its first two losses and won its first game of the season.

The city teams grew accustomed to long road trips to attend games: the three schools played only four games against in-county opponents and three of those games were against each other. In addition to driving from the west side of the Indiana to the east side to play fellow NIHSC teams, LaPorte played in Culver, Terre Haute, and Vincennes. But nobody traveled as extensively as St. Mary's.

Many local schools hadn't bothered to schedule St. Mary's in the past because the school had been barred from official IHSAA competition. All-black high schools were not permitted in the IHSAA statewide tournament either due to their "exclusive enrollments." In 1942 the IHSAA finally ended the ban and admitted all high schools. But the main idea behind the trips was to let the boys bond and to see other parts of the Midwest. The team traveled to Niles and Benton Harbor, Michigan; Rockford, Illinois; and Milwaukee and Racine, Wisconsin. The boys rode the famous Burlington Zephyr train to Dubuque, Iowa, for a game even. But the road trips were tough. "I ran into some tough times," Coach Steve Pavela recalled. "When we played Racine [St. Catherine] and saw how tough Wisconsin was—very tough school, St. Catherine—we didn't have a great deal of success [against] them, but that was part of the learning experience."

While the city schools traveled throughout the state and the Midwest, the county schools rarely ventured past the county lines to play a game. Combined, the twelve county schools traveled more than twenty-five miles to play a game on only eight occasions. They played a total of 247 games throughout the season.

With twelve teams in one conference—and all of them in the same county—the attitude might have been: Why bother traveling any further than need be? Another explanation might have been that many of the county school kids lived on farms. Extracurricular activities such as basketball or the school play came second to chores that needed to be done at home. Keeping games close to home was a practical matter. A business decision, you could say. Then again, considering the condition of the county school buses, it probably was a good thing the teams didn't travel far.

When the state police conducted bus inspections in the fall of 1949, the LaPorte County schools had the worst record in the state. Sixty-three of ninety-one county school buses had been tagged "in need of repair," a full twenty buses more than the second-worst offending county in the state. But it didn't end there. The state police condemned another nine buses considered beyond repair.[12] Little won-

12 For comparison sake, the neighboring three counties combined had 252 buses—fifty-three needed repairs and only four were condemned.

der. In one of the strangest arrangements of the time, townships owned the body of the bus, while the bus driver owned the chassis that included the frame, wheels, and motor. It wasn't uncommon for drivers to detach the body from the frame during the summer months, and then use the chassis on the farm to move hay, wheat, or even livestock. These buses oftentimes were well-used.

Even when the buses were in good standing condition, riding school buses on country roads could be an unpleasant experience. The Werner farm where Dean grew up marked the end of the bus line for Union Mills School and none of the roads that led into town were paved—they were all dirt. When the school bus driver started his route in the morning at the Werner farm, he backed the bus up to the milk house where two full buckets of water waited for him. The driver threw open the back door of the bus and dumped the water onto the floor in an effort to contain the dust that rose through the floorboards as the bus rattled over the rutted dirt path on its way to school every morning. At the end of the day, the driver paid Dean's younger brother Bobby a nickel a day to drop him off at the corner a quarter-mile away to save time and to avoid turning around in the driveway.

In Springfield Township, one of the local farmers had a contract to drive a bus for the school—$125 per month. One morning the tie rod broke on the bus, leaving the farmer unable to steer. The bus rolled into the ditch and tipped over. All of the kids tumbled to one side against the windows. In a true sign of a different era, the students simply crawled out of the bus, brushed off the dust, and walked the rest of the way to school.

On a typical Indiana winter morning, those buses got downright frigid. If the school bus had a heater onboard, it would have consisted of a single blower fan right next to the driver. Anybody sitting more than one row back relied on a warm coat, warm hat, wool socks, and shared body heat to keep warm. That would have made for a miserable trip on a cold December night to and from a basketball game.

Most county school basketball teams chose not to travel by bus. Only the fan bus carrying students and cheerleaders made the trip to away games. Players and coaches found their own transportation. They traveled in the family car with their parents or caught a ride with a neighbor or teammate's family. The night before a game, Union Mills Coach Park Sanders had one last piece of business to conduct at the end of practice. Sanders sat down all of his players and one by one asked them how they were getting to the game.

Ray, you riding with your parents? Good.

Dean, your mom and dad taking you to the game? Okay.

Tony, do you have a ride?

What about you, Sherm?

Warren, how are you getting to the game? Whole family's coming? Great, that will help fill our side of the stands.

Gene, how about you?

If a player wasn't sure, or didn't have a ride, the team worked out arrangements on the spot. All things considered, maybe it was a good thing that the county schools played close to home and didn't rely on the buses any more than need be.

Most people paid little attention to the drama swirling around the school bus inspections. Instead, a looming deadline captured their attention. As December 1 grew closer, Americans wondered whether the United Mine Workers would strike again, as John Lewis had promised. The large coal companies still refused to concede to the union's demands. They pressed President Truman to intervene, but he refused to do so until the miners struck and the strike proved dangerous to national health and safety. When Americans got home and unfolded their afternoon newspapers, they read some encouraging news.

Coal miners did strike at midnight as planned, *but* Lewis ordered the men back into the pits that morning. Americans would not have sympathized with the striking workers weeks before Christmas and a strike would have frustrated union members who needed the income to get through the holiday season. But rather than show up five full days every week, Lewis' miners worked only three days per week. This move kept coal trickling out of the mines and into American homes and businesses and kept the U.S. government from invoking the Taft-

Hartley Act that would have forced the miners back to work. In the ongoing chess match between mine operators and the United Mine Workers, this move belonged to the workers.

10

A Kid Named Goog

I asked former Stillwell head coach Hobart Martin about one of his players: Everett Dunfee. "Oh, he still lives in Stillwell," Martin said. "Of course, everybody called him Goog. Still do."

When I called Dunfee's house, I asked to speak to Everett—a dead giveaway that I wasn't a close friend or relative. Probably a telemarketer, or a scam artist of some sort. "He isn't here," a terse voice told me. When I mentioned his old high school basketball coach, Hobart Martin, he turned out to be home after all. When we met, he stuck out his hand and said, "Nice to meet you. Everyone calls me Goog."

Goog loved to joke, smile, and laugh. He marched to the beat of a different drummer and was a genuinely nice guy. Thinking back on their years together in school, Lila (Ames) Hagenow couldn't help but laugh. "Between him and Gene Jones, they were *out* of trouble less often than they were *in* trouble for one thing or another." Yes, trouble and Goog Dunfee always knew where to find each other. He could tease a fellow student as well as the next person and he was always good for a laugh. Even teachers found him and his co-conspirator's shenanigans difficult to resist.

Flatulence has remained one of the greatest elementary school gags for hundreds of years. As the class clown and ring leader, Goog sat with the other boys next to the windows in the old Quonset hut classrooms. Suddenly one of the boys would start calling, "Woo, woo, woo!" and another would rush to the windows and throw them open.

Their behavior tore their teacher in half. On one hand, she desperately wanted to laugh, but on the other had she had to maintain order and was furious with them. She almost cracked a smile, but managed to maintain her composure.

After the new school building had been built, Goog and a couple of buddies grew bored one day and wanted to get out of class. Rather than sneak out of the building or fake an upset stomach, the boys hatched an idea. A coal furnace powered a boiler, and steam from the boiler heated the school. First, the boys turned up all the radiators in the building. Next, they urinated in a large tin can and, finally, they tossed the can into the flames of the furnace when nobody was looking. Anybody who ever urinated on a campfire knows what happens next. An awful stench filled the classrooms and hallways of Stillwell School. The plan worked. The principal cancelled classes and sent students home for the rest of the day while he figured out what had happened—and it didn't take long to find the culprits. "We got caught and ended up in the principal's office for that," Goog said.

Boys weren't allowed in the gymnasium during the girls' physical education class, which only piqued Goog's curiosity more. "A couple of us decided to see what the girls looked like, so we crawled underneath [the stage] on our bellies and looked through the louvers, but that didn't last either," Goog said. They got caught. Time after time, Goog Dunfee pushed the envelope and time after time, he got caught. But he didn't make excuses. When he got caught, he got caught. Sure, he liked to stir things up a little bit, but he generally accepted responsibility for his actions. When trouble came, he knew its call and he took his lumps. And he earned plenty of lumps.

Outside school, he loved to goof off when he had the chance. Goog worked at the local grain elevator and made good money: twenty dollars per week. "Some people came up from Kentucky in an old '36 Ford and I bought that for ninety dollars," he said. "We rolled it over I don't know how many times and I always had kids climbing all over it. They were made solid!" When Goog landed a date, he didn't dare roll up in that battered jalopy—he borrowed his dad's 1946 Pontiac instead. He'd take his date to LaPorte and park along Pine Lake and before long, boys from LaPorte High School would find him. They'd shine their bright lights in his rearview mirror, run into the rear bumper, and tell him to get out of their town. Yeah, yeah, Goog would say, and then he looked for somewhere else to hide.

Goog was a hard worker and a dedicated teammate. He was one of the boys who ran four miles before school to stay in shape for basketball season. He was a good athlete, but never put himself before the team. It was always about the team winning first and foremost. Everything else would fall into place if he worked hard. Well, except the time he *did* put himself before the team and he paid a heavy price that changed everything for the season.

"They were supposed to be in at a certain time at night," Coach Martin said, "and I had heard that Goog was doing what Goog wanted to do—that time didn't mean anything to Goog in a way." Martin suspected Goog wouldn't make curfew, "And I caught him on a Saturday night."

It was a night Goog never forgot. He and a teammate had gone on a double date and the boys were running late. His teammate got nervous, but Goog told him to relax. Nobody would be looking for them. "Of course, we screwed up and I took Gael home first and [Coach Martin] wasn't around Gael's house." Goog thought he was in the clear, but when he turned the corner, Coach Martin sat in his Ford alongside the road in front of the Dunfee house. "I thought, 'Oh shit,' and I hurried and closed the door and just stayed inside the garage." Martin had Goog cornered, so he got out of his car, walked up the driveway, and knocked on the garage door. In his baritone voice Martin calmly said, "Goog, I know you're in there. You might as well come out and face the music." Goog froze and didn't make a sound. The night air was cold and Martin had no intention of waiting him out, so he laughed to himself, walked back to his car, and drove home. When Goog heard the car door slam, he went into his house and went to bed, but he knew he'd been caught and would take some lumps for this one as well.

Monday morning, the principal called Goog into his office. There sat not only the principal, but Coach Martin and a number of other

teachers. The makeshift committee suspended Goog the next basketball game and then it would be up to his teammates to decide whether
his suspension would continue or if he'd be allowed back on the team.
When the next game came, Goog thought he'd stay home—too embarrassed to show up and not be allowed to play. "Nope. You're going
to sit right there, buddy. Right beside me," Coach Martin told him.
"You'll know what you did."

The team traveled across the county line to play North Liberty and
Goog sat right next to Coach Martin. He didn't play a single second
and watched helplessly as his team lost by a single point: 38 – 37. The
Vikings' perfect season ended and its record fell to 6-1.

"That killed me. That killed me," Goog said. Had he played, undoubtedly he would have scored the needed two points to pull out the
win and maintain his team's perfect season. Now his place on the team
was up to his teammates.

The players and especially the senior class were a tight-knit bunch.
When it came time for the boys to vote on Goog's fate, it was unani-
mous. "Of course, we all [voted for him] and he played. I don't think
he missed any curfews after that," Bill Singleton said with a laugh. He
toed the line the rest of the season because he didn't want to let down
his team again. He never squealed on his teammate and fellow senior,
Gael Swing, who was with him the night they broke curfew, and Coach
Martin never found out.

And what about that unusual nickname—it had to be the result of
some nonsense he'd gotten into or trouble he'd caused, right? Nope.
When he was a baby, somebody gave him a bite of a banana and he
liked it so much that he went all googly-eyed. The name stuck. Goog.

11

Bill Yates: Voted Most Talkative

The LaPorte County Coaches Association held its first meeting of the year at a tavern in Westville: the Westpoint Inn. First order of business: election of new officers. Clinton Township Coach Noel King replaced John Dunk as president. Charles Park Sanders was elected vice president and Harlan Clark, secretary-treasurer. The County Coaches Association was composed of the twelve county school coaches whose teams made up the LaPorte County Conference.

"We would meet there once a month and talk over all kinds of stuff and all the coaches, I thought, got along together pretty well. Everybody wanted to win naturally, but it wasn't a dog-eat-dog thing either," Coach Hobart Martin said. But ask any of the surviving coaches what official business was conducted during these meetings, and none could remember any specifics. Rolling Prairie Coach Harlan Clark thought hard on it for a while. "I don't quite remember," he said, "but whatever it was, I'm sure it was darned important!" A wide grin grew across his face.

None of the county schools employed athletic directors, so duties were shared between the coaches and the principals. Together, they worked out the schedules for twelve schools in three sports: baseball, basketball, and track. Once the schedules were completed, the primary tasks at the meetings fell to socializing, drinking, and giving each other a good ribbing from time to time, and no member was better at that than Bill Yates, the new Springfield Township coach.

At one County Coaches Association meeting, Noel King left the table for a minute. Yates snagged a couple of cigarette butts from an ashtray on a vacant table—cigarette butts with lipstick on them—raced out to the parking lot, tossed the lipstick-laden butts in the ashtray in King's car, and ran back inside the tavern before King returned to the table. When King's wife later found them, she was furious with her husband. "Noel got into all kinds of trouble over that!" Hobart Martin said with a laugh. But all of the coaches were good friends, so there never were hard feelings or a grudge. It was a clever prank, they had to admit.

Bill Yates had taken the job to teach and coach at Springfield Township High School in the fall of 1949. When he and his wife moved to LaPorte County, they lived at 107 Illinois Avenue in Michigan City. It was just steps away from the Lake Michigan beach and he quickly found a friendly neighbor he could confide in. St. Mary's Head Coach Steve Pavela and his wife lived next door at 105 Illinois Avenue. Yates taught shop and indicative of the kind of person he was, he made a pair of bookends for his new neighbor: one marked with an *N* and the other with a *D* in honor of Pavela's alma mater, Notre Dame. "He was the nicest guy," Pavela said. "We used to shovel our drives out together to get to school."

Yates grew up in the town of Bluffton, Indiana. He was one of four kids living together in a small house. The family never had much and together they struggled, but together they got by. Rather than complain about what he didn't have, Yates appreciated what he did have. The house was always well-kept and his parents maintained strict discipline. While in school, Yates had a job shoveling coal, but that was no excuse to dirty up the house. His shoes needed to be cleaned and polished and set outside at the end of the day.

At Bluffton High School, he played second base on the baseball team and was a member of the football team[13] that recorded its best season ever: seven wins, one loss, and one tie. The Bluffton Tigers shut out three opponents and its sole loss was a one-point decision. Still a

---

[13] Bluffton played six-on-six football.

scrawny teenager, Yates played guard at five-feet-six-inches tall and 125 pounds. What he lacked in size, he made up in grit and determination. Like every Indiana boy, Yates loved the game of basketball, but Bluffton had an outstanding group of players and didn't need a player with his size—or lack thereof—so he never made the team. Undeterred, he played intramural basketball all four years of high school.

The kids at Bluffton High School always knew where Bill Yates was. He loved to laugh, make a joke, and clown around. His classmates voted him the most talkative boy of the senior class and beneath his yearbook picture it read, "A rival of Joe E. Brown."[14]

When Yates graduated high school, he knew exactly what he wanted to be: a coach. But he and his family couldn't afford college tuition, and a year later he found himself working for the Estey Piano Company rather than working on his degree. Two more years passed and when the United States entered World War II, Yates enlisted in the Marine Corps. Stationed in Alaska, his body had grown from an undersized high school football player to an all-Pacific Marine Corps basketball and football player. When the war ended, Yates finally had the means to realize his dream of becoming a coach and teacher. He used the G.I. Bill of Rights to attend Ball State University.

Years later, Hobart Martin was on a golf course in Florida when he met a man from Bluffton, Indiana. Martin asked the stranger if he'd ever heard the name Bill Yates.

"Bill Yates? Yeah, I knew Bill Yates," the stranger said.

Martin told him that Yates was a teacher and a coach in LaPorte County. The man stopped dead in his tracks and a surprised look came across his face.

"He went to college and graduated from college? You know, for that guy to go from where his family was in Bluffton and graduate from college—that just amazes me that Bill Yates did that."

Bill Yates *did* do that. He worked hard. He never complained and he made the best of what he had. He persevered. He was a fighter. He

---

[14] Joe E. Brown was an actor and popular American comedian in the 1930s and '40s. He was most-known for the broad smile that stretched across his face.

never gave up. When he arrived in Springfield Township, he immediately captured everyone's attention. When he entered a room, people knew he was there. Even though he taught shop class, he dressed sharp. Every night before going to bed, Yates stood at an ironing board, preparing for the following morning. Shirts starched and pressed. Every day. Perfect pleats ran down his trousers. Every day. Shoes shined. Every day. His hair neatly combed. "Shoes shined. Terrific. Always dressed nice. All the time—not just once in a while—all the time," said Stan Nedza, a Springfield senior.

Just like his days growing up in Bluffton, Bill Yates was a talker when he arrived at Springfield High School. He was always talking and teaching, teaching and talking. His message ran beyond shop class. He wanted young men and women to excel. He wanted his students to do something with their lives and to take advantage of their education. He wanted them to seize opportunities and make something of themselves. Before class, passing period between classes, lunch hour, after school, Bill Yates was always talking and teaching, teaching and talking.

"You could not walk by him without having a conversation with him," Stan said. "If you wouldn't mention something, he'd make a comment. He'd talk about how important education is and how important obeying orders is, how important it is to appreciate your family, without the hard work of your father and mother you wouldn't be here and you wouldn't have this opportunity to have such a good education or get as much out of school that you possibly can."

During basketball practice and even during basketball games, the chatter continued unimpeded. Talking and coaching, coaching and talking. Teaching and coaching. Yates's voice carried and he frequently slipped into the habit of talking like a Marine. Talking and coaching, coaching and talking. But sounding like a *full-fledged leatherhead*. His antics caught some people off-guard and others disapproved of the words that sometimes flew out of his mouth, but his Springfield players quickly learned when to let the words soak in and when to let them slide off like too much rain. As animated and as loud as Yates might have gotten and as much as he carried on, he always encouraged his boys. "Even if it was a bad play, bad this, or bad that, he always stressed [that] you'll have another chance to better yourself," Stan said. "And all the ball players, they just came up and did the best they possibly could."

No doubt about it, Bill Yates could get quite animated. His antics quickly earned him the nickname *Wild* Bill Yates. "On the sidelines, you knew that Bill Yates was the coach," Stan said. "He showed a lot of interest in how you were playing and he was excited about certain plays that were made and he made you feel good. As a coach, you wouldn't see him sit down! Not Wild Bill! He was always on the play. All the time. As Wild Bill as he was, he never got thrown out of the game."

"Yates was a character, but a good character," said Coach Harlan Clark. "He was always capable—I always felt—of crossing the line sometime or another. I don't know whether he did or not. I think he always stayed pretty well on the line (laughing). I do remember that!"

Through all the chatter and the antics, Yates remained a strict disciplinarian. Jim Strakowski was a freshman and got an opportunity to play on the first team when another player broke a leg. "I was a good outside shooter. We were supposed to work the ball inside, but I had an open shot and I took it and made it. We won the game by two. Well, I had to sit three or four games after that long shot." Rules were rules. Listen to your coach, play as a team, demonstrate respect, be disciplined. The lesson was learned.

But one thing was clear about Bill Yates. "He would do anything for somebody," Hobart Martin said. "I think it was just the way he was raised up. He had a pretty big heart."

The big heart, the constant talking, the enthusiasm, the excitement, talking like a Marine, the fun-loving nature, and the practical jokes—Bill Yates fit right in with the County Coaches Association and they loved him.

When he arrived at Springfield, he had accepted a very difficult job. The Springfield Indians basketball team had a perfectly imperfect season the previous year: zero wins and seventeen losses. In only three of those games did the team manage to keep the negative point spread to single digits. Union Mills beat them 66 – 14. Westville pummeled them

72 – 20. In the county tourney, Clinton Township—the smallest school in the county—annihilated the Springfield Indians 55 – 8. The year before that, the team managed just one win over the last two months of the season. Since basketball was the only game that mattered, morale was at an all-time low in Springfield Township. But Bill Yates knew what it meant to be the underdog and he rose to the occasion.

"Yates Works Wonders With Indian Quintet," read the headline. The story continued, "Yates has injected some new spirit into the Indians and the war paint is on and the tomahawks are waving this season." Not only had Yates' team managed to win three of its first eight games, but it nearly upset Stillwell on Stillwell's home court. The people of Springfield Township were eager to see their boys play a home game against a top-notch opponent and on December 16, they got their wish. Union Mills—possessor of Herman, the traveling trophy—would appear in Springfield to play a conference game right before Christmas break.

The night before the big game, the County Coaches Association met at the West Point Inn. The men opened the meeting, discussed old and new business, enjoyed dinner, drank, smoked, and needled one another over who had the best team. At that point, Yates announced to all of his fellow coaches and at least one member of the press that if Springfield beat Union Mills the following night, he personally would mount Herman on top of the Springfield Township School. All of the men laughed. Undoubtedly they were unsure what was funnier: the fact that he thought his team had a chance to beat Union Mills, or that he was brazen enough to declare something so foolish. Nobody took the threat too seriously—least of all, Union Mills' coach Park Sanders.

The Springfield Indians

Back row: Coach Bill Yates, Dick Robbins, Louie Perschke, Ed Schnick, Gerald Woodrick, Ron Zila, and student manager Gene Russell. Front: John Hoffmaster, Stan Nedza, Al Gloy, Marion Waldo, and Dick Manthey.

12

Park Sanders Returns to Springfield

With so few students available, a county school coach had to recruit every able bodied boy for the team, and Park Sanders grabbed every kid he could get his hands on. Of the eight boys in the senior class at Union Mills High School in 1950, six of them played on the basketball team. As for the remaining two boys, one ran track and served as the official score keeper for the basketball games while the other played baseball.

So small were the county schools that everyone was expected to participate in extracurricular activities and everybody *did* participate. It was a matter of need as much as school and community pride. While Gene Goad loved sports as much as any kid in the twelve county schools, there was one problem: his body never grew. He stood four-feet-nine-inches tall. Playing sports—even at such a small school—wasn't a realistic possibility. But Coach Sanders wouldn't let any student sit on the sidelines if he could help it and he knew Gene could be an important part of the team. Besides, Sanders needed his help. There was only one thing that stood between the coach and his new student manager: Gene's father, Shirley Goad.

Sanders approached Gene in the hallway at school and asked him if he could count on him to help him out with the basketball team as the student manager. As badly as he wanted to say yes, Gene couldn't.

"I don't know if Dad will let me because of chores," he told the coach. Like most farm kids, he had a full load of chores that had to be done every morning before school and every night after school. Milking cows came first. End of story.

"Well, can I talk to him?" Sanders asked.

"Uh, well, yeah," Gene replied, but he had a realistic expectation how it would end up and it wasn't good.

That night Park Sanders stopped by the Goad farm. Gene's dad shook the coach's hand and invited him inside, "How about a plate of beans?" he asked.

"Yeah, Shirley, that sounds good," Sanders replied.

Gene's mother had prepared corn bread and beans for dinner that night. It was Sanders' favorite meal.

The two men made conversation while they enjoyed dinner, but Gene couldn't eat a thing. Sanders still hadn't said a word about why he stopped by and Gene's nerves turned his stomach in knots. He knew what his dad was going to say and his words rolled over and over in his head, "Nope, he's got to do chores," and that would be that.

Finally, when the men finished their meals Sanders stated his business, "Shirley, I need your boy to help me with basketball."

Every muscle in Gene's body tensed up. He knew exactly what his dad would say and he dreaded to hear the words come out of his mouth.

Shirley Goad replied, "Well, if that's the way it's gotta be, that's the way it'll have to be then as long as he gets his work done."

Gene was shocked and elated. He darted from the table, raced upstairs and changed his clothes, tumbled back down the staircase, and flew out the door and jumped into Sanders' car.

Sanders thanked the family for dinner, headed out the door, climbed into his sedan, and drove himself and Gene to the gym for basketball practice.

It marked the beginning of a four year relationship between student manager and head coach, and for all his hard work Gene earned four stripes on his letter sweater sleeve before graduation: one for each year he'd earned a varsity athletic award. Of course, when he got his sweater the sleeve was so long the stripes fell below his elbow rather than on his bicep. The home economics teacher shortened the sleeve to put the stripes back where they belonged.

Dick Tillinghast was a junior at Union Mills that season and attended basketball games in other towns with Gene. Not only was Gene short, but he also had a childlike face and people inevitably stared at him and the four stripes on his sleeve. Dick and the other boys loved to play a joke on the curious onlookers. He'd grab the gawkers' attention, nod at Gene and say, "This guy here is on the basketball team. He jumps center for us. You ought a' see him. He's got one helluva vertical leap!" The staring strangers never knew what to say. Some laughed and others anxiously looked away. What did the boys care? They had fun and it served people right for staring for nothing.

But Gene didn't need anybody's protection. Oh, no. He could run his mouth with the best of them. Once when the team was having dinner together, he was on a roll and getting particularly smart with the guys. When he excused himself to the men's room, the other boys called over the waitress and had a quick word with her. When Gene returned, the waitress asked in a motherly tone, "Are you the little boy who was asking for a high chair?" He was speechless for a change and the team busted up with laughter. They truly *were* a team. Family. Brothers. Every one of them.

As student manager, Gene kept busy. "Back then you didn't buy a dozen basketballs. If you got one new one year, you were lucky. So, you took care of what you had. I'd go down to Hicks' grocery store and get shoe polish, and of course I had to get chewing gum for the guys—they all chewed gum when they played—and then I'd scrub the basketballs. But, when they came out on the floor, they'd shine like you wouldn't believe. I scrubbed them, then waxed them with shoe polish, and then put them in a gunny sack and [shake them back and forth in the sack] and that shined them." The basketballs shone like a well-polished eight ball and Coach Sanders said, "Goad, we may not have new basketballs, but we've got the shiniest ones."

Friday night as Park Sanders drove to Springfield School for the basketball game, he looked forward to the familiar faces that would be in the stands. His former Springfield students had graduated, but parents, brothers, and sisters of those students he'd taught before the war would be there. His team was 6-1, with the only loss at the hands of a nonconference opponent by a single point. They sat on top of the County Conference standings. Christmas break was a week away and a victory over the Springfield Indians would keep Union Mills on top going into the New Year. Furthermore, his wife Florence had just given birth to their first child four days earlier. Joe Eyler had written that "Coach Charles P. Sanders of Union Mills is the proud papa of a young cheer leader. Sanders claimed it was easier than most ball games but undoubtedly Mrs. S. would disagree there." Things definitely looked good for Coach Sanders and the Union Mills Millers.

While Sanders drove in his car, his student manager Gene was struggling to make it to the game. After the final bell at school rang, Gene hurried home, milked the family's cows, fed the cattle, cleaned the barn, finished his chores, got cleaned up, scarfed down his dinner, and loaded the team's equipment into his dad's car. The sky had grown dark and the clock was ticking fast. Gene had planned to catch a ride on the fan bus. The driver knew Gene's predicament and had agreed to meet him a couple miles north of town. As his dad sped down Highway 6, Gene could see the headlights of the bus on a country road in the distance and he made it in the nick of time.

When he met the bus on the dark rural road next to the highway, Gene opened the trunk to his dad's car, pulled out the medicine kit and Coach Sanders' Army Air Corps duffel bag filled with the team's four basketballs, and then he struggled to haul Herman the massive traveling trophy up the steps onto the bus. The trophy was a particular challenge for him. "I was four-feet-nine at the time and the trophy was almost as tall as me and I had to carry that sucker." When Goad arrived at the Springfield High School gym, he stationed Herman at the end of the bench, placed the medicine kit nearby, and unloaded the team's four basketballs from the army duffle bag. As the Union Mills team ran through its warm-up drills, the basketballs outshone those of their opponent.

Shortly after the opening tip-off, Springfield opened up a 7 – 1 lead. Union Mills didn't panic and closed the gap, but Springfield continued its attack on the basket and ended the quarter up five points, 13 – 8. Springfield maintained the edge throughout the second quarter but Union Mills closed in. Trailing by three points with ten seconds left in the half, Union Mills forward Loren Uridel sank two free-throws. When the two teams headed into the locker room at halftime, Springfield led by a single point, but Union Mills had the momentum in its favor.

Coach Bill Yates was notorious for his halftime speeches. He was so lively that crowds gathered outside the locker room door to listen to his spirited words. Inside, of course, the boys listened intently and deciphered what to hold onto and what to let go. That night, he was particularly excited. "We had Dick Manthey. He was our center and a very good ball player," Stan Nedza said. "Bill Yates thought if we could hold down Hadella and control their center [Ray Rosenbaum], then we had a chance to beat them here. It was really something."

Of course, holding down Hadella or Rosenbaum was no small task. Hadella averaged nearly twenty points per game and led the conference in scoring while Rosenbaum averaged fifteen points himself. Yates had devised a strategy to win and his boys had executed it flawlessly through the first two quarters. If the team could hang on—if they could continue to *believe* in themselves—Yates felt the biggest upset of the season was sixteen minutes away. So, he did his best to fire up his team before they headed back out for the second half.

In the other locker room Park Sanders calmly talked his boys through the game and their adjustments. No doubt, he didn't expect Springfield to be this close, but his team had the momentum and his two stars, Hadella and Rosenbaum, had barely scored so far.

Yates occasionally led his team out onto the court after halftime by doing a backflip on the basketball court. Dressed in his suit and tie, shoes perfectly polished, he'd launch himself in the air off the run and turn head over heels right there in front of everyone. As for Sanders, he quietly sauntered out and took his seat on the bench with his favorite fedora on his head. He always wore his hat while the game was in progress and when he called timeout, he removed his hat and tossed it on Gene Goad's head.

When the game resumed, Union Mills quickly grabbed the lead off Eben Fisher's basket. There was that momentum Sanders needed and he relaxed a bit. However, those were the only two points the Millers scored in the third quarter and the Springfield Indians extended their lead to six points. The Springfield boys were in a state of euphoria as they entered the huddle before the final period. They couldn't believe the score. The boys were smiling. Giddy. But Yates forced them to focus. The game wasn't over, he reminded them. There were eight minutes yet to play and anything could happen.

Coach Yates "could get the last drop out of your veins and you'd still have a smile on your face," Stan said. And he squeezed those veins hard that night. Wild Bill coached from the sideline until the very end. Coaching and teaching, teaching and coaching. Always talking. Yates pointed, yelled, encouraging, jumped up and down, spun in circles, waved off the referees, threw his hands in the air, stomped his feet, and twisted his face. This was Springfield's biggest game and Yates could sense the pieces falling into place.

Always cool, calm and collected, Coach Sanders was irritated at his team's lack of offense. He looked down and saw Herman, the massive traveling trophy, at the end of the bench. Undoubtedly Yates' words the night before about putting Herman on top of Springfield's school echoed in the back of his mind. He pulled the starting five out of the game to open the fourth quarter and put his reserves in the game. Maybe *they* could do something in the game. The reserve players cut the lead to four points—not enough—and Sanders threw his starters back into the game. Rosenbaum and Hadella scored eight points in that final push, including five in the last twenty-five seconds, but Springfield matched the Millers point for point down the stretch.

When the final gun sounded to mark the end of the game, Springfield held Tony Hadella to eight points and Ray Rosenbaum to nine—eighteen points below their combined average. Yates' plan had worked. Final score: Springfield – 40, Union Mills – 35. The Springfield team never gave up and one reporter noted, "Any resemblance to the team which represented Springfield last year by the present group is strictly coincidental."

Union Mills was no longer undefeated in conference play. They no longer sat atop the County Conference standings. They no longer possessed the traveling trophy. If it was any consolation, at least Gene Goad didn't have to wrestle the oversized traveling trophy back onto the bus.

That same night, twelve other high schools played six more games inside LaPorte County's borders. LaPorte traveled to Michigan City to play for bragging rights. In the game, LaPorte missed nineteen free throws, prompting Joe Eyler to write, "They ought to take the 'free' out of the free throw for the Slicers—they are just 'throws' to our boys." The Red Devils led the Slicers through the final three quarters and won by ten points.

Half of the county school gyms were filled as they all matched up that night. Besides Springfield's triumph over Union Mills, Westville won its game. The struggling Kingsbury Kings upset LaCrosse. The Wanatah Midgets maintained its perfect record—zero wins and nine losses—when it fell to Hanna. Stillwell and Rolling Prairie both won, giving the two teams perfect conference records and together they sat on top of the County Conference.

Charged with the task of covering all of those games were two sports writers: Joe Eyler and Bill Redfield. In Michigan City, Redfield employed a high school kid part-time to help during the basketball season: Roger Bixler. Like many Friday nights, the two worked late at the office to track down all the basketball game information throughout the county. The coaches held the official score books and the only way to get the basketball stories into the newspaper. "Of course, when some of the coaches would lose, they would be pissed off and they wouldn't call [the scores] in," Roger said. "So, we'd have to get on the phone and start calling babysitters and small bars in these little communities trying to track them down. Westpoint Tavern—that was one we'd call. We had a list of taverns we'd go through. We'd get them."

When they finished working the phones and gathered all of the scores and highlights, Bill Redfield sat down and wrote the story. Oftentimes they worked past midnight, but they always got the story. When the paper hit newsstands the following day, the sports page included the box scores and highlights for all seven games held in the county that night. They also published details from a Michigan City Moose game, two Porter County games, and a game played by the New Buffalo, Michigan, high school team. And to think: all that information—plus a lot more—could be had for the tidy sum of just five cents.

13

Fire

A new spirit and energy swept through Springfield Township. After going twenty-two months without a single win, the Springfield Indians had won four basketball games in just a few weeks. They had a new coach who believed in his players and the team gave him everything they had. "When Yates came along, he taught us how to shoot, dribble, and got you in shape," said one player. "He had a big job [as basketball coach] when he came to Springfield Township and he did it. We didn't have a team—we didn't win any games the year before." Those who hadn't attended the game had heard the news and read about it in the newspapers. Springfield had just beaten the top team in the County Conference. The team possessed Herman the traveling trophy. Things were looking up.

Monday morning, as the school buses rocked down the rutted dirt roads toward Springfield Township School, the student body's excitement and pride insulated them from the cold winter air. The buses parked in front of the school as they always did, but when students took that last step out the door, something caught their attention. On top of the school building, a shiny gold basketball glimmered in the early morning light. Students pointed up, smiled, and laughed in disbelief. There it is! Herman the traveling trophy. Bill Yates had kept his word.

As soon as class attendance was taken, the principal called a morning assembly and the entire student body—all 102 of them—filed into the gymnasium. Herman sat front and center, flanked on both sides by the basketball team and the cheerleaders. Coach Bill Yates gave a speech in which he replayed the game's finest moments for everyone to hear, explained how proud he was of the team, and thanked the students who cheered them

Courtesy of Marilyn (Marquart) Buerger

on and supported the boys. Everybody in attendance cheered in unison.

Maroon and white, fight-fight!
Maroon and white, fight-fight!
Who fights? We fight!
Maroon and white, fight-fight!

Christmas break was three days away and the school would hang onto the massive traveling trophy into the New Year. Hurray! Throughout the remainder of the day, teachers, students, the principal, secretaries, custodians, and the cooks had a spring in their step and held their heads high. Good feelings and newfound optimism had taken over. The kids at Springfield couldn't have asked for a better Christmas.

The following morning, Jane (Shippee) Lindborg and her sister woke up and got dressed for school as usual. They walked down the driveway to the road and stood in the cold morning fog expecting the school bus to arrive any minute to take them to Springfield High School. But the bus never came. Growing cold and tired, the two girls walked back up the driveway and sat in their farmhouse and looked out the window. Apparently classes had been delayed, they thought. They couldn't call the school to find out—the family didn't have a telephone. So, they waited.

Four hours earlier, around 3:30 a.m., the first South Shore passenger train traveling from South Bend to Chicago passed through Springfield Township. In the distance the train engineer saw a bright yellow light piercing the morning darkness. Fire! The engineer relayed a message to the dispatcher who called the volunteer fire department. By the time firemen arrived at the scene with their equipment and a five-hundred-gallon water pumping truck, the flames had torn through the halls and classrooms of Springfield Township School. The roof had collapsed and by the end of the day one of the exterior brick walls fell too. The school recently had installed a new floor in its gym and the basketball team played only four games on the new home court. It was destroyed. The principal confirmed that all records, school books, supplies, and athletic equipment were gone. The fire spared nothing and somewhere in the twisted wreckage—charred and melted—rested Herman, the trophy that traveled no more.

With nowhere to attend classes, Christmas break arrived three days early at Springfield Township School, but nobody celebrated. Instead, students gazed gloomily at the remains of their school. A reporter interviewed two students who showed up to survey the damage that morning. "We liked school," one of them said, "and this has to happen just when our basketball team was getting good."

Courtesy of Gerald Woodrick

14

Life Goes On

When classes broke for Christmas, holiday tournaments fed Hoosiers' collective basketball appetites. Michigan City Elston traveled to Hammond to play in its annual tournament at the Civic Center. Four of the six tournament teams belonged to the brutal NIHSC athletic conference in which seven of its teams ranked in the top twenty in the state, including Elston's first opponent: Hammond High School. The boys gave Hammond everything they could handle, and then some.

With the score tied at forty-three points apiece and the clock ticking down the final seconds, Elston had the ball. At the same moment the buzzer sounded to mark the end of the game, the referee blew his whistle. Foul! The boys had shot well from the free throw line that night and senior Joe Tanski had a chance to win the game, but his shot missed its mark and in overtime Hammond scored three baskets to Elston's two. Final score, 49 – 47. In the consolation game, the team faced another NIHSC rival, Hammond Clark, and lost another heartbreaker, 52 – 51.

Back in LaPorte County, three different schools hosted holiday tournaments. LaPorte invited Elkhart, Rochester, and Bloomington to the Civic Auditorium and racked up two straight wins to capture its own tourney title, much to the delight of local fans. "LaPorte's Slicers pulled themselves up by their bootstraps last night and took a 39 to 37 thriller from Elkhart," wrote Joe Eyler. The Slicers showed signs of improvement and celebrated New Year's Eve with an even record: five wins against five losses.

The other two tournaments took place in south county. LaCrosse invited Westville and out-of-county opponents San Pierre and Wheatfield to its tourney. There, Westville beat a talented Wheatfield team in the first game and then breezed past LaCrosse in the school's own brand-new gymnasium. Hanna hosted Union Mills, Clinton, and Wanatah. Union Mills won back-to-back games with ease to capture that tourney title. The Wanatah Midgets lost both of its games by a combined thirty-two points and its winless streak continued. On December 31, 1949, the final county school standings read as follows:

County Team	League Games	All Games
Stillwell	6-0	7-1
Rolling Prairie	5-0	7-2
Union Mills	5-1	9-2
Westville	4-1	7-2
Hanna	3-3	6-6
Springfield Twp.	3-3	4-5
Clinton Twp.	2-4	5-5
Mill Creek	2-4	3-6
Union Twp.	2-4	2-5
Kingsbury	2-4	2-6
LaCrosse	1-5	2-7
Wanatah	0-6	0-11

Back in Springfield Township, the smell of smoke still lingered in residents' hearts and minds. Everyone believed the basketball season was over for the Indians. The team had no basketballs to practice with and no gymnasium to practice in. The team's uniforms went up in flames. The soles of the boys' Chuck Taylor All-Star sneakers melted in the bottom of their lockers.

While students mourned the sight of the school's charred skeletal remains, the first spark of good news rolled out of the ashes. "We'll outfit the team with new maroon and white uniforms, jackets, shoes, socks, and sundry equipment," declared the chairman of the Michigan

City merchants. By noon the following day, Michigan City retailers had raised more than four-hundred dollars necessary to equip the team. The boys borrowed a nearby elementary school for practices and played its remaining home games at Rolling Prairie High School. The basketball team would continue its season. However, one big question remained: where would the school hold classes? Without classes, there was no school for the basketball team to represent.

Area officials and building owners quickly cornered the county schools superintendent, Springfield Township trustee, and school principal Vernon B. Craig. The Methodist church of Rolling Prairie offered space in its meeting rooms for classes. Michigan City building owners offered vacant space. LaPorte School's superintendent offered several rooms in its city schools as well.

Although Springfield School was growing like an adolescent school boy, people tossed around that dirty word rural residents despised: *consolidation*. Many people suggested the small schools combine to create bigger schools with better curriculum and reduced costs spread across more and more students. Economies of scale in education. It was possible the thought of consolidation motivated LaPorte's superintendent to offer class space. Luring the township to LaPorte schools would boost enrollment and increase its coffers with Springfield Township tax dollars.

A representative of the Indiana department of public instruction visited the area to view the fire's damage and to assess the township's situation firsthand. Besides, the department had to sign off on any temporary school. Rumors favored the old Elston High School in Michigan City, which still stood. It would have been a relatively short trip to get to classes and the building had five rooms to house grades seven through twelve. However, the final decision surprised almost everyone. Grades four through six used space in one of LaPorte's school buildings. Grades seven through twelve attended classes in abandoned buildings in Kingsford Heights—in the far opposite corner of the county. "The school day will not be lengthened for any student," the Springfield Township trustee explained. "Pupils will be returned home at the regular time." Principal Craig eliminated gym class to accommodate the longer travel time all the way to Kingsford Heights, and why shouldn't he? The temporary facilities had no gymnasium.

On the morning of Wednesday, January 3, 1950, classes resumed for the kids of Springfield Township. One-hundred-forty-five students squeezed onto four buses that picked them up at the regular time and then made the long drive to the new school, but students were less than thrilled. "It was a farce," said Jane (Shippee) Lindborg. "We spent more time on the bus than in school. And, oh, was it cold!" The buildings weren't a school in the traditional sense. They were Quonset huts like the ones Stillwell had used after its fire in 1941. Every room had a door to the outside. An old oil heater stood in the corner of each room and the huts had little if any insulation.

Many students felt they didn't learn a whole lot under the circumstances. "We gutted it out," Stan Nedza said of the temporary school. "Our whole class was proud that we had the opportunity instead of going to Michigan City or going to LaPorte to finish—we had the opportunity to finish high school together. Our principal, Mr. Craig, had a lot to do with that."

Stan, who played an important role in the victory over Union Mills, had made a significant sacrifice to finish school at Springfield High School. After his junior year, his parents found work in Chicago and moved there. While the family rented out their house in Springfield Township, Stan and his brother carved out a little space to remain in the area. "We were living in the basement of our old home with three inches of water on the floor and walking on two-by-fours." All because he wanted to finish school with his classmates—his lifelong friends—rather than finish his senior year "at some strange school."

"Mr. Craig, he would bring me home, he would pick me up. He was home. He was like a father to me. He was great and he didn't have to do this."

Seeing Stan Nedza's sacrifice firsthand, Principal Craig understood the importance of doing everything in his power to keep the school going. "He was a man who kept everybody together. He found this, he found that, he found where we were going to finish out school, he found where we were going to practice, and where we were going to play our games. Mr. Craig was right on top of it."

Kingsford Heights might not have been the ideal location, but given the circumstances, it was the best Vernon Craig could find to keep the state happy and to keep everybody together. Despite everything he'd done, there was always something else. School supplies such as typewriters and science equipment still needed to be sourced and he welcomed all possible donations the area communities could make.

As Springfield tried to get into its new groove, other schools resumed familiar routines. Farm kids woke before dawn, walked out to the barn and then shoveled silage out of the siloes, fed the cows, put the milkers together, milked the cows, lugged the milk cans into the cooling tank, cleaned all the equipment, went into the house, and ate a hearty breakfast prepared by their mothers. But they weren't done yet. They trudged back out to the barn, shoveled manure, spread fresh straw for bedding, went back into the house, washed up, and changed into school clothes.

Then, they gathered their books and marched through a path in the snow to the side of the road where the school bus picked them up at the usual time and drove the same path to school and parked in the same familiar spot.

History, English, typing, algebra, lunch, Latin, chemistry, and shop.

Midafternoon, the buses met students in the same parking spot and took them back home at the usual times where the boys did the afternoon chores. They fed the cows, milked the cows, lugged the milk cans into the cooling tanks, cleaned all of the equipment, shoveled manure, spread fresh straw for bedding, walked into the house, and washed up again. In the evening, the kids enjoyed a huge dinner with the family, followed by a little homework while listening to the radio in the living room. The next morning, the process repeated itself.

Of course, many city kids had jobs and small chores of their own that needed to be done before and after school—caring for younger siblings, helping out around the house, taking out the garbage, collecting bottles and cans, working at the local grocery store, sweeping the floors in a local barber shop, or delivering newspapers—and most of these kids walked to class as opposed to taking a bus. But in every corner of the county when the sun settled at night, it was time to listen to the evening radio and read the evening newspaper to catch up on everything that had happened in the world over the previous twenty-four hours.

With classes back in session, basketball coaches resumed their demanding schedules as well. The city schools could afford coaches who specialized in each sport. Dee Kohlmeier and Norm Hubner coached varsity basketball. They even had assistants to coach the junior varsity squads. But when a county school coach signed his contract before the start of the school year, the contract specified teaching *and* coaching. That meant he was *the* coach.

"You coached everything," Harlan Clark said. "No assistant. Nothing. Just you. So I had cross country, baseball, basketball, track—you name it."

An assistant for the junior varsity squad? Forget it. No county school would pay for that. If some fool wanted to volunteer his time, that was up to him, but he wouldn't get paid. Not a chance. As *the* coach under contract, these men coached the junior high teams as well. It was the same story at all twelve county schools. The county coaches faced each other on the baseball diamond, on the basketball court, and again on the track field. It was a good thing they all got along so well. Some of the coaches felt like they saw their players more often than they saw their own families.

Park Sanders had a typical schedule of a county school coach. He woke up early in the morning and arrived at Union Mills School by 7:30 a.m. before the school buses arrived. He taught classes from 8 a.m. to 3 p.m. He patrolled the cafeteria during lunch time to ensure everyone behaved. At 3:15 p.m. Sanders ran the junior high boys through their basketball practice. Calisthenics, running, shooting drills, dribbling drills, passing drills, conditioning, and more running. Sanders taught the boys the proper defensive stance, how to meet your pass, boxing out, and rebounding, the pick-and-roll, zone defense, full-court press, half-court press. And hustle—always hustle.

Sanders knew who his future varsity players would be: *these* boys. There was no getting around it. So it was critical they understood the fundamentals of the game; thus he groomed them and honed their skills. Not only did Sanders need to keep his players in shape physically, he needed to keep them in shape mentally as well. He believed in a good education, but many of the boys didn't see the value of a high school diploma. Most of them did want to be a part of the varsity basketball team though. Almost every boy wanted to run out onto the floor with his teammates in front of the home crowd as fans cheered. He wanted to see his name in the newspaper the next morning. He wanted to read what Bill Redfield and Joe Eyler had to say about how he and his team had played the night before. School boys idolized players like Ray Rosenbaum in Union Mills and Bill Hannon in Westville. Adolescent boys studied their idols and practiced to take their spot on the varsity floor in three or four years' time, but if grades couldn't be maintained, that dream would be dashed in a heartbeat.

Sanders kept close ties to the small cadre of teachers at Union Mills School and when one of the boys—junior high or varsity—began to slip academically, he knew it immediately. At practice that night, Sanders would set out two chairs facing each other and he would have a good heart-to-heart conversation about that young man's behavior and performance in class.

After Sanders sent the junior high boys home, he caught up on some school work, ate a sandwich he'd brought from home, and tried to get a short nap on an old military cot. Since half the Union Mills team lived on farms, Sanders had to give the boys plenty of time to do chores after school or he wouldn't have a team. As a result, the varsity and junior varsity practiced at night. At 6 p.m. the boys who lived in town were expected to be in the gym for practice. The farm boys got extra time to finish milking cows, scarf down dinner, and get back to the gym by 6:30 p.m.

At 8:30 p.m. practice ended, the boys showered and headed home, and Park Sanders settled on a bar stool at Novak's Tavern in downtown Union Mills for a couple of beers. An hour later, he walked out of the tavern and ran into the junior high boys, killing time as boys do.

He told them it was time for everybody to call it a night. The boys who could afford bicycles pedaled home while others hitched a ride on the handlebars. The rest walked along the cold, wet roads. Then, Park Sanders climbed into his Studebaker sedan and drove home, only to repeat the process the following day.

Every other Friday was payday and the township trustee would knock on Sanders' classroom door and give him a hand-written check. For all his work and all his sacrifices, the township paid him the whopping annual sum of $3,492. To earn that kind of income, Sanders had several years of teaching experience. Men with less experience like Bill Yates, George Bock, and Hobart Martin earned less. Martin's salary that year was $2,970.

And to think, most of the coaches had a wife at home, and life for her wasn't an easy one. Struggling to get by on that meager salary while raising kids, these women coped with the schedules of a busy husband and the demands of being a coach's wife in their own ways.

"I had a baby and was at home alone all the time," Betty Clark said. "We didn't have any money." Being the coach's wife in a small town presented an additional set of challenges. Not long after the Clarks arrived in Rolling Prairie, Betty ran into a mother of one of the boys on the team at the local store. When she said hi, the woman ignored her. What had she done? Why didn't she like me, Betty wondered? When Harlan got home, she was close to tears she was so upset. After hearing the story, Harlan knew what was going on and he told her that he had disciplined the mother's son at school—that's why she was sore.

Each woman found a way to make things work the best way possible. "Well, you just tried to please everybody and be good and be agreeable and that's it," Betty said. At one game, Harlan was punishing two of his starting five players by sitting them on the bench. One kid's big brother sat right behind Betty. When Harlan finally put in the little brother the big brother yelled, "Why didn't you tell him to go to hell?" Betty wanted to tell big brother exactly where he could go and who he could take with him, but she knew what kind of trouble that would have started. Instead, she bit her tongue and "just sat there all nice and didn't say a word."

The wife of Clinton Township Head Coach Noel King employed a different strategy to avoid the heat directed at her husband. When the team played in a tournament, she and her boys sat near the top of the gymnasium, far from the team's bench. When irritated fans dragged her husband over the coals and hurled bitter criticism at him, her boys sat safely out of the line of fire.

Every team practiced basketball every night and almost every former player insisted his team practiced harder and had tougher conditioning than anybody else. In Michigan City, the Elston team scrimmaged against the Michigan City Moose, a talented independent league team captained by Head Coach Dee Kohlmeier. The Moose weren't just good. They had won the Indiana state tournament three years in a row and the boys learned just how rough and tumble the game of basketball could get as the Moose tossed the boys all over the court, literally and figuratively.

"We scrimmaged against them one time," Gene Gielow recalled. "Our coach felt that our guys needed to scrimmage against them to get an idea of what it was like with the bigger, older guys. It was a disaster, but it was fun!"

Despite that eye-opening experience, all Gene really wanted at practice was a drink of water. "Scrimmages were tough. One thing I remembered is that he [Coach Kohlmeier] would run us for forty-five minutes to an hour without a break—just run, run, run. You would want water so bad, but he just wouldn't give you a break. You would just keep running. I didn't mind the running so much, I would just get so thirsty." It may seem like cruel punishment, but it wasn't that strange. In that era many believed water might make you sick when playing a competitive sport, or give you a disadvantage, so water intake was kept to a minimum.

The boys in nearby Springfield Township talked about their hard practices too. Each one of the boys had to earn his playing time before every game and Coach Yates treated all of them equally. "There was no means of somebody better than you or whatnot, he just went right out and everybody had an equal chance to win their position or be a back-up player. Same thing in practice, it was as if we were playing the game." Yates liked to keep players on their toes. He didn't have access to a whole troupe of bigger, stronger players like the Moose to condition his boys. So, the twenty-nine-year-old Marine would jump into a drill or scrimmage himself and mix it up with the boys. Show them how the game could be played more physically.

In Westville Coach Charles McComas dragged an old jukebox into the gym. After the boys practiced shooting, dribbling, running drills, and scrimmaging, McComas fired up the well-used jukebox and cranked up the volume. While the music played, the boys ran. Lap after lap around the gym they went while the jukebox played song after song. Around they ran and the juke box played. When the twentieth and final song finished playing, practice ended.

After the Westville boys had gone home, the Clinton Township basketball team arrived at their own gym. They practiced from 7 to 9 p.m. to accommodate the farm schedule. Coach Noel King had the boys start with twenty laps around the gym, followed by loops in which the boys ran up twenty-four stairs, through the auditorium on the second floor, down twenty-four more stairs, then passing through the gymnasium back to the other side again. They did that six times every night. That was just part of their conditioning to get them warmed up. And to think, eight of the ten Clinton boys lived on farms. They already shoveled silage out of the siloes, fed the cows, put the milkers together, milked the cows, lugged the milk cans into the cooling tank, cleaned all the equipment, shoveled manure, and spread fresh straw for bedding. Then they sat through History, English, typing, algebra, Latin, chemistry, and shop. When the bus took them home, again they fed the cows, milked the cows, lugged the milk cans into the cooling tanks, cleaned all the equipment, shoveled manure, and spread fresh straw for bedding. They'd already put in four to five hours of physical labor before racing off to the gymnasium for practice. And *then* the coach felt the boys needed to *warm up*.

Then there was Union Mills. For decades, local legend held that Park Sanders knew he was going to have a good team in 1950, so he got the boys summer jobs working on the railroad to make them stronger. To toughen them up. The story wasn't true—half of the boys grew up on farms and spent their summers engaged in back-breaking manual labor, making hay, feeding cattle, cleaning barns, and harvesting wheat. But the myth about the railroad jobs wasn't without merit. Sanders was a calisthenics instructor for the Army Air Corps during World War II. Throughout his entire life he held onto his army-issued training manual: *FM21-20, War Department, Basic Field Manual, PHYSICAL TRAINING.* In it were hundreds of pictures demonstrating a myriad of calisthenics, strengthening, and conditioning exercises. And Park Sanders' military training reflected in his practice regimen.

"We will be in shape," he told his players. "We may not be the best players in the world, but we will be in shape and we will run their ass off and then we will beat them."

Sanders spoke those words so often that his players could hear the words ringing in their ears sixty years later. Sanders knew the way it went in these small schools. If you were lucky, you had a talented group of boys, but then it could be years before it happened again. He figured if he kept his boys in excellent condition—military, war-ready condition—he could win more games than he lost. It was his only hope for a competitive advantage.

Every practice started with thirty minutes of intense calisthenics that came straight out of the War Department's physical training manual. Push-ups, deep knee bends, planks, trunk rotations, burpees, stomach crunches, balance exercises, core-strengthening exercises, squats, sit-ups, and then the leg lifts. The boys lay on the floor, side by side, in an orderly line and then Sanders gave the word.

Up!

The boys lifted their heels off the floor just a few inches and held them there, waiting for instructions to put them back down. Sanders lectured them on the importance of conditioning and teamwork while they held that position. Stomach muscles convulsed. Leg muscles twitched. Back muscles quivered with fatigue.

And down, Sanders called. After a short rest, the call came again.

Up!

The heels of their canvas sneakers hovered a few inches off the floor while Sanders walked on the boys' stomachs. Yes, *walked!* One end of the line of boys to the other. Varsity and junior varsity. Twenty stomachs in all. His own human boardwalk.

And, down!

Sanders drew only a couple of plays, but the team ran drills until every movement became second nature. Pure instinct. When one of the boys made a mistake he knew the rule. He picked up a medicine ball in the corner of the gymnasium, lifted it over his head, and ran laps. "That was tough to do," Eben Fisher said. "You knew you were gonna get it some time or another. And that's how he trained you. He trained you to be disciplined. That's what he wanted and what he got." Sanders never raised his voice. If a player screwed up, the look on Sanders' face and the tone in his voice said it all. You had disappointed him and nobody wanted to disappoint Coach Sanders. They respected him too much for that.

"He was one great coach. I admire him so much, it's pathetic," Loren Uridel said. "It was great to have a coach like that, that you can admire." Indeed, it was great! Not everyone has experienced a coach like that: someone they could trust, someone they could count on, someone they could admire. Too many young men could have used a Coach Sanders in his life. The boys were lucky to have a coach like him and Sanders was lucky the boys respected him so much because he sure put them through the paces during practice.

Like every other team in the county, the Millers ran. When weather permitted, the boys ran a three-mile loop around the small town of Union Mills. Sanders led the way on his bicycle and the boys tried to keep pace. "Practice was push-ups, sit-ups, run, and run, and run," Loren said. "We never got tired [in a game]."

"He'd run you to death," Eben Fisher said of Park Sanders. "I'd rather play a game than practice. Practice was harder than the ball games. We could run [opponents] to death and we still weren't breathing hard. That's the way he wanted it. He wanted us to keep running with the ball."

So, Union Mills Millers ran, and ran, and ran. Around town, they ran. Back and forth, they ran. Around and around in circles in their tiny little gym, they ran. When the boys weren't running, they did calisthenics until their muscles ached and their bodies exhausted. By the time practice ended, they were physically wasted and ready to go home and go to bed. The boys hit the showers and for many of the county school kids, hot running water, a shower, and an indoor flushing toilet were not taken for granted. These standard bathroom fixtures represented actual luxuries, a perk to all of the punishment imposed on them during practice. If asked what he or she wanted more than anything else in the world, many rural kids would have said indoor plumbing. Sure, a radio, a television, or a car would have been nice, but give me a hot shower and a private toilet *inside*, would ya?

While indoor plumbing had improved dramatically over the previous ten years, rural households still lagged behind those of city dwellers. As a matter of public health, cities connected houses to running water and sewage systems. Out in the country—where a half-mile or a mile separated neighbors—it was a different story. Some rural residents viewed indoor plumbing as an unnecessary luxury. Others couldn't afford it. Some actually regarded an *indoor* toilet as totally absurd—why would anyone in their right mind want to do *that* inside the house? They were people, not barn animals, for Pete's sake.

U.S. Census data captured the plumbing discrepancy. In LaPorte and Michigan City, ninety-seven percent of households had indoor flush toilets and ninety-one percent had an installed bath tub or shower. In the small towns like Westville, Wanatah, Rolling Prairie, and Union Mills, those numbers fell to seventy percent and sixty-three percent respectively. On the rural farmsteads that dominated areas like Clinton Township, only fifty-eight percent had an indoor toilet and fifty-five percent had installed a tub or shower.

In Union Mills the Clindaniel brothers, Bub and Ron, lived without indoor plumbing. During the summer months, the boys relied on the swimming hole that sat adjacent to Mill Pond. Ron and two of his buddies walked there with a single swim suit between them. Being resourceful young men, this didn't present a problem. The first boy jumped into the water with the trunks on, then peeled them off and threw them to the second member of the group who changed into the swimming trunks, dove into the swimming hole, and passed the trunks onto the last boy. Once they finished horsing around—and felt they were sufficiently washed up—the swim trunk process reversed itself and the boys made their exit. The swimming hole served as their favorite spot for a summertime bath, but northern Indiana winters closed the public bath, forcing the boys to bathe in a tub in their own kitchens.

Goog Dunfee was sixteen when his family got indoor plumbing in Stillwell. "We originated back in the old tub days. Goddamn, that was something else," he said. Water was boiled on a stove and then poured into a metal tub that was hauled into the kitchen. A screen was put up to imitate the idea of privacy and then everybody took their turn stepping behind the screen and stripping down for their weekly bath. "My sisters and my one brother—take your turn in the kitchen. In the winter time—colder than hell. All we had was an oil stove."

Ah, but the school had a locker room and the locker room had a shower with hot water. And if you participated in sports, you got to use the showers. The boys luxuriated in the modern accoutrements the school provided after practice and games. "That's why I liked sports," Ron Clindaniel said, "I could take a shower."

Stillwell cheerleaders Lila (Ames) Hagenow and Myrtle (Allmon) Skinner often spent the night at each other's houses. In the morning waiting for the school bus to arrive, a run to the outhouse was in order, but not without a proper plan in place. One girl ran to the privy while the other served as the lookout, standing firm in the driveway, eyes squinting into the horizon searching for a cloud of dust and a yellow school bus approaching from the distance. You didn't dare let the kids on the bus see you coming out of an outhouse! And for good reason. Jane (Shippee) Lindborg and her two sisters grew up on a farm in Springfield Township. "We had an outhouse and the three of us were pretty girls. The neighbor boy would see us go into the outhouse and run over and throw big rocks at it while we were in there. The noise would scare you, that's for sure!"

For those who have never experienced an outhouse, imagine snow falling, drifts forming, and you stare longingly out the window at that small, unheated, unlit outbuilding—the privy, the outhouse—where the wind forced its way between the cracks in the walls. A difficult choice must be made: use a chamber pot, or face the bitter air and walk through the snow. Despite these challenges, outhouses stood proud across the scenic rural countryside, but not all outhouses were created equally. Some of them were built a little bigger to accommodate more than one seat. People are different after all and not everyone wears the same size pants. Different derrieres demanded different seat sizes. A large man compared to a small child, for instance. It was a matter of comfort as much as safety. There was no need to risk getting stuck or, worse yet, falling in. As a result, one hole, two hole, and even three hole outhouses popped up, for those willing to spend a few more dollars. And those with real money? They bought indoor plumbing and a septic system.

"Those were the good old days," one old farmer used to say, "Glad they're past."

15

Basketball Heats Up

In January, the days were short and winter weather gripped the landscape. But basketball carried on indoors and as the season heated up, games provided a welcome escape from the cold, dreary days and nights.

Properly outfitted with new shoes, socks, uniforms, warm-ups, and basketballs, the Springfield Indians seemed ready to go, but the long break and its recent challenges of finding a new school building took a toll on the team. In its first game of the New Year, Springfield traveled to LaCrosse where the home team played its best game of the season and won handily. Springfield's possession of Herman—both the real one and the ghost trophy—was short-lived.

That same night, the two County Conference leaders, Stillwell and Rolling Prairie, faced off in front of a packed house and the game treated fans to a thrilling contest. It was nip-and-tuck to the very end: 4 – 5, 14 – 15, 26 – 23, and finally, 33 – 31. Stillwell won and sat all alone atop the standings, the sole undefeated team in conference play. But it was a precarious perch. Union Mills, Westville, and Rolling Prairie each had a single loss and in one week, Stillwell would host Union Mills.

Michigan City Elston experienced more tough luck. The team had a two point lead with three minutes to play against Elkhart, but couldn't hang on. Final score: Elkhart – 42, Michigan City – 40. But the boys never gave up. They picked themselves up and took a long road trip to Brazil, Indiana.

Coach Kohlmeier wanted his team to push the ball up the floor and attempt seventy shots against Brazil. The boys focused on the shot chart and that was a good thing, because Brazil's scoreboard mystified them. "I remember the scoreboard down there in the Brazil fieldhouse," Gene Gielow said. "It had been made back in 1910 or something because I could not figure it out. They put the numbers up, but the rest of the stuff—like fouls or any other information—I did not have a clue what it was about."

The boys might not have been able to interpret all the lights and other distractions on the scoreboard, but the final score was clear: Michigan City – 51, Brazil – 42. That night the team stayed in a hotel in nearby Terre Haute and the next morning rode the South Shore bus back home.

As basketball action heated up on the court, so did the words on the newspaper pages. After Hammond High beat LaPorte, *Hammond Times* sports editor John Whitaker went on the attack: "Norm Hubner, the LaPorte coach who rates with many of his colleagues as a 'Weeping Willie' seemed reconciled to the 70 – 50 beating at the hands of Hammond High."

But Whitaker wasn't satisfied until he insulted the rest of LaPorte County. "Michigan City is also down this season and none of the smaller schools in that area have shown much . . . Fortunately for Hubner, he doesn't have so-called 'small school' opposition from the likes of Portage, East Gary, Hobart and Griffith."

Joe Eyler came to the county's defense and fired back. In his column, he retorted, "We'll stack 'our' Stillwell, Westville, Rolling Prairie and Union Mills up against your 'small' schools anytime and give you all the basketball you care to see. Careful you don't tread on Michigan City's toes either. Can't say that Hammond High looked exactly like world beaters after eking out an overtime win over the Devils."

A week had passed and the moment had arrived for the Stillwell Vikings' next big test as the team hosted Union Mills in a contest for

county school supremacy. Union Mills needed the victory to stay in the
County Conference race and to create a tie for first place. Stillwell
needed to win to stay atop the standings all by itself. Five-hundred fans
quickly filled the seats inside the gymnasium and more people stood in
corners, along walls, in doorways, and down corridors.[15] Anything to
catch a glimpse of the action or overhear what was happening. Fans
could hardly wait for the game to unfold and nobody went home
disappointed. After one quarter of play, Union Mills led 13 – 10, but
Stillwell defended its home court and closed the gap to two points at
halftime. After three quarters of play, the score was tied, 36 – 36. Each
team knew what was at stake. Each team wanted to win that game
more than any other and eight minutes separated each team from its
destiny.

Park Sanders felt the fourth quarter was the time that his boys
shined. He conditioned them for moments like this against a tough opponent and he trained his boys not to break. And they didn't. Union
Mills poured in nine straight points and that's when things got ugly.

In the restricted period—the last three minutes of the game—a
Stillwell player attempted a free throw but missed the basket completely. An air ball. The referee gave the ball to Union Mills and Stillwell
fans screamed.

Wait a minute! Not so fast!

They knew all about the new rule that gave the team a free throw
and the ball out of bounds whenever a player was fouled during the
restricted period. With the most important game of the year on the
line, fans got caught up in the intensity of the moment. This idiot, this
buffoon, this *knucklehead* gave the ball to the wrong team! The home
crowd hurled insults and obscenities at the official, but the call stood
and the ball went to Union Mills, much to Stillwell fans' frustration.
Stillwell managed to score three more points, but the damage had been
done. When the game ended, Union Mills prevailed, 48 – 42.

In his summary of the game, Joe Eyler wrote that the official was
"abused verbally and pushed around a little physically by some fans

---

[15] The newly organized Stillwell band played its first basketball game that night.

after the game." The official swore not to file a complaint with the IH-SAA, even though he had grounds to do so, but he wouldn't hesitate if it ever happened again. Eyler never wrung his hands deciding whether to call out his readers for displaying anything but the best behavior during sports contests, and he had no problem taking the Stillwell fans to task. He pointed out that the official had gotten the call correct. When the shooting player violated a free throw rule—such as missing the basket entirely—the ball went to the opposing team. *Even during the restricted period.*

"The above is all in the rule book if you take the trouble to look it up," he wrote. "The Stillwell players and Coach Hobart Martin made no complaint whatsoever because they knew the rule. It's a pity that more fans don't attend free basketball clinics where such technicalities are demonstrated and explained."

"It would be unfortunate if the action of a few hot-headed fans, who are too lazy or too sure of themselves, to get acquainted with the rule book would cause the suspension of any team."

Union Mills had forced a tie for first place with Stillwell and things got even better for the team. The high school grew its enrollment to sixty-five students with transfer student Joe Merth, who was a regular contributor to the Hanna High School basketball team. Eager to get every last student involved—especially one who had scored seventy-six points in the season—Coach Sanders immediately included Joe in practices and expected him to add depth to an already talented lineup. Two weeks later, Joe broke his hand and his basketball season came to an end. Such was life in the county schools.

Westville and Rolling Prairie were tied for second place in the county standings and now it was time for the two teams to play their make-up game. The first time they met back in mid-November, it was considered the biggest game of the young season. Fans packed into Westville's gym filling every seat, nook, and cranny where a sight or a sound of the game could be picked up. Even more basketball fans stood outside, unable to squeeze inside the building. With everybody ready to go, there was just one problem: one of the officials didn't show up. An illness in the family kept him from attending and somebody forgot to send a substitute in his place.

Coach Charles McComas frantically dialed one telephone number after another trying to find an official nearby who could make the trip and feed the hungry crowd's appetite for basketball, but it was no use. It was a Friday night, after all, and Friday nights in Indiana meant every team was playing basketball and every official was working in a gym somewhere. The game had to be rescheduled. As fans exited the gymnasium, they each received fifty cent refunds—the price of admission. The Rolling Prairie players saw the people lining up to collect their change and got an idea.

"The boys were getting paid on the way out the door when they hadn't paid to get in," Coach Harlan Clark explained. "They just stuck their paw out there on the way out the door and the people put fifty cents in it. Well, I found out about that and had to tell them to give it back. (Laughing) Goes to show you, kids are still kids and things haven't changed all that much. The boys thought it was pretty funny after that. And it was!"

Now it was time for the make-up game and this time there were two officials present. The game also had added significance. The winner would be tied for first place in the County Conference while the loser would fall out of the championship race.

On January 17 fans again crowded into Westville's gymnasium. Doors opened onto mid-court where the free throw circles intersected the center circle. Pillars rose up from the floor along the nearest sideline, backed by five rows of bleachers. Above the bleachers, those pillars continued their climb up to the high ceiling and held up a balcony where four more rows of fans looked down on the playing floor. The other three sides of the gym were brick walls that marked out-of-bounds. Five-hundred people crammed into that space and found seats while late arrivers stood in the doorway and outside the gym itself.

Rolling Prairie jumped to an early lead before Westville took control. The hometown Blackhawks led the rest of the way and Bill Hannon paced the winners with twenty points. The margin of victory shocked everyone, including Bill Redfield. "Last night's 69 – 36 win over Rolling Prairie stamped Westville as a potent club for sure. The Blackhawks have height and their first five—Bill Hannon, Don Layton, George Thompson, Don Wozniak and Bob Spencer—is a top unit. Without a doubt, any one of the group could break into the starting team of any NIHSC unit."

That same night, Joe Eyler was back in Stillwell to cover its game against out-of-county opponent Grovertown. Since chastising the Stillwell fans for misunderstanding the rules and abusing an official after the Union Mills game, Eyler worried that he might be run out of the gym upon arival: "The Jotter was pleased to learn that he hadn't been hung in effigy when he reported to Stillwell to cover the Vikings-Grovertown game Tuesday night. We found the Stillwell folks just as hospitable and nice as they always have been."

"We can't remember a game that we enjoyed seeing any more than that one. The teams were a dead even match, the crowd behaved itself and we were treated to some of the finest long-distance shooting we have seen in a long time."

The shooting display was no surprise to Coach Hobart Martin. One night after practice, Martin asked Goog Dunfee, Stillwell's perennial troublemaker, to wait up.

Uh-oh, what did I do this time? Goog wondered.

"Put your shoes back on and I'll shoot a few buckets with you," Martin said. So, dressed in bib overalls, Goog put his sneakers back on and he and Coach Martin shot baskets together. Martin taught him how to shoot the long-range set shot that was popular during that era. If a player could shoot a long shot with accuracy, it gave his team a significant advantage. Under Martin's tutelage, Goog got good. *Real* good. One night Martin told him, "If you ever get to a point where you wanted to go somewhere and you would want to shoot a long shot, don't ever hesitate because you have good balance and you learned how."

Goog had been given the green light to shoot from anywhere on the floor and he showed off his skills that night against Grovertown, a team that had gone undefeated and beaten four LaPorte County Conference teams. The Stillwell Vikings avenged the county school's previous losses. "Stillwell unlimbered its twin howitzers, Gene Jones and Ev Dunfee, along with jumping jack Gael Swing to snap Grovertown's winning streak at 13 games," Eyler wrote. "Jones and Dunfee rang in eight of the 30-feet variety between them to keep the Grovertown defense on the fluid side."

Meanwhile, the Wanatah Midgets lost their fourteenth straight game in Union Mills' cigar box of a gymnasium, 63 – 19.[16] And lest anyone accuse Union Mills of unsportsmanlike behavior and running up the score, Eyler included the following comment, "Union Mills used 12 players against Wanatah but still couldn't keep from running away with the game."

Union Mills, Westville, and Stillwell crowded the top of the County Conference and all three teams were peaking at the right time. "County fans are smacking their lips in anticipation of a possible match between Westville and Stillwell in the county tourney," Eyler wrote. "These two teams can fast break like a herd of antelope and if they meet on Michigan City's large floor, watch for a corker."

Ah yes, the county tourney. Basketball fever rose as county school fans anticipated the most important event of the year: the LaPorte County Conference Basketball Tournament.

---

[16] After the game a dance was held in Union Mills' gymnasium. Carl Gumbert's Melody Masters supplied the music.

16

Controversy and the County Tourney

Michigan City had its fair share of top-notch entertainers pass through town. Gene Autry—movie star, television star, theater star, radio star, song writer, singer, cowboy, and rodeo entertainer—was one of America's greatest performers at the peak of his stardom when he rode into town in January 1950. Autry led a parade down Franklin Street and the cowboy performed two shows in his only stop in Indiana that year.

Professional wrestling came to the city as well. Thousands filled the Michigan City High School gymnasium to watch Rudy Kay, Cyclone Anaya, Jumping Joe Savoldi, and Mike Mazurki toss each other around the ring. Other spectators showed up to catch a glimpse of former heavyweight boxing champ Jack Dempsey, who refereed the event. Promoter Tex Nunnally promised there'd be enough tickets to go around and proceeds went to LaPorte County's March of Dimes fund to fight polio.

Autry's shows sold out and the professional wrestlers almost did the same. But nothing drew as many spectators as the game of basketball and the last week of January was county tourney time.

In the hearts and minds of the small-town cheerleaders, fans, and players, the annual county tourney maintained top billing. Even Michigan City and LaPorte residents couldn't help but sense the county tourney's unique aura. On a date with a county school boy, Elston junior Elsie (Kuszmaul) Burns was awed by the environment. "There was more unity there," she said. "At the Sectional there was a BIG LaPorte

Group and then a BIG Michigan City group and then the rest of the schools. But the county tourney—it had a whole different feel to it."

The county tourney was *the tourney*. The Sectional? It was a triumphant season finale where teams went down in a blaze of glory and then waited to hear which big city school won the whole thing in Indianapolis.

When Park Sanders gave Union Mills senior Wes Heironimus the choice to dress for either the county tourney or the Sectional as the team's tenth man, it was an easy choice. The team at least had a chance *to do something* in the county tourney. The Sectional? Yeah, right. Wes made the commonsense choice and left the Sectional tournament to junior Bub Clindaniel to be the team's tenth man.

"The county tournament was a bigger deal than the Sectional," Bill Hannon said. "I don't think we ever had much vision of winning the Sectional and you go from little Westville to play big LaPorte and Michigan City. . . the conference and county tournament were the biggest in my mind. It was exciting to play in the county tournament."

"Well, to us it was more important because most of the time you didn't have a chance against LaPorte or Michigan City in Sectionals, or nobody had in the past," said Bob Spencer. The Sectional was "nothing like the county tournament in importance. I mean, you wanted to do good, but you weren't figuring on winning too much."

But Westville did figure on winning plenty against its county school opponents. In 1949 the Blackhawks won the County Conference championship and the county tourney. In 1950 the boys were on top of the County Conference standings again, tied with Union Mills and Stillwell. They possessed Herman, the traveling trophy yet again. "Yeah, we expected to win it again," Bob said matter-of-factly. And if there was one thing Coach Charles McComas knew, it was winning county tourneys. He'd won three Porter County Conference tournaments as the head coach at Portage High School in 1942, 1943, and 1944. He'd also won the LaPorte County tournament in 1947 and 1949. Things looked good for Westville.

The location of the 1950 LaPorte County Basketball Tournament surprised many, not least of which was the city of LaPorte. The tourney had always been held in LaPorte, but for the first time ever Michigan City played host in Elston High School's gymnasium. But why had it moved?

In years past, some county school fans believed that the LaPorte Police targeted *their* cars with parking tickets during the tournament. Others thought that the operators of the LaPorte Civic insisted on selling the concessions. It had always been managed by students of the various schools and the revenue split between them. Another rumor posited that the cost to insure the event at the LaPorte Civic grew too high. Still others felt that LaPorte took the tournament for granted and assumed it belonged in the county seat and, therefore, it would never leave.

And if LaPorte did have an attitude, who could blame them? Not a single county school could host a twelve-team tournament. Even La-Crosse's brand new gym didn't have the capacity to handle half the crowd that attended the annual county tournament. Michigan City? All the way in the far corner of the county by the lake? Much too inconvenient! Why on earth would the county folk want to drive all the way over there? LaPorte was smack-dab in the center of the county. It was only logical to host the event at the Civic Auditorium. Besides, it was LaPorte's Lincolnway Avenue that attracted most of the farmers on the weekend. That's where the small-town residents chose to do their Friday night shopping. This is where the tournament will stay. This is where it belongs. This is its home.

It was true. Friday was payday and Friday night was shopping night. Rural residents drove into LaPorte to buy goods and services they couldn't get in their small-town general stores. Bright advertising signs lit up Lincolnway Avenue at night. Lights shone through the plate glass storefront windows and illuminated the sidewalks outside. Merchants, taverns, and restaurants stayed open late and the warm lights casting shadows on the sidewalks and streets lured shoppers.

Cars crowded the downtown thoroughfares. Fords and Chevys and Plymouths dominated the streets. Those who had a few more dollars

drove Pontiacs, Buicks, Packards and Chryslers. Others preferred a local product—a Studebaker made in nearby South Bend with its split
windshield and big chrome bullet projecting from the center of the
hood. These cars flashed wide, teethy grins with mouths filled with
chrome. Alluring. They tempted you to slide behind the wheel and take
them for a spin. Their lines flowed down the long sides of the heavy
sheet metal with rear decks sloping toward the ground. Chrome hub-
caps and wide whitewall tires flanked all four corners. The cars were
big and bulky and beautiful.

Drivers navigated their cars down the streets looking for elusive
parking spots near the shopping and all the bright lights. Nobody
wanted to park near the Allis-Chalmers plant, where the streets were
dark and the excitement dimmed. Not only was it a longer walk, but
nobody could see the shiny grin of your car.

Parked along curbs, men lounged in their cars listening to the radio,
or leaned against the fender while smoking a cigarette or chewing to-
bacco, hats rested crooked on their heads. Other men gathered in taverns for a couple of cold ones while women ran through their shopping lists in the various stores. Children sat in backseats or were towed
along like unwilling sheep as their mothers made their rounds. Other
kids roamed alone, exploring the city's streets and alleyways. The lucky
ones had a few pennies to pick up some cheap candy in a confectionery
or five-and-dime.

While the merchants welcomed shoppers spending money in their
town, some LaPorte residents held a grudge against the out-of-towners.
"Those farmers are messing up the streets and everything," one complained. "It's all dumb farmers." Some took offense to these words,
but most shrugged it off with a laugh. It was part of the back-and-forth
between the city folk and their country cousins that had gone on for
decades.

But there was growing frustration among the country cousins with
regard to *their* tournament and the small schools and small towns held
the biggest bargaining chip of all: the LaPorte County Conference Basketball Tournament. When Michigan City merchants got wind of the
growing malcontent among county school fans, they smelled a golden

opportunity and they knew where to make their sales pitch: a tavern in Westville.

"Well, you know. The county tourney was always in LaPorte," said Stillwell Coach Hobart Martin. "At a county coach's meeting at West Point—it ended up the County Coach's Association was the one that started to get it moved to Michigan City. A guy who was the head of a bank was a big pusher getting the tournament [there]. I know some of the people in LaPorte had the idea it couldn't be played anywhere but LaPorte, but it was. Ultimately, I think it had something to do with revenues . . . there was a fee to play at the Civic in LaPorte and in Michigan City, it was zero. Nothing. Why would we pay if we don't have to? Then we better go to Michigan City."

Michigan City welcomed those dumb farmers with open arms. The city wanted to lure the county's rural residents away from Lincolnway Avenue by showcasing its own business district: Franklin Street. The retail merchants of Michigan City applied a full-court press on the coaches and principals. Not only was Michigan City willing to host the tournament in its high school gym—which sat twelve-hundred more fans than the Civic Auditorium—but they wanted these fans to come to Michigan City, have a good time, visit their businesses, and most of all spend some money. In an aggressive move to gain the upper hand, the city rolled out the red carpet.

In the Michigan City newspaper, retailers took out large advertisements accompanied by pictures of the basketball teams and cheerleading squads. Up and down Franklin Street, stores decorated their businesses with signs and letters cheering on the county schools.

GO TROJANS! read the paint in the window of Hirsch's Department Store while Buchanan's Dry Cleaning painted, GOOD LUCK, CLINTON TWP! in its storefront. A newspaper ad that featured pictures of the team and the cheerleaders enticed fans with $1.69 men's denim dungarees and 75¢ nylon hose. The other eleven teams got the same treatment.

Arnie's Griddle and Sears Roebuck & Company pulled for the Wanatah Midgets.

The 8th Street Café and Lakeshore Cement made the Hanna Panthers feel right at home.

If Coach George Bock and the Union Township Tigers were hungry, they found a friendly face and a sign reading, WELCOME, UNION TOWNSHIP TIGERS! in the window of The Original Kitchen of the Italian Village.

Ideal Paint and Wallpaper ran an ad saying, "Hi, Neighbor! Bring your Painting Problems to us!"

The Bulldogs of Rolling Prairie found Blackmond's Jewelry and Montgomery Ward glad to see them. Montgomery Ward ran a three-day special on wool-lined rayon ties (77¢) and Sanforized flannel work shirts ($2.28).

The Hickory Pit and City Television and Radio welcomed the Union Mills Millers team, cheerleaders, and rooters to town.

LaCrosse residents looking for a new watch should have stopped by Olsen and Ebann Jewelry. Not only did their storefront root on the Tigers, but it held a "Dime a Day Watch Sale" during the tournament, while The Ladies Shop tempted women with a woven gingham plaid shirt for $2.98.

Kresge's Store and Michigan City Electric Company welcomed the Stillwell Vikings to Michigan City, Indiana!

L. Missal Decorating welcomed the Mill Creek Wildcats to town as did the Eastport Laundry & Dry Cleaning.

JC Penney and Grieger's Clothing Store encouraged the Kingsbury Kings to give it their all in the county tourney.

The windows of Korn's Televisions and Smith's Shoes pulled for the Westville Blackhawks and, last but not least, Cush & Ginther Men's Store wished the Springfield Indians well in a *full-page ad*.

In the newspaper pages, the local theaters beckoned fans to catch a movie during the tournament. The Tivoli ran *Chicago Deadline* with Alan Ladd and Donna Reed. The Lido Theater featured Tyrone Power and Al Jolson in *Rose of Washington Square* or Mickey Rooney and Wallace Beery in *Slave Ship*.

Yes, the county tourney was a big deal and Michigan City matched the county school fans' enthusiasm notch for notch. It was a whole new environment compared to the previous year's tournament. Players and fans noticed the merchants' efforts and they loved it.

"Stores would decorate their windows with one team or another," Bob Spencer said. "In those days, everybody would have a store window and there would be a basketball with pictures of Westville or Union Mills or somebody. There was a lot of action like that. It was kind of nice because you would get a little notoriety and whether or not they were supporting a team, they would get a buck out of the fans. Michigan City did that. LaPorte didn't really do that."

In the ongoing battle between the two cities, Michigan City scored a major coup.

Year in and year out, the LaPorte County Basketball Tournament promised excitement, and for good reason. Ten of the twelve schools had won the tourney at least once. It had been won back to back seven times. Bill Homan, a junior at Clinton, explained that "In the county schools, it was just a matter of the boys you had that year. If you had a couple good players, you were the good team and the next year it'd be somebody else."

Hobart Martin made the same point: "I was fortunate having a bunch of good guys. I can still remember Lou Holtz making the remark that if you get a real good quarterback on your football team, that makes a good coach. (Laughing). I think that is the same old thing. You have to have players."

Get a talented group of boys growing up together and they would dominate the county their junior and senior years. When that bunch graduated, it was somebody else's turn.

Only Kingsbury and Clinton had never had the players at the right time to win the county tourney. Tiny Clinton, the smallest school in the county, had such a shortage of boys in the high school that they couldn't field a proper B-team to play the preliminary game before the varsity in 1946 and 1947. So the coach improvised. The junior high boys suited up and played on the B-team. "And we beat them from time to time," Jim Smoker noted.

In 1949 Clinton came as close as it ever had to capturing the elusive county tourney trophy. The Trojans entered the tournament with a strong record and advanced all the way to the championship game. But as luck would have it, Westville had a good group of players too. Fans overwhelmingly backed the hapless Trojans. Everybody loved an underdog and everybody in the gymnasium rooted for Clinton. Everybody wanted to see them win their first tournament. Everybody wanted—no, they *demanded*—the parity that the county tourney had afforded them. Everyone felt that Westville didn't need a seventh tourney title. It was Clinton's turn and they had the boys to do it too! Or so the fans had hoped. Despite the overwhelming support, Clinton lost by five points. Fans booed—yes, booed!—the Westville Blackhawks as they accepted the championship trophy.

Joe Eyler reminded readers of the previous year's tacky display and pushed fans to change their behavior. "Westville's appearance in the gym brought on the 1950 chapter of 'the world against Westville.' Last year the 'Hawks were roundly booed when they stepped on the floor to receive the title trophy. If last night was any indication, they will get more of the same throughout this tourney unless fans begin to act like adults."

The tournament opened on Wednesday night and Wanatah faced its arch rival LaCrosse in the first game. The Wanatah Midgets had been the only team to win the county tourney three consecutive years, but 1950 wasn't their year to recapture those glory days some sixteen years earlier. The team still hadn't won a game. So, Coach John Dunk gave his one true scorer the freedom to take every possible shot he could find. "Stars were many, but certainly none outshone Arnold Rosenbaum of Wanatah who was high point man for the night with 27 markers," wrote Joe Eyler. "He proved to be a driving, ball-hawking demon who seemed to be everywhere at once. He was given a tremendous ovation by the crowd when he fouled out in the fourth quarter."

While Rosenbaum stole the show, LaCrosse's Ralph Meiss proved to be the difference maker in the game. In the Tiger's eleven-point victory, Meiss made twelve of the sixteen free throws he attempted. Wanatah fell to 0-15 on the season.

In the second game Rolling Prairie's big men—Bill Rehlander (6'2") and Walt Zolman (6'4")—vastly outsized Hanna, whose tallest boy was five-feet-ten-inches tall. But Hanna's head coach had a plan. He deployed a shifting zone defense that kept Rolling's big men away from the basket and created a number of successful fast breaks. Hanna scored the tournament's first upset as it rolled to a nine-point victory.

In the nightcap, the Springfield Indians played Mill Creek. The Indians trailed the Wildcats for three straight quarters. Then Coach Yates got his boys riled up for the final quarter. Yates stood up, sat down, and pounded his hands together. He hollered at the officials, and he hollered encouragement to his players. Coaching, coaching, coaching. Talking, talking, talking. *Wild Bill* Yates worked the sidelines like nobody had ever seen. He toed the line—no, he *danced* on the line—between acceptable and unacceptable behavior, all the while sharply dressed with his shined shoes gleaming under the gymnasium's bright lights. The Springfield boys matched their coach's intensity and pulled out a seven-point victory. Yates couldn't have been prouder of his young men and he let them know it.[17]

But Springfield's victory couldn't salve the wound that had been inflicted that week. The headline spelled out the bad news: "Available Funds Insufficient For New Springfield School." The township was short $100,000 to rebuild its school that had been destroyed by the December fire and state law restricted its ability to raise additional taxes or to borrow more money to close the gap. The Springfield Township trustee received letters from the state superintendent of public instruction as well as Indiana Governor Schricker informing him that no other government fund sources would be available either. More meetings would be held, but unless the township could come up with $100,000, the future of the high school looked bleak.

Joe Eyler again mentioned the dirty word—consolidation—in his column: "One thing that has been turning over in the minds of county

---

[17] Springfield's win led Bill Redfield to write, "Mrs. Dee Martin, wife of the Stillwell coach, is a teacher at neighboring Mill Creek, and they are rivals all the way. With Mill Creek out of the tourney, she can pull for Stillwell now without becoming an outcast."

basketball fans recently is the problem of consolidation and what it would do to the net sport among county schools."

Sandwiched between Michigan City, LaPorte, and Rolling Prairie, the township's location seemed ideal for it to join with another school. As a fellow county school, Rolling Prairie might have sounded like a good partner, but it was quickly outgrowing its own space. As Eyler pointed out, "It is equally obvious that Rolling Prairie will have school children literally falling out of the windows and doors when the war baby crop hits in a year or two."

It was a familiar story all across the county. Township school buildings were old, outdated, and undersized. They couldn't accommodate the baby boomers who were about to start first grade. Eyler spelled out his vision for a whole new set of schools that included football teams, "tennis and golf teams as well as top notch baseball and track teams." He saw the county schools competing with out-of-county opponents with bigger and better athletic programs, rather than the same eleven opponents that sometimes had difficulty filling a roster. "We can continue the dream to the point where the 12 LaPorte county schools have been consolidated into four. Think of the athletic material available under such setups."

Eyler wanted everyone to know he was loyal and dedicated to the county school teams and he'd come to their defense in the past,

> But no one can escape the fact that county schools face an almost overwhelming task of winning in the LaPorte sectional. It took Rolling Prairie 17 years to win the first bunting for a county team and it could be twice that long before another county school comes through.
>
> At the present rate of sectional tourney winning by county schools it would take some 300 years before each of the 12 could win once. We don't want to wait that long, do you?
>
> To further our argument for consolidation of county high schools for purely athletic reasons consider these figures compiled by Ray Bevington, coach at Tippecanoe:
>
> Of 1,280 sectionals in the past 20 years, 73 per cent have been won by schools with enrollment of more than 200. In addition, 91 per cent of the regionals, 99 per cent of

the semifinals and 100 per cent of the finals over the last 34
years have been won by so-called large schools.

He pointed out that nineteen schools had dominated the state championship and the average enrollment of the winners had been 1,092 students. Meanwhile, the twelve county schools averaged just sixty-eight
students.

His words made perfect sense, of course, but county school fans
dismissed Eyler's ideas just as easily as they had ignored Professor
B.B.'s (Carl Sanders) call for larger, safer gymnasiums. The farmers and
small-town residents had no interest in consolidating. They lived for
those small-town rivalries and if that cracker box of a gym was good
enough for them twenty years ago, why, it would be good enough for
next year's team as far as they were concerned. Furthermore, they just
didn't like change all that much. If it ain't broke, why fix it?

While the players competed to win the county tourney on the
basketball floor, the cheerleaders competed too. A cheering award and
accompanying trophy went to the best cheer. The Clinton Township
yell leaders' new skirts were ready just in time for the team's game on
Thursday night. Every school took its yells and cheers seriously and the
county tourney was the venue to showcase their skills. With the student
body standing behind the cheerleaders, they chanted in unison, "We
are the Trojans, the mighty, mighty Trojans!"

In Union Mills, developing original cheers was serious business, as
Pinki (Haspel) Bowman explained.

> We would go down in the gymnasium and we would prac-
> tice. Whenever you had an idea, you would show it to the
> other girls and then you would work the routine out and
> then go from there.
>
> There was more of a competition. It was just the way
> the boys were with the teams. They didn't like the other
> boys. They would be cordial and friendly and everything to
> them but—the cheerleaders—I would not have anything to
> do with (laughing). Just meet them and say hello and that
> was it.

And then if they showed up with a cheer that was simi-
lar to ours, and they did some of the same things we did, we
would whine and complain about it. It was especially irk-
some when they would come up with one of your cheerleading routines. Everything that we would be saying, they
would be saying on their side of the floor. It was like,
"Where did they get that? They stole that from us!

Stillwell's cheerleaders also practiced in the middle of the day, since
none of the girls had a car and few lived within walking distance of the
school. "For us it was very important to be there and people cheered.
They really did! It was a lot of fun. We just loved it," said Lila (Ames)
Hagenow. The girls carried a large cone-shaped megaphone to amplify
their voices. "We did the same things over and over and over again.
We would try and think of something new, but we didn't do any acro-
bats like they do today." That was left to the girls in Springfield.

Marilyn (Marquart) Buerger and her sister Elaine were the pioneers
of acrobatic cheerleading in LaPorte County. They led the way in getting their fans excited to cheer loudly and to back the boys on the
court. The girls yelled out the cadence, *Two bits, four bits, six bits a dollar!*
All for Springfield— and at that point Elaine leapt into the air, landed
squarely on her sister's shoulders, then thrust her hands up with a big
smile—*stand up and holler!* Springfield fans jumped to their feet and
threw a barrage of hoots, hollers, yells, and applause.

In the second round of the county tourney, Springfield faced Union Mills. Just as fans recognized Wild Bill Yates for his unbridled enthusiasm on the sidelines, fans knew Coach Sanders when he sat on the
bench. "Charles Sanders, Union Mills coach, stood out as he again kept
his hat on during the entire game. He may check his coat, but never the
hat," Bill Redfield wrote. Having been upset by Springfield right before
Christmas break, Union Mills had no intention of letting that happen
again. Union Mills led from the opening tip-off to the end of the game
and beat Springfield by ten points.

The county tourney prepared the boys for the manic pace of the
Sectional tournament and by the end of Friday night, twelve teams
played eight games in four days. So far, Hanna represented the lone

upset in its win over Rolling Prairie and only four teams remained: Westville, LaCrosse, Stillwell, and Union Mills. The teams would play Saturday afternoon and then after a five hour break, the two winners played in the championship game that night. This gave fans ample time to do their weekend shopping in Michigan City instead of LaPorte.

Kids from the twelve county schools gathered in Michigan City for the biggest event of the year and they saw pictures of their teams posted in storefront windows. The names of their schools appeared everywhere. Those county fans owned the town that weekend and they reveled in the excitement. It was a giant celebration. Mardi Gras in the frozen air of northern Indiana. They celebrated their own religion—the Hoosier religion—basketball.

The county school kids stormed Franklin Street, undeterred by the bitter cold winds that whipped off Lake Michigan. Their letter sweaters kept them warm. Yes, the letter sweaters! Sturdy wool that weighed heavy on the shoulders with thick bands at the waist and wrists. Each one sported a letter of the alphabet that beamed pride for your school and town. There were letter sweaters in every color of the rainbow.

Purple sweaters with a golden *S* stitched to the front, or black with a golden *K*. Maroon and white with a giant *U*, orange with a blue *MC*, black with a white *H*, gold with a blue *RP*. Maroon with a white *S*. White with a royal blue *C*, green with massive *L*, red with a giant *W*, gold with a blue *UT*, and orange with a black *W*.

Those sweaters seemed to be everywhere because they *were* everywhere. Nearly every boy had to participate in one sport or another out of necessity in the county schools. The girls wore them too as the letter sweater was the dominant cheerleading uniform coupled with a long skirt, a Peter Pan collar, and saddle shoes. "Try cheering in one of those things," Marilyn (Marquart) Buerger said. No easy chore, she'd have you know. Jumping up and down, running this way and that, cheering your little heart out in a crowded gymnasium full of lights and fans and sweating basketball players and all that weight of virgin wool draped around your torso.

A colorful alphabet soup bobbed in and out of the downtown restaurants, businesses, and movie theaters Wednesday, Thursday, and

Friday nights. And if someone held a grudge against the dumb farmers who crowded downtown streets on shopping night, some of the students did little to dissuade those opinions.

A movie theater would fill with so many kids from so many different schools, it was impossible to keep order as they frittered about in the dark. The theater manager would shut off the projector, turn up the lights, and ask everyone to stay quiet, but it never lasted. Unwitting adults who happened into the theater that day got more than they bargained for. Invariably they would ask for their money back and management politely obliged.

Sorry, the kid behind the register would say. It's county tourney week, you know.

One year, a couple of farm boys captured a bunch of sparrows and stowed them in a feed sack. After the movie started, one of the boys pulled the sack out from under his wool jacket and released the birds. Confused and disoriented, the sparrows fluttered in front of the flickering light, the birds' wings flapped madly as they tried to figure out which way to go. Feathers and bird droppings rained down on the audience as people screamed in the dark. The sparrows eventually clung to the silver screen wondering what to do next. The film stopped, the lights came up, and the manager investigated the scene. It was all in good fun and the businesses endured the shenanigans as their cash registers sang.

17

Rematch

With all of the rural residents watching basketball and experiencing the sights and sounds of Michigan City, LaPorte's Lincolnway was quiet on Friday night. Since the Civic Auditorium had an empty weekend on its calendar, LaPorte scheduled back-to-back home games on Friday and Saturday night. Friday was a rematch with its hated rival: the Michigan City Elston Red Devils.

The two cities competed for business. They competed for visitors. They competed for workers. They competed for shoppers and the two newspapers competed for readers. And when it came to basketball—the most beloved game in Indiana—the two cities were fierce rivals. The teams made up two of the ten schools in the Eastern Division of the NIHSC and all ten teams played each other once a year, but that would never do for LaPorte and Michigan City. No, siree! Neither school trusted the other to play just *one* game. They needed two games—one on each home court. So, one game served as the official conference matchup and the other was the grudge match. The chance to even the score or double the pain. And the opportunity to fill the athletic department coffers because the game always sold out.

"It was a true, true rivalry," Ralph Jones said. "I am sure they didn't like us and we didn't like them. It was the game of the year type of thing, each of them." Twenty-five years later, Jones attended a game as a fan and couldn't bear the bitterness if Michigan City won. And

vice versa, the men from Michigan City couldn't stand a LaPorte victory either.

"Ah, the rivalry with LaPorte—I think that was a history," Lawrence Witek said. "You grew up with that. As a freshman or sophomore you would hear this little quiet talk, 'Well, we've got to beat
LaPorte.' Why? Why not Gary or somebody? So that rivalry was just
ingrained in you, only because it was always talked about."

Fellow senior Joe Tanski felt the same kind of pressure. "Constant,
man. We always went at each other. There was no love loss between
each other. There was always a rivalry in every sport no matter what
you played—football, basketball, baseball—you name it. When we met
each other, there was always gonna be a grudge game no matter what.
That thing has never calmed down through all the years. This was the
two big cities going after each other and you were gonna play your
heads off to knock each other off."

Elston had taken the first game between the two schools and now
they met in the Civic Auditorium to play their heads off.

Compared to Elston High School, the LaPorte Civic was a great
place to watch a game. Sure, it wasn't as big, but it had individual stadium seats with seat backs. Although it was comfortable for the spectators, the playing floor wasn't as great and provided a home court advantage for the Slicers. At least as far as Michigan City senior Gene
Gielow was concerned, it did. "The Civic had an absolute dense floor.
When you dribbled, you had to work at it to get the ball back up. It was
a bad, bad floor." Dealing with a dead floor was one thing, but the
home town crowd did its part to make the game unwinnable too.
"There were these pipes bolted to the floor to hold the baskets in place
and there were kids shaking the pipes of the basket when the other
team was getting ready to do something," recalled Elston sophomore
Jerry Jones.

As the players felt the intensity on the court, it was just as intense
between the people who *watched* the game and emotions sometimes
boiled over. Elston junior Elsie (Kuszmaul) Burns experienced the rivalry first hand when she sat next to a LaPorte fan. "At the Sectional
one year I was a student sitting next to an adult from LaPorte. The

game was back and forth and this guy bet me a box of popcorn LaPorte would win. In the end Michigan City pulled it out. He was so mad, he just stormed out! I never did get my popcorn, but I sure would have paid up if I'd lost the wager. That's how intense the rivalry was."

A capacity crowd filled the Civic. As game time approached, the Slicers lined up in the locker room, climbed the steps to the main foyer where fans cheered on the boys as they shot through the tunnel and into the crowded auditorium. The pep band sounded their arrival and a sea of black and orange pounded their hands and feet in unison. The Slicers cheering section taunted the Michigan City team and fans. They clapped their hands in unison and chanted over and over again:

There ain't no City, but the ci-ty dump!

There ain't no City, but the ci-ty dump!

Joe Eyler captured the spirit of the game: "Last night's 'contest,' to use the term with levity, was a typical donnybrook between the two old rivals at the Civic auditorium."

The tension was thick as the two teams stormed up and down the court. Back and forth they went. Up and down the hardwood floors the players sprinted. Each team wanted to gain those ever-so-important bragging rights. The two teams traded baskets and Michigan City held the upper hand throughout most of the game. But in the end, LaPorte came from behind and redeemed itself with a six-point victory.

At least those singing cash registers back in Michigan City helped minimize the sting of that bitter loss for some fans, even if just a little bit.

Saturday afternoon the final four county teams squared off. In the first game, the LaCrosse Tigers gave Westville a better fight than anybody had anticipated. LaCrosse's Ralph Meiss put in another outstanding performance from the free throw line, hitting ten of twelve shots. The kid had a knack for getting to the free throw line (thirty-six times during the tourney) and he was better than anybody in the county when he got there. In an era when good free throw shooters averaged fifty percent, Meiss converted seventy-eight percent. But the

Blackhawks maintained a narrow lead throughout the whole game and won by five points.

In the second afternoon game, Stillwell and Union Mills met for the second time. Only two weeks earlier Union Mills delivered Stillwell's first conference loss and the Vikings wanted redemption. The two teams proved to be equal matches as the score seesawed back and forth with several ties and lead changes. In the fourth quarter, Union Mills' conditioning showed as the Millers poured it on, but Stillwell fought back. Back and forth, the two teams sprinted up and down the floor. Defense was tenacious. Neither team wanted to give an inch. This was the biggest tournament of the year. Nobody had a chance of winning the Sectional. If they wanted to take home a tournament trophy, it would have to happen here. It would have to be now!

When the game ended, the scoreboard captured the spirit of the contest, 46 – 44. Advantage: Union Mills. The championship game would be a rematch between Westville and Union Mills.

As for Stillwell, they had advanced to the county tourney semifinals two years in a row and both times the boys fell short of advancing to the championship game. They were three points shy in 1949 and just two points shy in 1950.

That afternoon, Norm Hubner attended the county tourney and "was more impressed by Ray Rosenbaum of Union Mills than any other cager in the county tourney," reported Joe Eyler. "Hubner particularly liked the way 'Rosey' pivoted and shot with either hand."

That night, Hubner was back to work in the Civic as his boys hosted the Archers of Fort Wayne South Side. Before the game, a ceremony honored the 1925 Slicers team that advanced to the finals of the state basketball tournament in Indianapolis. Hubner was a sophomore at LaPorte then and played with several of those men the following season when LaPorte repeated its success and advanced to Indianapolis the second straight year.

In front of two-thousand fans, the LaPorte Slicers won by five points and Hubner beamed with pride. His boys had beaten the hated Michigan City Red Devils in an official conference affair. The team scored a win against a tough Fort Wayne South Side team in front his old teammates. He was proud of the level of basketball his boys had played and must have felt they were now the favorites to win the up-coming Sectional tournament.

Back in Michigan City, thousands of fans made their way back into Elston gymnasium for the championship game at 8 p.m. The first meeting between Union Mills and Westville had proved to be a big one. The two schools tied for the conference lead and in head-to-head battle, the Millers held the upper hand. Westville had only gotten tougher as the season progressed. This time, they met on the big floor—not that puny excuse for a gymnasium in Union Mills—and the Blackhawks had revenge on their minds. The big prize—the LaPorte County Conference Basketball Tournament trophy—was up for grabs. Westville looked to extend its dominance over the rest of the county schools and win its eighth tourney title. Union Mills wanted to close the gap and capture its fourth title and reclaim Herman the traveling trophy in the process.

As the game drew near, Park Sanders prepared his Millers the same as usual. He kept the mood light. "Park Sanders always had us ready," Eben Fisher said. "He'd make you feel comfortable before the game. He would relax you. Maybe he would tell you a joke or something he used to do in the service, but he'd give you a real down-to-earth calm-ness before a ball game. He'd get you thinking you could beat anybody and you did. We got to thinking that way—we could win this game. That's the attitude he got us into."

Sanders stood calmly in the locker room and told the boys a funny story about how young GIs wooed British girls with panty hose and chocolate from their C-rations during World War II. The boys would need every bit of confidence they could muster. They needed to feel they could beat anybody. In the other locker room sat a hungry Westville team. They hadn't forgotten that early season loss at Union Mills and Coach McComas kept his boys focused on the prize: the county tourney championship.

The game started with star centers Bill Hannon and Ray Rosen-baum trading points. Westville took the lead. Union Mills closed the gap. Westville finished the first quarter with a four point lead. Westville nearly doubled up the score on Union Mills early in the second quarter, 15 – 8. Union Mills took over: two points for Loren Uridel, four for Tony Hadella, and two more for Rosenbaum. Hannon countered. Westville up by one. George Thompson added two more for Westville, then Uridel tied it up. Thompson scored again. Rosenbaum countered. Westville hit the last shot of the half and that gave them a two point advantage. Union Mills found itself caught in its second tight contest of the day.

The crowd hustled to the concession stands and back to their seats. This battle of champions would go down to the wire and nobody wanted to miss a minute of the action.

When the game resumed in the second half, Union Mills quickly tied the score, but Westville struck back and recaptured the lead. Back and forth it went and the crowd couldn't believe its collective eyes.

What a game! What a battle of great teams! What a battle of talented big men!

Two great centers, Hannon and Rosenbaum, fought for rebound after rebound, hook shot after nifty pass. Rosenbaum held Hannon to six points on the game, but don't forget the other guys! Don Layton scored eighteen points for Westville. And Tony Hadella, the tough-nosed little forward from Union Mills, showed why he led the county in scoring. Union Mills finished the third quarter with a five-point lead. As the fourth quarter opened, evidence of the Millers' extensive condi-tioning showed. Union Mills could not be worn down and the lead grew to eight points.

What happened next was a matter of some debate. Park Sanders instructed his team to hold the ball. After all, victory seemed imminent. But there was just one problem. "Hadella wouldn't do what the coach told him to do," recalled senior Wes Heironimus. "He wouldn't just hold the ball. He kept dribbling and shooting it. That gave Westville an opportunity to get back into the game and win it."

Bob Spencer remembered it differently. "We weren't shooting. I didn't think we were that far down. I was taking the ball away from Tony Hadella most of the time."

Regardless the details, the door opened and Westville capitalized. With 1:05 to play in the game, Westville's Don Layton tied the score, 41 – 41. He was fouled on the play and he missed his free throw, but since the game was in the restricted period, Westville retained possession of the ball. Seconds later, Hannon scored a jump shot. 43 – 41, Westville. On the other end of the court, Westville fouled Woody Jacobs, who made his free throw. 43 – 42. The Millers kept the ball with just seconds left in the game and set up a final, game-winning shot. The ball went to Ray Rosenbaum. He moved, took a hook shot, and missed—but he was fouled! Westville fouled him with seconds left in the game! Ray stepped to the free throw line to tie the score, but he missed. In the few remaining seconds of the game, a scramble for the ball ensued, but nobody scored. Westville held onto a one-point victory to capture its eighth county tourney title.

A game like that deserved no winner and no loser. Even Charles McComas, the victorious coach, felt it was a shame one of the two teams had to lose and thought it was too bad the trophy couldn't be sawed in half. But it could! It could be sawed in half! But nobody would go for that and McComas knew it as well as everybody else. In sports, somebody must win and somebody must lose. And that night, in the game that mattered most, Westville won and Union Mills lost.

Bill Hannon accepted the tournament championship trophy on behalf of his team and Ray Rosenbaum settled for the sportsmanship award. The dejected look on Rosenbaum's face said it all. While the Blackhawks celebrated and cut down the nets, the Millers were awarded the game ball as a consolation prize. That was it. The biggest shot at a tournament championship the boys had dreamed possible had slipped through their fingers.

The emcee presented one final award that night. The cheer award went to the Springfield High School cheerleading team. The Marquart sisters' acrobatics earned the team the trophy and all five girls received a corsage, courtesy of the Michigan City Retail Merchants.

When the Union Mills team returned to school, Gene Goad added the consolation prize (the game ball) to the three practice balls in Park Sanders' army duffle bag. Then, the worst-for-wear practice ball—coated in shoe polish—was placed in the school's trophy case with the words COUNTY TOURNEY RUNNER-UP 1950 scrawled in white grease pencil on one of its panels.

Two weeks later, the twelve county school principals met in LaPorte at the Wildwood Inn to take inventory of the tournament and divvy up the receipts. Nine-thousand fans attended the tournament, but profits dropped more than twelve percent from $2,831 in 1949 to $2,480 in 1950.

A delegation of LaPorte businessmen from the Chamber of Commerce and Business Bureau attended the meeting and appealed to the principals and coaches to return the county tourney to its "home" in LaPorte.

Joe Eyler pitched in to help and wrote, "It is interesting to note that despite claims of superior seating capacity and many gifts by Michigan City, this year's county tourney failed to attract as many people and made less money than last year's show at the Civic auditorium. Most county schools would be unable to operate their athletic programs without the profits of the county tourney. This year each school got about $30 less than last year which hurts because of the tight situation."

Eyler even acknowledged his city's neglect of the county schools and implored them to look at the facts. "Admittedly, LaPorte slipped badly in past years. The county tournament had become such a fixture here that laxity allowed Michigan City to move in and take over this year. The Michigan City Chamber of Commerce and Retail Merchants association spared no effort to get the tourney and keep it with free banquets, free fire and police protection, free this and free that. Despite the fact that the county schools were given more elaborate treatment this year they should remember that their revenue was down."

That same day, Bill Redfield reported the same financial results but pointed out that "The difference in the school split can be traced to season ticket sales. At LaPorte in 1949 it was just about necessary to buy a season ticket to get a seat. With the local gym seating 1,000 more, many fans from schools whose teams are down decided to see just their own team play and they didn't have to buy a season book to be sure of getting in." Redfield was right. Individual session tickets had swelled to 3,094 in Michigan City, compared to 1,925 the previous year.

Beyond that statement, Redfield was quiet on the whole affair of where the county tourney belonged. In his daily column he did not appeal to county school officials to keep the tourney in Michigan City. He made no sales pitch to the public. Two weeks earlier while the county tourney was in full swing, Redfield had invited the twelve county coaches and their wives to his apartment in Michigan City. When the coaches arrived, they discovered Redfield's bathtub filled with bottles of ice cold beer.

The twelve county school principals met in the county school superintendent's office on February 14 and, acting on advice from their coaches, cast their votes.

The 1951 county basketball tournament would remain in Michigan City.

The LaPorte Chamber of Commerce and Joe Eyler never stood a chance.

Arnie Rosenbaum of Wanatah
wins the opening tip-off against
LaCrosse to start the county
tourney (top).

Gerald Masterson of Hanna
grabs a rebound against Rolling
Prairie (left).

Clinton fans cheer on their
mighty, mighty Trojans at the
county tourney (below).

*See Notes & Information at the end of
the book for more names.*

Ray Rosenbaum grabs a rebound against Springfield in the county tourney (above).

Bill Hannon cuts down the net after Westville won the county tourney (left).
Courtesy of Bill Hannon

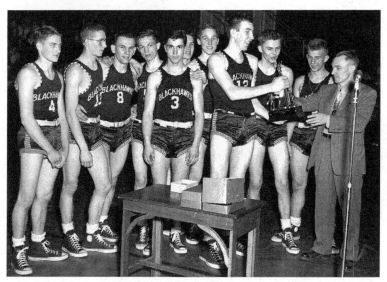

Westville receives the county tourney trophy after defeating Union Mills. Left to right: Bob Elliott, Bob Spencer, Jerome Sawicki, Roger Pearson, Don Layton, Joe White, George Thompson, Bill Hannon, Ron Wozniak, Bill Swift, and Coach Charles McComas.

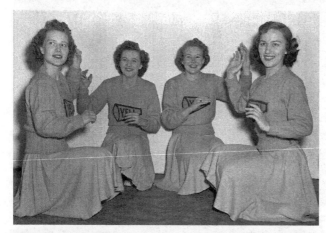

Springfield cheerleaders (top).
L to R: Elaine Marquart, Gloria Benford, Barbara John-ston,
Pat Gipprich, and Marilyn Marquart.

Stillwell cheer-leaders (middle).
L to R: Beverly Dunfee, Wilma Bartz, Lila Ames, and Myrtle Allmon.

Union Mills cheerleaders (bottom).
Laverne "Pinki" Haspel, Phyllis Scott, and Mildred Frank.
Courtesy of the LaPorte County Historical Society.

LaCrosse School's new gym on opening night (top). Courtesy of the LaPorte County Historical Society

Opening tip off of a LaPorte game in the Civic Auditorium (left). Courtesy of the LaPorte County Historical Society.

Wanatah yell leaders. Bonnie Marks, Bessie Prowant, and Shirley Scholz.

Kingsbury Kings cheerleaders (top). L to R: Leona Solmos, Norma O'Dell, Darlene Schoof, and Betty Griffin. Courtesy of the LaPorte County Historical Society

Elston's Gene Gielow guarding Bernie Hoogenboom in practice (left). Courtesy of Gene Gielow

Dorrance "Dee" Kohlmeier (below left). Courtesy of Kirt Kohlmeier

John Dunk (below right).

Coach Steve Pavela instructs the
St. Mary's team (top).

Mill Creek cheerleaders (right).
Mary Tarnow, Betty Stombaugh,
and Genevieve Piotrowicz.

The Rolling Prairie team gathers
around Coach Harlan Clark (below). Courtesy of the LaPorte County
Historical Society

The Stillwell Vikings. In the V from left to right: Gael Swing, Ev "Goog" Dunfee, Don Bradfield, Bill Turnham, Richard Gillen, Bill Loucks, Allen Dickson, Dean Robison, Gene Jones, and Bill Singleton. Center L to R: Gerald Kerchner, Coach Hobart Martin, and Robert Ferris.

Coach George Bock and the Union Township Tigers. Standing next to Bock are Bob Wittchen, Ted Daube and Herman Koch. Sitting L to R: Bob Goens, Larry Eastman, Harlan Kepcha, and Gene Peeples.
Courtesy of Ted & Irma Jean Daube

Ray Rosenbaum of
Union Mills (above).

Stillwell Vikings vs. Kingsbury Kings in the county tourney (top left).

Hanna cheerleaders Marilyn Fair, Doris Mulloy, and Janet Merth (middle).

Tony Hadella pointing out a foul to the referee during the Sectional (below). Courtesy of the LaPorte County Historical Society

18

Luck of the Draw

As the biggest high school athletic tournament in the United States drew near, two questions loomed: would there be coal and where to find a ticket?

When Michigan City finished construction of its gymnasium in 1937, it had the largest seating capacity in LaPorte County. However, the IHSAA made the local Sectional tournament bounce back and forth between Elston High School and the LaPorte Civic Auditorium every year. With the Civic's seating capacity at 2,200 fans compared to Elston's 3,400, it was reasonable to wonder why the tournament traded locations. Perhaps LaPorte held an ace card: Arthur Trester.

Known as the czar of Indiana high school basketball, Trester was first elected to the Board of Control of the IHSAA in 1911 and then served as secretary before becoming the organization's commissioner. In 1941 *News-Dispatch* sports writer Jim Walters lamented the poor officiating in the Sectional held at the Civic Auditorium in LaPorte and lashed out that "little Artie Trester of the IHSAA picked them [the officials]." Walters also made readers aware that the first round drew nine-hundred fewer fans than the event held in Michigan City and alerted readers who was to blame: "Another thing little Artie picked was the sectional cite [sic]—LaPorte." Walters undoubtedly remembered that Trester was once the school superintendent in LaPorte.

Nine years later, little had changed and the dispute between the two cities continued to play out on the pages of their newspapers. The sports writers sparred over who deserved to host the Sectional tournament and seating was a central tenet of the Michigan City argument. Bill Redfield called the alternating-host arrangement "ridiculous" and made sure no one mistook where he felt the tournament belonged. "Why LaPorte should have the tourney is the question," Redfield wrote. "Attendance is certain to be 1,000 less per session because of seating capacity. It would make good sense to keep the sectional here every year, where it belongs."

Joe Eyler defended LaPorte's claim. "When Bill Redfield of The Michigan City *News-Dispatch* isn't busy turning blue in the face over officiating he's seen this year, he is generally trying to slip over some sly digs at LaPorte. We don't know Redfield's basis for saying the tourney 'belongs' in Michigan City but quicker than you can say 'Bernie Hoogenboom' we can tell you why it might 'belong' here. LaPorte has won the sectional title 16 times to Michigan City's nine and possession is nine points of the law."

Two days later, Redfield retorted that there is "some strange reasoning from LaPorte. Regardless of what LaPorte in general thinks, the other sectional schools are going to voice some strong opinions . . . The 1,000 who can't attend the sectional every other year deserve consideration, too."

Few people would have argued against the point that the ticket situation was a major problem. The demand to watch tournament basketball action far exceeded the capacity of any gym in the county. Coach Steve Pavela was in his second year as head coach at St. Mary's. Playing baseball at Notre Dame University exposed Pavela to a loyal, enthusiastic fan base, but the Indiana basketball scene was entirely different. "It was rabid," Pavela said. "I remember people would line up the night before at Beebe's Sporting Goods store to be the first in line to get tickets to the Sectional. I remember that vividly. That was the enthusiasm. Boy, I tell you—Indiana, right away, right from the very beginning, the lowest rung on the ladder which was the Sectional—that was very, very evident that the people really were interested and took their basketball very seriously."

With a large and enthusiastic public chomping at the bit for basketball tournament action to commence and more than three-thousand
students enrolled in the high schools set to compete in the local Sectional, deciding how to distribute tournament tickets challenged many
high school principals. To be as fair and impartial as possible, many
principals resorted to applications and lotteries. LaPorte High School
reserved half of its ticket allotment for students and the other half for
adults. Anyone from LaPorte—student or adult—hoping to attend the
Sectional games had to fill out an application. When demand exceeded
supply, as it always did, a drawing was then held to determine who got
the right to buy a ticket.

   If you weren't lucky and didn't score a ticket from the high school,
you would have been wise to attend the opening night of the Sectional
and stand outside in the cold, waiting for the losing team's fans to de-
part and then press them for their remaining tickets. With full-session
passes priced at $2.40, scalped tickets drew a premium over their face
value and many fans who had no intention to return after their team
got beat turned a tidy little profit.

   Nobody entered the Sectional without a ticket and disbursements
were divvied up in order of importance. Players, coaches, school administrators, and the press got the first allotment. Beyond that, 3,160
seats remained and each school started with twenty tickets apiece.
Then, the distribution was based on student enrollment and the alloca-
tion of tickets told a compelling story all by itself:

Michigan City Elston	1011
LaPorte	869
St. Mary's	236
Rolling Prairie	164
Springfield Twp.	111
Mill Creek	96
Westville	84
Union Mills	80
Union Township	79
Stillwell	70
Jackson Twp.	69
Wanatah	66

Hanna	65
Kingsbury	61
LaCrosse	53
Clinton Twp.	46

If you were tempted to feel sorry for Clinton Township and its measly forty-six tickets, you needn't bother. Clinton was the luckiest school in the whole tournament. Each of the ten players received a full-session pass. So did the student manager. With only eighteen students remaining in the entire high school, Clinton had two tickets for every student, *plus* ten more seats to sell! Poor Michigan City and LaPorte—they didn't even receive enough tickets to give one to every student.

Thursday, February 16, 1950, was an important day. Hoosiers tuned in to their local radio stations waiting for the news to break while others raced home to pick up the afternoon newspaper. That was the day the IHSAA announced the pairings of the first round of the Indiana state basketball tournament: the Sectional.

Incredibly, 766 high school principals mailed 766 tournament RSVPs to the IHSAA. Yes, our team will participate in this year's tournament, the returned entry form proclaimed. Seven-hundred-sixty-six Indiana communities, large and small, had a stake in the outcome. Who would our boys play in the first round? What would be the path to win the Sectional tourney this year? Would we get to play more than a game or two?

In LaPorte County, people opened the folded newspaper to read the first page. There, front and center beneath the newspaper's masthead, was the Sectional bracket with all the teams, matchups, dates, and times of every game. Fans quickly sized up who their boys would play. However, foreboding news threatened the entire tournament that very same day. The coal situation had worsened.

Industry officials, government labor officials, senators, and congressmen met with President Truman. Coal shortages had become dangerously low, they said. People were nervous, they warned. The Bu-

reau of Mines director said a national emergency existed, or would
soon exist. They pleaded with Truman to invoke the Taft-Hartley Act
to force the miners to return to a five-day workweek and to restore full
coal production. But the President spurned these appeals. *He* would
determine when the situation constituted an emergency and when that
day arrived *he* would act against John L. Lewis and the United Mine
Workers. *The buck stops here*, Truman reminded everyone.

Meanwhile, wildcat strikes popped up. Week after week, dizzying
numbers flashed in daily newspaper reports.

69,000 miners in seven states walked off the job.

64,000 coal miners in six states walked out.

88,500 mine workers walked out.

"67,000 Coal Miners Defy Lewis, Continue Walkout," read the
headline on another day.

There was no explanation and no warning. Many miners vowed to
stay out of the pits until something was done once and for all. Coal
miners' patience had run out. They had been working without a contract for eight months. Frustrations mounted. Enough was enough,
men insisted. Give us a new contract, or no coal will be mined, many
proclaimed.

But rather than coming closer to a deal, the two sides seemed to be
more entrenched in their positions. Negotiations with John Lewis reopened, but the operators stood firm that all of their conditions be met.
While the nation screamed for mercy, nothing had changed.

Finally, President Truman asked the two sides to agree to a truce
while a government fact-finding mission investigated the impasse to
help broker an agreement. One condition of the truce was that the
miners would return to the pits and agree not to strike. Of course,
mine operators approved the idea and dashed from the negotiation table. The miners were less enthused with the deal.

On February 6, 400,000 coal miners went on strike. Within days
President Truman invoked the Taft-Hartley Act and a federal judge
issued an injunction ordering miners to return to work. But the United
Mine Workers ignored the injunction and workers refused to enter the
pits. For the men who carried their lunch buckets deep below the

earth's surface and who toiled in the filthy, dangerous coal mines, enough was enough. Give us a contract, or go to hell.

Violence erupted. A dynamite explosion shook the earth for fifteen miles around Uniontown, Pennsylvania, as the blast wrecked two power shovels. Roving pickets enforced the strike and drove nonunion miners from their coal fields as well. Three men were beaten in Richwood, West Virginia. In the predawn hours outside a mine near Derry, Pennsylvania, someone fired a shotgun at a picket, sending two men to the hospital.

On the home front, meager coal supplies dwindled. Public buildings in LaPorte reported no *immediate* threat, even though the courthouse was down to a nine-day supply. The nation's stockpiles reportedly had been reduced to less than an eleven-day reserve and one local business, LaPorte Corporation, shut down operations indefinitely due to its depleted coal supply. The New York Central Railroad cancelled six trains that serviced a line from Chicago to LaPorte, angering commuters along the route. As the strike lingered, coal-dependent businesses across the country sent men and women home. Steel mill workers. Railroad workers. More than 134,000 people were laid off. Another 100,000 employees worked shortened schedules or faced potential layoffs.

Meanwhile, winter held a firm grip over Indiana. People continued to shovel coal into their furnaces. Factories burned coal to power their equipment. Energy plants burned coal to fire street lamps and shop windows up and down main streets. Coal supplies in Indiana had reached historic lows.

If something didn't change, the Indiana Fuel Commissioner believed, the Indiana state basketball tournament would have to be postponed to conserve precious coal. Yes, postponed! Even Indiana Governor Henry Schricker weighed in on the seriousness of the situation. He announced that he was "confident such a postponement would be necessary."

L.V. Phillips, IHSAA commissioner, made it clear that he would comply with the governor's request to postpone the tournament, if he made it. Furthermore, he declared that if any one of the sixty-four Sectional sites reported it didn't have enough coal to host local games, the whole tournament would be delayed. With the state basketball tournament scheduled to start in five short days, its launch looked doubtful.

The dour news shook the boys in Stillwell, but it wasn't the coal shortage that provoked feelings of gloom and doom. It was their first-round Sectional opponent.

"Coach Martin said when they had the drawing for the tournament, 'I will take LaPorte or Michigan City.' We all thought he was out of his mind!" said senior Bill Singleton. "We wanted to play as many games as we can play and if you played LaPorte or Michigan City—you were only going to play one. Well, we got LaPorte."

That's right! The Sectional pairings had been announced! The news everyone had been anticipating revealed that Stillwell was slated to play LaPorte in its opening game of the tournament. The Slicers had amassed a perfect record, 58-0, against county school opponents in tourney play. As sports editor Joe Eyler wrote, "No matter how poor a team LaPorte has it will always, within an infinitesimal fraction of one percent, win out over a county team."

Key among Eyler's reasons included the fact that LaPorte High School had four-hundred more boys to field a basketball team, the school could afford to scout other teams rather than rely on a single coach for everything, and—hey, let's face it—bigger schools competed against top-ranked opponents on full-sized courts before capacity crowds. The small county schools played each other in Cracker Jack boxes in front of four or five-hundred friends and relatives.

Even when a county team had LaPorte beaten, victory was far from imminent. In the 1930 Sectional tournament, Union Mills led LaPorte with one minute left to play and the game became of the most disputed in county history. The scoreboard indicated the number of minutes remaining in the game but didn't show how many seconds were left. The official time was kept at the scorer's table. Fans were sure sixty seconds had ticked off their wristwatches since the one-minute light on the scoreboard had turned dark, yet the official time-keeper sat silent. A few seconds after LaPorte finally scored a basket to take the lead by a single point, the timekeeper sounded the buzzer to mark the end of the game. Union Mills felt cheated. Fans screamed in outrage but there was nothing anybody could do. The fact that the game was held in LaPorte's own gymnasium only fueled peoples' suspicions.

No, things definitely looked bad for Stillwell, and the Vikings squad was disheartened. They had lost out on the LaPorte County baseball championship title by a single run. Two years in a row they'd lost in the semifinals of the county basketball tournament by the narrowest of margins. They finished second in the LaPorte County Basketball Conference in 1949 and the week after the county tourney, they lost to Westville, locking them into second place in the County Conference for the second straight year. Any chance of being recognized, winning a trophy, or leaving their mark and being remembered by anyone had been dashed.

Things just never seemed to work out for Stillwell. Why couldn't they just manage to get a fair draw and possibly live to play a second or third game in the Sectional? And to top it all off, the players had a crazy coach on their hands who was ready to end the season as soon as possible! What was their crazy coach thinking, anyway?

"To win the Sectional, at some place along the line, you're probably gonna play one of those schools [LaPorte or Michigan City]," Coach Martin said. "You might as well play them at the beginning as well as the end."

His point was simple: if you're going to play in a tournament, play to win it all. One question remained: could he convince his boys—who were feeling like perennial bridesmaids—to buy into his thinking? He had a couple of ideas in mind, but would they work?

All in all, the tournament pairings were evenly balanced and everybody living outside Stillwell was excited to get things started. The top two county schools, Westville and Union Mills, were split between the top and bottom halves of the bracket. Tournament favorites Michigan City Elston and LaPorte also were divided between the top and bottom halves.

Joe Eyler acknowledged the county schools' "chances seem a little brighter than usual with LaPorte and Michigan City finding the going tough this season," but there was no doubt how it all would end. "No matter how thin you slice it, it still looks like the Slicers and Red Devils in the final game Saturday night," he wrote.

Surprisingly, he and Bill Redfield agreed on that. "County schools figure this may be their year to win the sectional here," Redfield wrote. "With an 'on' night, one of the county conference's top clubs might be able to swing it. While it's not probable to have a county school take the title, it's not impossible."

While fans got worked up about the upcoming Sectional—if it started at all—most of the teams had one last chance to play a game before the pressure of win-or-go-home took over. The Stillwell Vikings were scheduled to play a March of Dimes benefit game in the LaPorte Civic Auditorium on February 14. Stillwell's gymnasium only sat five-hundred people and the auditorium seemed a better location for a polio fundraiser. However, an explosion at LaPorte's Washington Street utility plant cut off power to large parts of the city, including the Civic, so Stillwell faced out-of-county opponent the Hamlet Tigers two days later.

For Joe Eyler, the game had added meaning. A month earlier Hamlet played the Kingsbury Kings and Eyler smelled a rat.

> Seldom do we take a high school coach to task but this is one time where we can't let what we consider an injustice get by.
>
> We have nothing personal against Hamlet High School or Coach Gene Little. . . but we fail to see what his Hamlet cagers accomplished by crushing Kingsbury, 88 to 27.
>
> As near as can be ascertained, however, Hamlet regulars played the entire game until they fouled out. Three of them fouled out in the fourth quarter before any reserves took the floor. Only eight players were used by Coach Little.

He called on Stillwell to redeem their fellow County Conference team. "Wouldn't it be nice if Coach Hobart Martin decided not to play his boys double and took the wraps off his big team. We'd like to see a little 'principal' paid off the Kingsbury debt."

When the moment arrived for Stillwell and Hamlet to play, Martin spotted LaPorte Head Coach Norm Hubner in the audience before the game. Hubner wasn't taking any chances against the seemingly outmanned Stillwell Vikings his team would face in the first round of the Sectional. He scouted the team himself to ensure LaPorte's perfect streak against the county schools extended to fifty-nine straight wins.

Much to Joe Eyler's chagrin, the Kingsbury "principal" wasn't paid back. The Vikings looked terrible and never held the lead. Hamlet handed Stillwell its worst defeat of the season: 46 – 32. So underwhelmed was Hubner with Stillwell's performance that midway through the game, he packed up his pen and notebook, pulled on his coat, said, "Well, I think I have seen enough of this," and left the auditorium.

The game raised $168.20 for the March of Dimes, but the Stillwell faithful were terribly disappointed. Here on the big floor in front of LaPorte fans and everybody else, the team was embarrassed. This was hardly the best time, or location, to start playing so poorly.

Thirteen area schools played on that last Friday of the season and residents opened the Saturday afternoon sports pages to see how the teams had fared. The results shocked lots of readers. Westville and Union Mills, co-champions of the County Conference, each ended their regular seasons with a loss.

As part of Charles McComas' plan to build a more rigorous schedule, the Westville Blackhawks traveled to North Judson and lost a heartbreaker. Bill Hannon chipped in thirty-three points to force overtime, but it wasn't enough as the Blackhawks lost to a very tough North Judson team, 67 – 65. Westville finished the season 17-4 and time would soon tell whether McComas' strategy of playing tougher teams would pay off.

Union Mills and Hanna played a last-minute matchup to keep their teams fresh. The Millers led for three quarters and Hanna's Gerald Masterson scored half of his team's points, but it was an up-and-coming freshman, Jack Werner, who sank the game-winning shot to upset Union Mills by a single point. The Millers' record fell to 16-4.

But the box score surprises continued. The Wanatah Midgets had maintained a perfectly imperfect season. The team had played eighteen games and lost eighteen games. Arnie Rosenbaum was the star of the Wanatah team and every opponent would tell you that he was tough—damn tough—but his teammates weren't able to provide much scoring support. Throughout the season, Wanatah played very few close games. Sixteen of its losses came by double-digit point spreads. The Midgets scored fewer than thirty points eight separate times. They had been beaten twice by Union Mills by a combined sixty-six points. They lost twice to Hanna, twice to LaCrosse, and twice to out-of-county opponent Morgan Township.

In the final game of the season, the Midgets scored a come-from-behind victory against the Kingsbury Kings, 33 – 31. The losing streak was over *and* Wanatah and Kingsbury drew each other in the first round of the Sectional tournament. The basketball gods worked in mysterious ways.

As for the city schools, Michigan City Elston finished its seasons on a high note when it traveled to Bernie Hoogenboom's childhood home of Goshen, where he had grown up before moving to Coldwater, Michigan, and then Michigan City. "It was a tough game but fun to see sisters and brothers in the Goshen crowd," Bernie said. He led his team in scoring that night as the Red Devils beat a conference opponent. The St. Mary's squad finished its own brutal schedule on a high note as well. The team beat a difficult opponent: Chicago Fenger. The wins gave both Michigan City teams momentum going into the postseason Sectional tournament, but would the coal miners' strike postpone, or even cancel, the whole event? Only time would tell.

PART III

19

Please, Let There Be Coal

As the coal situation grew more and more precarious, cities and utility providers implored residents and businesses to cut back their usage of the fuel, and some residents experienced rolling brownouts. Many businesses closed early or opened late, others turned off their store front lights. Building owners closed off rooms that weren't in use and turned off the radiators. Not only was there less and less coal to go around, but supply and demand kept prices creeping up and up. While a few nonunion mines kept coal trickling in, some area suppliers refused to pay the inflated prices, depleting their coal supplies even further. To save money, thermostats slid lower and lower to conserve the coal that remained. The outlook was grim.

Twenty-four hours before the state basketball tournament was scheduled to begin, IHSAA Commissioner L.V. Phillips conducted a telegraph survey of the schools scheduled to host the sixty-four Sectional tournaments. When he got his replies, it was nothing short of a basketball miracle! Every school had enough coal on hand to heat their gymnasiums for the tournament games. After conferring with Governor Schricker, it became official: the basketball tournament would start as planned. Confronted with a national coal emergency, Hoosiers still had their priorities.

As teams made their final preparations, fans contemplated who would beat whom and in taverns and coffee shops, people made friendly wagers. The previous year, Joe Eyler accurately predicted the outcome of thirteen of the fifteen Sectional games, so this year he assumed the role of lead prognosticator and calculated the odds for every team to win the Sectional and then presented his numbers for everyone to read. The favorites were clear and his odds-making ran down like this:

Michigan City Elston	2-1
LaPorte	3-1
Westville	10-1
Union Mills	10-1
St. Mary's	12-1
Hanna	15-1
Stillwell	25-1
Jackson Twp.	25-1
Rolling Prairie	30-1
Mill Creek	40-1
Springfield Twp.	40-1
LaCrosse	50-1
Clinton Twp.	75-1
Union Twp.	80-1
Wanatah	100-1
Kingsbury	100-1

As part of tournament preparations, each team practiced in the host gymnasium. Scheduled to face Michigan City Elston on opening night, the Clinton Trojans didn't expect to play past that first game, but they were entitled to practice in Elston's gym just like everybody else, and well, it was an excuse to get out of school for a couple of hours anyway. Monday morning, the Clinton Township principal dismissed the basketball team from classes. In true county school style, the players piled into two cars driven by two boys on the team, Jim Smoker and Don Goetz. The cars jumped onto Highway 421 and drove north to Michigan City.

That evening, Wanatah Midget Head Coach John Dunk prepared for a different game. He packed his Chuck Taylor sneakers and other equipment in his car and drove to Valparaiso to play against the Harlem Globetrotters in a polio benefit game, which pitted the Porter

County basketball coaches, plus Dunk, against the world-famous Globetrotters. The coaches were no match for Nat "Sweetwater" Clifton, Jumpin' Johnny Wilson, and Reece "Goose" Tatum. The Globetrotters jumped to an early 33 – 7 lead and cruised to their 113th consecutive victory.

The following night the Lakers ended the Globetrotters' win streak at the Chicago Stadium. Maybe—just maybe—the coaches wore down the Globetrotters. Then again, maybe not. The coaches' twenty-three total points didn't pose much of a threat and few of them made it into the scorer's book at all. With his poor eyesight, it was little surprise Dunk didn't manage a field goal against the world's greatest basketball team. However, Dunk made his mark. The box score read as follows: Dunk - 0 0 0 1. He did the only thing he could against a team as great as the Globetrotters: he committed a personal foul. And into the official scorer's book he went.

Michigan City Elston's mediocre record was misleading. Having lost six games by a combined nine points the team just as easily could have been 14-6. Furthermore, Michigan City faced stiff competition all season long, including top-ranked teams such as Hammond, Mishawaka, Frankfort, and South Bend Central, as well as six eventual Sectional champions and two eventual Regional winners. Indiana University Head Coach Branch McCracken acknowledged as much and sent a telegram to the team. It read, "Having lost three western games by a total of 4 points we at Indiana can appreciate your tough season. We would welcome the chance to get even with several of our opponents. In your case you have that opportunity in the coming tournament. Best of luck and go get 'em."

When you played the kind of schedule Elston had, the regular season record didn't tell the full story. Eager to reverse its fortune, the team was poised to put together a string of victories when it mattered most and it was going to be a tough opponent for any team.

LaPorte High School played an equally difficult schedule and faced seven opponents who were ranked in the top twenty in the state that season. Their opponents also included seven eventual Sectional champions and three Regional winners.

No, win-loss records meant nothing come Sectional time, especially when comparing the city schools against the county schools. In 1949 LaPorte (12-6) beat the county tourney champs, Westville (16-5), by fifteen points. In 1947 Westville had amassed a 19-2 record, but Elston (12-8) defeated them by eleven points. In 1944 the county tourney champion, Springfield Indians (13-4), were badly beaten, 40 – 12, by an Elston team that had won only *five games* all season long.

Joe Eyler already said it: LaPorte's rigorous schedule provided an advantage that gave any county school less than one-percent chance of victory. He figured LaPorte would battle its way to the championship game and defeat the Michigan City Red Devils based largely on the team's strong reserve players. He pointed to the Stillwell-Hamlet polio game as an example of other teams' week reserve units: when Stillwell's Gael Swing fouled out of that game, Stillwell "practically collapsed," he noted.

As far as Coach Hobart Martin was concerned, any chance LaPorte could lose was good enough for him. His Stillwell Vikings had won fifteen games and lost only five and missed a share of the County Conference championship by a single win. So, he started to put his plans into action. Martin asked the cheerleaders to make signs and banners. BEAT LAPORTE posters hung all over the school's hallways. Martin removed the bleachers from the school's gymnasium, expanding its width to a full fifty feet, to get his players accustomed to playing on a full-sized court. Finally, figuring it might help, Martin scheduled his team's official Sectional practice for 11 a.m.—the exact same time his team was scheduled to play its first-round tournament game on Friday.

As a teaser, the state basketball tournament officially started with twenty games smattered around the state on Tuesday, February 21. From there, things accelerated. On Wednesday, 105 games were played throughout the state. Thursday, 145 games. Friday, 240 games, followed by another 192 games on Saturday. In total, over 7,000 Indiana high school boys played 702 games over five days of Sectional play across the state. Within five days, the field of 766 teams would be whittled down to sixty-four.

In LaPorte County, the Sectional tournament began on Wednesday night. As basketball fans entered the Elston High School gymnasium, crepe paper marked off the seating that separated the cheering sections of the sixteen different schools. Orange and black. Green and orange. Maroon and white. Black and gold. Green and white. Purple and gold. Two-hundred-sixty-four seats cordoned off by blue and gold twisted streamers marked St. Mary's cheering section against the black and white streamers for Hanna's sixty-five fans.

When the first game started at 7 p.m., two-thousand people turned out to watch St. Mary's and Hanna play. St. Mary's had a mediocre record (7-11) but the team traveled extensively to play one of the most difficult schedules around. On the opposing bench, Hanna had a better record (13-7) and had just knocked off county leader Union Mills. Who would prevail: the team with the better win-loss record, or the team with the more rigorous schedule? St. Mary's quickly proved its schedule to be more valuable as the city team dominated the boards and allowed Hanna only three field goals in the entire first half. Most fans expected Hanna to win, but the St. Mary's Blazers manhandled the Panthers, 43 – 32.

Fifteen minutes later, Clinton Township and Michigan City Elston tipped off. And what a sight that was to see! Forty-six seats carefully cordoned off with blue and white paper streamers for the Clinton Township faithful on one side of the gym, while red and white streamers draped a section of 1,011 seats for Michigan City Elston fans. An intimidating sight, one would expect.

Clinton didn't expect to win, but intimidated? Never! Bill Redfield noted Clinton's unique playing style: "Clinton went out on the floor completely relaxed." That was an understatement. The Elston Red Devils were caught off-guard at first and confused by the unusual play of the Clinton Trojans. Junior Bill Homan explained. "That was the most fun game we ever played in. We didn't have a snowball's chance in winning. If you made a mistake, you just laughed about it right there on the court. We'd run up to the guys from Michigan City, look up at them, and say, 'How you doing up there!' We went to have fun and that's what we did." After all, if it wasn't fun, what was the point in playing at all?

Elston overcame its initial surprise and got in a rhythm. Even though the starting five sat on the bench the entire fourth quarter, the Red Devils sailed to victory over the Trojans, 59 – 30. And yes, the Clinton boys *did* have fun.

Right off the bat, St. Mary's and Elston demonstrated what everybody knew all along: the tiny county schools and their County Conference schedules were no match for the larger student populations and the more difficult schedules played by the city schools.

Thursday night meant two more games. The first game brought Mill Creek and Jackson Township together. Jackson Township sat in the neighboring county and was brought in to make it an even, sixteen-team tournament. As the only out-of-county team, the taller Jackson Panthers were favored to win. However, Mill Creek sent the Panthers back to Porter County with their tails between their legs in a decisive win. As quickly as that, the foreigner was expelled and the Sectional was restored to an all-LaPorte County tournament.

Westville and Springfield played in the nightcap. The Springfield boys found hope in an energetic young coach, Wild Bill Yates, who encouraged them to believe in themselves. Following one of the biggest wins in school history over county co-champion Union Mills, their beloved school burned and students were forced to travel thirty miles south every day to attend classes in worn-out military Quonset huts. The basketball team practiced at an elementary school to the west of the high school's ruins and held home games to the east in Rolling Prairie.

Despite their hardships, the boys kept battling and they weren't done fighting yet. The team stuck together and the students backed their team all the way. Senior Stan Nedza recalled, "We had a good fighting ball club. Team work all the way around and that's thanks to Bill Yates. With all the situations that were around us, we kinda stuck together and made it through." Even Joe Eyler recognized the "fighting Springfield team" in his daily newspaper column.

Westville opened the game by blanking the Indians 12 – 0, but Springfield battled back and closed the gap to 14 – 10. Springfield kept picking away at the lead and refused to give up. Springfield double-teamed Westville's star center, Bill Hannon, and the strategy worked. Hannon managed only eight points in the game but Westville had too much depth. Teammates Don Layton and George Thompson combined for thirty-six of Westville's forty-eight points.

Springfield did its best to keep the game close and kept Westville on its toes, but in the end, Westville just had too much talent. Springfield might not have set any records and it might not have had a winning record, but the season was a success. Despite everything the young men had gone through, the Indians finished with seven wins— that was seven more than they had won the entire previous season.

At the conclusion of the first two nights of Sectional play, four teams moved on and four teams had been eliminated. With only two days remaining, the first round of tournament play was still only halfway done and there were eleven games yet to be played before a Sectional champion would be crowned. The pace was about to pick up.

20

Friday Morning Blizzard

There are few certainties in life. Death, taxes, and change round out the list of guarantees people routinely have agreed on. However, Hoosiers from northern Indiana have argued there is a fourth certainty: whenever the Sectional tournament picked up, bad weather hit the area.

Old Man Winter didn't disappoint anyone in 1950. Following recent temperatures in the mid-thirties, the mercury plummeted to single digits, causing wet surfaces to become sheets of ice. An overnight blizzard covered the ground with snow and the wind howled with gusts reaching thirty-five miles per hour. The white stuff piled up fifteen to thirty inches. The storm wreaked havoc on the roads. County and state highway employees worked around the clock to clear the miles of streets, highways, and country roads being overrun by the worst winter storm the area had seen in years. Stranded motorists were pulled from snowdrifts. People were advised to stay off the roads and to be careful if they did venture out. Commenting on the storm, area weather observer Herbert J. Link predicted, "The blizzard will continue too . . . There is no relief in sight and snow and cold weather will be with us over the weekend." The Sectional wouldn't have been the same otherwise.

The cold snap exacerbated the problem of dwindling coal supplies and LaPorte County School Superintendent J. Harold Tower pointed out that "scores of students will be attending the tourney," so why not just cancel classes? That's exactly what the twelve county school principals did. Surprisingly, Michigan City's Elston High School held classes that day, but with 237 students attending basketball games and 142 others simply not showing up, classes were sparsely attended.

With little motivation to face the outside climate, residents fed their stoves and fireplaces with wood kindling or shoveled their shrinking supply of coal into a furnace. Then, men and women huddled around the family radio. Basketball tournament action was broadcasted live from Michigan City all day long on local stations WLOI and WIMS. Anybody with a ticket, or the wherewithal to scalp one, braved the weather and treacherous roads and headed to Michigan City's gymnasium. For at least one student, staying at home to listen to the game on the radio was not an option and her journey to the Sectional tournament was anything but simple.

Lila (Ames) Hagenow was a cheerleader for the Stillwell Vikings. The senior class grew up together and were as close of friends as any group of students ever were. Lila wanted to attend their last basketball game together against the LaPorte Slicers. No, she *had* to be there, but getting there was a big problem.

"We were really snowed in," Lila said. "Super cold and bad and we couldn't get out. I was going to get there if I had to walk!"

Given the distance, walking wasn't a real option. Besides, the road in front of her house had drifted shut. One can only imagine the scene of an eager teenager cooped up in an old farmhouse with the biggest event of the year taking place that very day. Lila was determined to get there, and her father, one way or the other—God help him—was determined to send her.

Tom Ames trekked out into the frozen air, shoveled a path through the snow to his trusty old Allis-Chalmers tractor, pushed in the hand crank and gave it a turn. Nothing happened. He pulled the choke, fiddled with the throttle, and turned the crank some more. When he paused, the only sound he heard was the wind blowing snow all around him. Determined, Tom turned the crank again and again until it sparked and the machine fired to life.

"I know my dad had to dig out, get that tractor out and that was the only way I could get there, by the tractor and in my cheerleading outfit, freezing to death!" Lila said. With her dad on the steel seat behind the steering wheel, Lila climbed aboard and held on tight as the tractor lumbered west, crossing into fields where the snow drifted too high in the road. Mind you, tractors didn't have cabs then and there was nowhere to hide from the brisk morning air. When the two of them reached Highway 35, Tom flagged down a bus and watched his daughter board. The bus resumed its northbound route to LaPorte and Tom rambled back to the drafty old farmhouse. Once Lila reached LaPorte, she connected with a shuttle bus specially set up for the basketball tournament that took her to Michigan City. But how would she get home? She had no idea, nor did it matter. The important part was just being at the tourney and Lila, dressed in her cheerleading uniform and with ticket in hand, was on her way.

The Michigan City Sectional could be a brutal schedule for some teams, depending on the luck of the draw, or the lack thereof. Any of the eight teams in the bottom half of the bracket hoping to take home the Sectional title needed to win four games in two days. Friday morning, those eight teams played their first-round matches. When the first round finally wrapped up, second round games started at 2:30 p.m. when the four winners in the top half (who had already played Wednesday and Thursday nights) played. Those two winners advanced to the semifinals on Saturday. Friday night, the four winners from the morning sessions played again to advance to the Sectional semifinal.

Nobody liked to play the Friday early morning game and in 1950 the daybreak contest pitted Tiger against Tiger. The unlucky duo, the LaCrosse Tigers and Union Township Tigers, groggily tipped off at 8:30 a.m. and it was an easy game for the boys from LaCrosse. Union Township had struggled all season long. One player had been struck with polio and another with a broken finger, which kept the team from ever having more than eight boys to field a team. LaCrosse ran away with a convincing victory.

The second game was another county school matchup, but this time between basement dwellers, the Wanatah Midgets and the Kingsbury Kings. Starting at 9:45 a.m., the game entertained the morning audience. A mere seven days earlier Wanatah secured its single precious win with a come-from-behind victory over Kingsbury. This time, Wanatah led from the opening tip to the fourth quarter. The game wasn't exactly a barn burner. The two teams together shot seventy-five free throws and converted only twenty-eight times. As the game wound down, four Wanatah players had fouled out of the game, leaving John Dunk with only six players, forcing him to go deep into his shallow bench to keep five players on the floor. Kingsbury rallied late in the slow-paced contest, but in the end, Wanatah managed to hold onto victory, 29 – 27. Sure, both wins came against the same opponent one week apart, but the determined Midgets were on an actual winning streak!

While the players warmed up during their pre-game drills to start the next game, fans spotted a marked difference between the next two opponents. While the LaPorte Slicers had seven players at least six-feet tall, including Bill Phillips (6'4") and Ralph Jones (6'3"), Stillwell had only two boys that were six-feet-one-inch and the remaining Vikings stood short of the six-feet mark. But that wasn't the biggest factor that signaled just how small Stillwell was in comparison. It was the basketballs.

"We only had four basketballs and when we went out at halftime and the start of the game, they [LaPorte's team] had balls flying all over the place! Twenty balls—two to a player," Goog Dunfee said. "I told Gene [Jones] if one of those balls slide down here, keep it. We need another ball!"

Nobody needed to remind the Stillwell Vikings that LaPorte had a perfect record against the county schools or that LaPorte was the defending Sectional champions, but Slicers supporters didn't see any reason not to heckle the small-town players anyway. "They would call us farmers, hay fielders—but it didn't bother me. I told one guy up there, 'You probably wouldn't last an hour and a half on a farm.' He said,

'Look at this!' (pointing at his biceps and fists). That was some of it, you know," Goog said.

All of the schools had tremendous pride and the teams represented not just their school, but the community in which they lived. Nobody was willing to concede one inch to another school, and the county schools—perennial underdogs—weren't shy about firing back. Dennie Thomas was in eighth grade at Union Mills and described his interaction with some of the LaPorte fans. "LaPorte had a big sign—LPHS—and we'd say, 'Oh, you're advertising horse shit.' What do you mean? 'Your sign: Large Piles of Horse Shit.' Ohhh, man." In hindsight, it was all good-natured ribbing, but at the time, it seemed like serious business.

By the time the third contest of the day was warming up, the electricity in the air hummed with the energy of a capacity crowd. The seats had filled with spectators, while others stood in front of the full-length windows that surrounded the top atrium of the gym; their silhouettes overshadowed the seated fans below them. But, their shadows couldn't block out the sun as daylight struck center court and glared off the polished hardwood floor. The heat inside the gymnasium with so many people tightly packed into their seats provided a welcome sanctuary against the cold outside. Basketball served as a respite from the outside world and when Stillwell and LaPorte tipped off at 11 a.m., fans were hungry, as always, to see a possible upset. No matter how unrealistic it might be.

Off to a shaky start, the Vikings fell behind but rallied back. At the end of the first quarter, Stillwell was winning by a single point, 15 – 14. The restless crowd looked around at each other. After all, this was what they had come to see. In the second quarter, the LaPorte Slicers stepped up their defense and kept Stillwell from scoring a single field goal and built a convincing lead going into halftime, 25 – 18.

Stillwell Coach Hobart Martin's face was red as he led his young charges into the locker room to regroup. It was hot inside the building, yes, but that wasn't the cause. His boys knew he wanted this game, but there was more to the story.

Back in Martin's hometown of Young America—a town so small neither a railroad nor a river ran through it—the Yanks traveled to the county seat, Logansport, to play its Sectional. By his junior year, Logansport had waltzed through fifteen Sectional tournaments when Young America drew Logansport in the tournament. Martin's

LaPorte's Ralph Jones passes the ball against Stillwell.
Courtesy of Glen Rosenbaum

team nearly upset them and lost by only four points. He never forgot that game. Ten years had passed and Coach Martin damn-well *knew* a small school could beat a much bigger rival. He just needed to prove it and he burned to make it happen. The Stillwell boys wanted to win too, but their feeling was still that "this was LaPorte and we were over our head," Goog said.

When the two teams returned after halftime, LaPorte jumped all over the Stillwell bunch and the lead grew to eleven points at the end of the third quarter. The Slicers opened the fourth quarter and kept up the pressure as their lead expanded to thirteen points: 45 – 32.

The cheerleaders' signs in the Stillwell High School hallways. The Sectional practice time at 11 a.m. Removing the bleachers to widen the gym floor. Coach Martin's strategies appeared to have little effect. This game was going down as a typical route where the big city school dominated the little county school, just as Elston and St. Mary's had done on Wednesday night.

With victory imminent, LaPorte Coach Norm Hubner backed his team into a tight zone defense, forcing Stillwell to resort to long-range shots to win. "We planned on playing four games in two days," said Ralph Jones. "We were supposed to play two on Friday and two on Saturday and Hubner . . . decided that it was too many games because

we played man-to-man defense, so he changed it to zone for the tournament."

As fans looked at their wristwatches, the time was approaching
twelve noon and many of them wanted to get an early jump on the
lunchtime crowd that would soon overrun downtown restaurants. Everyone wanted to be back before the next game at 1:30 p.m. Bill Singleton was on the floor for Stillwell and remembered the disheartening
scene as he looked up into the stands. "The fans began to head for the
door. They were departing about like rats getting off a ship."

As Goog dribbled the ball up the court and the Slicers players
backed into their zone defense, he looked over at the bench. Coach
Martin's hand signals made it clear what he wanted him to do next:
stop and take the shot. "I would stand out there with the ball, dribbling, and think what the hell, you know? I would look over at the
bench and the coach would say (signaled with his hands) stop and
shoot it and LaPorte wouldn't even come out, so I just took my time."
POP! The ball cracked through the net. 35 – 45. Then Stillwell scored
again. And again.

    37 – 45.
    38 – 45.
    39 – 45.

Goog gashed the Slicers defense with two more long-range set
shots.

    41 – 45.
    43 – 45.

"Then LaPorte came out and that made us feel better because we
could fake off and let somebody go in for a basket," Goog said. The
Slicers scrapped the zone defense and scrambled to get the game back
under control. Stillwell went on an 11 – 0 run before LaPorte finally
staunched the bleeding. It was a *real* game now and Stillwell had all of
the momentum in its favor.

Fans responded to the run by standing and screaming. Stillwell's
cheering section—all seventy fans—was no match for LaPorte's 869
fans. But, *all* of the county school fans and Michigan City fans joined in
the fun and backed up the tiny Stillwell bunch to cheer on the town's

boys. Wrapped up in the enthusiasm, observers witnessed people grabbing ahold of fellow spectators and lifting them up off their seats. The recently departed fans heard the roar inside the auditorium and when it grew louder and louder, they knew something was happening. The next time Singleton looked up into the crowd, he saw an entirely different scene: "The people who started to leave when the lead began to disintegrate, many of them rapidly came back in and saw the end of the game and that was the buzz. The lead was down to six, the lead was down to four, and they were scrambling to get back into the building."

Minutes earlier the audience had drifted off, its hopes of an upset seemingly quashed, but now the crowd was running at a fevered pitch not seen nor heard since early in the second quarter. Everybody was on their feet. Union Mills' diminutive student manager, Gene Goad, was in the top row of the auditorium and had to stand on his seat to get a glimpse of the action, "I mean we were jumping!" he said. "To see, you had to get up on the bleacher because everybody was up and yelling. It was a standing ovation for the last three to five minutes because it was anybody's game."

Whereas the team might have given up under the previous head coach, Martin had inspired his boys and they weren't about to quit now. LaPorte found a few open shots and connected. Stillwell took the ball and scored on its end as well. With time running shorter and shorter and LaPorte leading by four points, something strange happened. LaPorte players *fouled* the Vikings. *Three times in a row.* Stillwell was a great free throw shooting team and took advantage of the newfound glimmer of hope and connected on all three free throws and received the ball out-of-bounds after each successful toss.[18]

46 − 49, 47 − 49, 48 − 49.

David was now within a single shot of Goliath and had the ball yet again. Who did the Stillwell team turn to? None other than Goog Dunfee, who connected on yet another long-range push shot. The crowd erupted with cheers. Feet rattled the bleachers. Hands pounded in

---

[18] Remember—the new rule gave the fouled team a free throw and the ball out-of-bounds during the final three minutes of the game.

unison. The noise tumbled down onto the court. Because of the noise, "You couldn't hear yourself!" Goog said.

With forty-two seconds left to play, Stillwell led by a single point: 50 – 49. Possession of the ball traded hands before Stillwell's Gael Swing was fouled and made good on his free throw. Stillwell, 51 – LaPorte, 49. The crowd hung onto every player's movement and every bounce of the ball. With the exception of the play clock and its few remaining seconds, time stood still. The blizzard and all other concerns in life were distant memories. The intensity was hot and everyone focused on the ball. Could this be the year? Is this really going to happen?

Then, Stillwell turned the ball over! While the crowd held its collective breath, the Vikings fouled the Slicers and fans cried in disbelief. LaPorte sank two free throws to tie the game, 51 – 51. Fans held their heads in the hands. The tension was unbearable.

Stillwell was running out of players—Robison and Bradfield had fouled out. Thirty seconds remained in the game when LaPorte inbounded the ball. Another twenty seconds ticked off the clock when Stillwell's starting guard Gene Jones committed his fifth foul, sending him to the bench for good. Why, oh, why would you foul *now*, the crowd groaned?

LaPorte Slicers' Joe Landis stepped up to the free throw line, took aim, and missed the shot! Twenty-four-hundred fans roared with hope. Stillwell was still alive. Eight-hundred-sixty-nine LaPorte fans winced, but quickly regrouped with supportive applause. The Slicers still controlled the game, after all. The city school had the ball with ten seconds to go. Make a basket or hit a free throw, and LaPorte's perfect record against the county schools would remain intact and its winning streak would extend to 59-0.

Before the start of the Sectional, Joe Eyler cited Stillwell's "definite weakness in reserve strength" as its main handicap and the team had just lost its third player—including two starters and their sixth man— to fouls. If LaPorte didn't win in regulation, it certainly would prevail in overtime. Victory seemed imminent. It was only a matter of when.

Coach Martin went deep into his bench and sent in senior reserve player Allen Dickson.

Along with his brothers and sisters, Allen grew up in a four-room house: a kitchen, a bathroom, a living room, and a bedroom. On the back of the house was a lousy lean-to where the girls slept. All seven of them. The five boys slept in the attic. It was crowded, but the family got by. They took no charity or any other assistance. Pride and a work-aholic father kept the Dickson family going.

In school Allen was a quiet kid who largely kept to himself. In sports, he played hard when he had the chance to come off the bench, but Allen had scored a mere twelve points all season long. In contrast, Goog Dunfee had just scored twelve points in the fourth quarter of this game alone.

With the clock ticking off the final seconds and the score tied 51 – 51, LaPorte set up a game-winning play and got off a good shot. Everybody watched as the ball arced in the air toward the basket and then caromed off the rim. Several players made hot pursuit after it. A scrum ensued and the referee blew his whistle. Foul!

Fans looked at one another. *Who has the ball? Who is that?* People rifled through their pockets and dug out their programs. *Who is number five?* Allen Dickson wore number five.

As the players walked to the other end of the floor, wild emotions fluttered around the nervous auditorium. Due to Stillwell's foul situation and lack of bench support, LaPorte would have crushed them if the game went into overtime. It was now or never. A smattering of applause skittered around the gymnasium, but nobody had confidence that Allen would make that shot—not even his own classmates.

Bill Singleton didn't mince words: "I didn't give him a chance in the world to make that free throw. I thought it just wasn't going to happen and it is not in the script that it *should* happen."

Stillwell cheerleader Myrtle (Allmon) Skinner was hopeful, but down deep, she knew better. "I was holding my breath thinking it probably wasn't going to work."

Coach Hobart Martin didn't have much confidence either. He let out a deep sigh, "Oh boy, *here goes.*"

Allen Dickson rarely expressed much emotion. To look at his face during a game, you'd wonder if he really wanted to be there. Always cool and straight-faced, many thought he wasn't interested in the game at all, like his mind was somewhere else. When Allen played, he played hard, but only his teammates knew his true enthusiasm for the game. The moment Allen stepped up to the free throw line was no different. He appeared completely unaware of the next shot's significance. He seemed indifferent about the whole thing.

The clock was stopped.

He stepped to the free throw line and took the ball from the referee.

The packed house stared at Allen.

Waiting.

And then . . .

The net cracked as the ball sang through the bottom of the basket. The shoulders of LaPorte fans slumped in dismay while the rest of the gym hollered together with joy. The noise and energy in the gymnasium exploded to levels neither heard nor felt before. Amidst the pandemonium, men slapped their foreheads with the palm of their hands and fedoras fell slack on the back of their heads, a look of amused bewilderment crossed their faces as they looked to one another.

Eyes widened. Eyebrows raised. Women knotted their hands together and tipped their faces upward in amazement.

Exuberance flooded the arena. Muscles twitched with emotion. People jumped up and down, shook each other vigorously, overwhelmed by the joy that besieged them. The gym was a sea of convulsing bodies and shining teeth. Oh, the teeth! They were everywhere! Grins stretched from ear to ear on every face in the crowd! One octogenarian fan declared, "This is the happiest moment of my life."

Those who weren't grinning held their mouths agape, screaming.

Yeessss! Yeessss! Yeessss!

Oh my, oh my, oh my!

This was what they came to see. *This* was what nobody saw coming and certainly nobody expected, but everybody hoped *might* happen. The Stillwell faithful were awestruck.

Can you believe that?

Allen did it! He actually made it! He did it!

The cheerleaders jumped up and down, screaming, with arms clutching one another.

The other schools joined in.

Atta' boy, Stillwell! At-A-Boy!

Take that, LaPorte!

Ho ho, that's the way it's done, boys, that's the way!

Spectators held hands, wrapped their arms tightly around the necks of fellow onlookers. Students stood on their seats, screaming, and thrust their arms high into the air—muscles locked solid in triumph as if they could actually grasp the rafters.

Yeessss! Yeessss! Yeessss!

Michigan City fans gloated.

Who's the city dump now, huh? Who's the dump now, Slicers?

Take that LaPorte! Dumped by the Stillwell Vikings! Ha-ha-ha-ha-ha!

Way to go Stillwell! Way to go!

Yeessss! Yeessss! Yeessss!

Tears streamed down faces. It was all too much. Just too, too much.

"When Allen hit that shot, everything was in an uproar. When we beat them, all hell broke loose. The place was crazy," Goog said. When "the [final] whistle blew, I was so goddamned happy!" His excitement got the best of him. Standing near LaPorte Coach Norm Hubner, Goog pointed to him and exclaimed, "We beat ya!" The look on Hubner's face was pure murder. But what could he do? What could he say? The scoreboard said it all and LaPorte's record against county school opponents fell to a tarnished 58-1.

While the Slicers retreated to their locker room with heavy hearts and long faces, the Vikings reveled in front of the admiring crowd. "That was the greatest sporting thrill I've ever been in," said senior Don Bradfield. "You never forget that," Lila (Ames) Hagenow said sixty-four years later. "And when the game was over, everybody was like, madhouse, because we won! It was a big event. Everybody in the county schools was close to each other, so we knew all the players and knew everybody, which made it fun."

"I don't remember much *afterwards*," cheerleader Myrtle (Allmon) Skiller said, "it's a blur. We were high with exhilaration!"

Two sedans carrying the Rolling Prairie basketball team rolled toward Michigan City to play their game against Union Mills at 1:30. The boys got quiet and turned up the radio that was tuned in to Sectional basketball action. The players couldn't believe what they had heard. Not only had Stillwell given LaPorte a tough time, but they'd actually won the ballgame.

Michigan City Elston's Gene Gielow was at the barbershop listening to the game. "We wanted to get to the Regionals, so we wanted the easiest way out. You were always worried about LaPorte. You wouldn't think about the county schools, it was always LaPorte. I remember getting a haircut that day and news came through that LaPorte had been knocked off and I thought, oh boy, we have a clear shot now."

Bill Singleton summed it up best: "Now here is a reserve player, didn't play many minutes, some games he probably didn't play at all, but he had that free throw and of course that was back when most of the free throws were shot underhand and he calmly put it in and we won by one point. LaPorte to this day cannot understand that. I don't either, but we won!"

Coaches Hobart Martin and Norm Hubner quickly shook hands and as Hubner walked off the floor he must have wondered, where was the Stillwell team he had scouted the week before that played *so badly* in the polio benefit game at the Civic against Hamlet? Where did all of that play in the fourth quarter come from? That Dunfee kid didn't shoot like *that* a week ago. Had Hubner witnessed a completely different team in the game he'd scouted? Had he somehow missed something?

When Hobart Martin saw Hubner in the audience before the Hamlet game, he huddled his boys together and gave them the following instructions: do not show anything tonight—lay low. He didn't want to give Hubner anything to put in his notebook that could help LaPorte beat his boys. The boys believed in their coach and followed his guidance. As a result, Goog Dunfee didn't sink any of the long-range shots he'd perfected and Stillwell turned in its worst performance of the season. That night at the Civic, Hubner witnessed a team that wasn't itself, and it wasn't itself on purpose. It turned out that Martin had one last trick up his sleeve and it just might have been the one that led LaPorte to its first defeat at the hands of a county school. Much like a rube taken in by a hustling pool shark, LaPorte's coach had been sandbagged.

Back in the Stillwell locker room, the team went crazy as Coach Martin proudly watched his boys focus their celebration around Allen Dickson. As his teammates hugged him, Allen's straight face finally broke and he cracked a little smile.

There would be ninety minutes before the next game started and Bill Redfield used the short break in basketball action to race back to his office and hammer out that afternoon's sports page. Not only did Redfield dislike the Slicers—he endlessly teased his wife, a LaPorte High School alumna—but he loved the small teams in the county almost as much as his Red Devils. Redfield could barely contain his joy, so he didn't bother. The rest of the News-Dispatch staff must have shared in his delight as well. In large letters the afternoon's front page headline read, "Stillwell Beats LaPorte, 52 – 51!"

That same afternoon, the *LaPorte Herald-Argus* felt area residents needed to be updated on international politics. Its front page headline read, "British Labor Party Nears Technical Majority of Seats."

Friday Afternoon Action

The Michigan City crowd couldn't have been more delighted with the fate of the Slicers. Elston sophomore Jerry Jones said of the game, "Oh yeah, most of us stuck around and enjoyed it. That game was not misery!" Stillwell had surprised the entire county and nowhere were the people more shocked than in LaPorte.

Bill Wampler missed the Sectional basketball games because he had been in Michigan all day with his uncle. "We drove back into LaPorte in the evening about seven or eight o'clock and I went into Smitty's Snappy Service there on Indiana Avenue," he said. "I walked in there and it was just—nobody was saying anything. It was dead. And I said, 'Who died?' And they said the LaPorte Slicers got beat by Stillwell. I said, 'I can't believe that,' but they said, 'Yep, they got beat by Stillwell.'"

Ralph Jones never forgot how he felt that day. "My dad was there and I felt just like hell. Honestly, I wouldn't have been surprised if we got booed walking down Lincolnway for losing that game."

But there was no need to make excuses. Joe Eyler wrote, "Attempts to explain the Slicer defeat are useless and silly. They lost to a better team. Any sane fan realizes that some games have to go down in the loss column. We would feel no disgrace in losing to a team which demonstrated its ability as well as Stillwell did. Tourneys may come and go but this one will be talked about for some time." He was right. People would talk about this tourney for years to come, but he couldn't have imagined how much more of the story had yet to unfold.

After its team lost, many LaPorte fans bailed out of Michigan City—they had no interest in sticking around their arch rival's town. "I can remember the place was packed," said Iris (West) Tillinghast. "We were stuck up on the stage area where we had our seats. The place was rocking that day we got beat. And we didn't go back for the night game. We said, 'You know what, we got beat, we're not going back.'" Eager fans from the other schools scalped the Slicers' tickets as fast as they could and then raced to a pay phone, slid a nickel in the slot, and told friends and family they'd scored a couple extra seats to the Sectional.

After Stillwell's miracle win, fans slammed the downtown diners and restaurants and chattered nonstop about the tournament's recent developments.

The county schools might be for real!

Maybe Stillwell was a fluke. The game sure played out like a fluke with all that last minute craziness, and, say, who was that kid who hit that last shot anyway?

I'd never heard of him.

I heard he only scored a coupla' points all season!

Wow, ain't that somethin'?

Anybody know his parents?

I heard they moved up from down south somewhere a few years back. Took one of the factory jobs during the war.

Hey, what about the Midgets? Wanatah is still alive, ya know!

It's true!

Ha ha, ain't that a hoot?

Both of those events back to back before twelve noon! What else could be in store?

Surely, Wanatah can't beat its south county neighbor, LaCrosse, this afternoon, can they?

Rather than satisfy the crowd's appetite for an upset, the pangs only got worse. Fans had just witnessed perhaps the greatest surprise victory in county basketball history, but they wanted *more* hard-fought games and *more* underdog stories. The excitement started building again as everybody geared up for another three rounds of basketball action back to back to back.

The Union Mills Millers recorded one of the school's finest regular season records: 16-4. The team butted heads with fellow County Conference champion Westville all season and narrowly missed the county tourney championship. The season-ending loss to Hanna stung and the Millers' fan base hoped their boys would bounce back and get to play a couple of games in the Sectional.

The Millers faced the Rolling Prairie Bulldogs in the first Friday afternoon game. The Bulldogs finished the County Conference with a 7-4 record and the team had two of the tallest players in the area in Bill Rehlander and Walt Zolman (6'2" and 6'4"). Most fans picked Union Mills to win, but surely the Bulldogs weren't going to just roll over. Everyone expected a competitive game and, given the way early contests had turned out, who knew what might happen?

At 1:30 p.m. the last game of the first round finally started and the auditorium again thrummed with the noise of raucous cheering, hands clapping, fans yelling, the ball bouncing, ears piercing from a referee's whistle, and the squeaking of sneakers on the hardwood floor.

Union Mills hammered the bigger Rolling Prairie squad and jumped to an 18 – 5 lead at the end of the first quarter and 33 – 12 at halftime. Coach Park Sanders' Millers never relented, ending any speculation whether the Millers loss to Hanna was a fluke or not. The Millers doubled the score on the Bulldogs, 48– 24, by the end of the third quarter and Sanders replaced his starting five with his five reserve players to finish out the game. That gave the Union Mills' starting five a chance to rest since it was apparent they would be playing a second game in a matter of hours against the tough Stillwell boys. "After we beat Rolling Prairie, we knew we were going to have our hands full with Stillwell," said Eben Fisher. "They were a good rebounding team. Michigan City was always the one that would beat LaPorte in the Sectional—it was always that way—and when Stillwell beat LaPorte, we thought, we've got a pretty good chance of getting down to the final now, we just gotta get by them [Stillwell]."

Second round action started at 2:45 in a rematch for city basketball supremacy as neighboring schools St. Mary's and Elston played. The game proved how tough the city schools were and the rivals battled back and forth. Elston slammed St. Mary's with nine points in forty-five seconds, but St. Mary's chipped away at the lead and closed the gap. With three minutes to go, the game was still up for grabs, but Elston controlled the ball to finish the game and won, 56 – 50.

Most fans were surprised, but not disappointed, to see the Mill Creek Wildcats send the Jackson Township Panthers back to Porter County. In the second round, they faced a more formidable opponent: Westville. The Blackhawks steadily worked the Wildcats and the county tourney champions were back in form as Bill Hannon led the winners with twenty-two points. Westville played all ten of its boys and seven of them scored points. While Westville's starting five rested on the bench during the fourth quarter, Mill Creek played only six boys the entire game. Westville easily won its only game that Friday, but if all went well, they'd play two games on Saturday, the second one being the championship final.

Around 5 p.m., fans exited the gymnasium for the second break of the day. With two hours to kill, people trudged through the snow and frigid temperatures and hurried in and out of the downtown businesses on Franklin Street. Many people crowded the nearby restaurants, cafés, and taverns for a bite to each before the final basketball session of the day.

In 1921, developers put together a plan to build a hotel on Franklin Street. They sold subscriptions to finance the project and raised $300,000. It was completed the next year and the seven story structure made the Spaulding Hotel the tallest building in the city and a landmark in the community. Ever faithful to the rivalry with LaPorte, rumor held that the seventh floor of the Spaulding was incorporated into the design so it would be one floor taller than the six-story Rumely Hotel in downtown LaPorte.

The Spaulding included several suites and hosted every conceivable event in its ballroom. The building was also the headquarters of the Miss Indiana pageant. On the back of its postcards, the Spaulding Hotel ran the following print:

> SPAULDING HOTEL
> MICHIGAN CITY, IND.
> Route 12 and Just Off Route 28
> Modern Fireproof Hotel and Health Spa.
> 200 rooms—Mineral Baths—Solarium
> Sun deck—Towne club dancing
> Duncan Hines recommended.

The hotel was just seven blocks from the gymnasium and the majority of the county school teams stayed at the Spaulding to rest between games. For most of the county school boys, staying at the Spaulding Hotel was a big deal. Most of them had never been on vacation or stayed in a hotel in their lives, especially one as nice as the Spaulding. "*Downtown* Michigan City," said Dick Tillinghast, a junior on the Union Mills team, "Living high on the hog. It was a nice hotel."

Anyone who expected the boys to actually rest quietly, focus on the game, and behave with some decorum didn't know a thing about teenage boys. "We'd hang out the windows and holler at the girls," Dick said. "The Sectional was a big deal. It was for *us* anyway." Some of the schools reserved a room for their cheerleaders as well. As acquainted as the county schools were with one another, all sorts of shenanigans occurred. Hobart Martin ordered his Stillwell boys to stay in their rooms. Unable to leave, girls slipped notes under the door and then the boys returned notes back into the hallway. One can only imagine the surprise an unsuspecting guest might have experienced if he or she discovered a note lying in the hallway intended for one of the girls.

The coaches knew staying at the Spaulding Hotel was a rare treat for the boys who had worked so hard all season long so most of them went along with the arrangement, knowing that all sorts of nonsense ensued. Coach Hobart Martin laughed, "Oh, well, you know with kids it wasn't a big deal [needing lots of rest]. It probably would have been better to let them go home. They didn't get so much rest at the hotel. They're young boys and that's the story. You just tried to get them to settle down a little bit. It's not an easy thing to do." Coming off the biggest win in county history, it was impossible to get the Stillwell boys to settle down.

The Sectional tournament was a boon for Michigan City businesses that welcomed folks from the sixteen Sectional schools. Just like they had done for the county tourney, businesses took out ads in the local paper that included pictures of the various teams and wished them all luck. For fans, there was no need to drive anywhere or move your car. You simply walked the block and a half from the gym to Franklin Street, then headed north. The next ten to twelve blocks comprised Michigan City's business district with hardware stores, department stores, restaurants, diners, cafés, taverns, and movie theaters—just about anything a person could possibly want. Everybody took in the sights and sounds and the city enjoyed the atmosphere the fans brought to town as well.

Three in a Row?

The sun provided little comfort to shoppers and diners who wandered the frozen sidewalks of downtown Michigan City. As the sun descended, players, cheerleaders, and fans hustled back into the gymnasium. Nightfall overtook the skyline and dispelled what little warmth the sun had mustered. The large windows that enveloped the upper perimeter of the auditorium and overlooked all the activity inside the gymnasium were blacked out by darkness. The fans no longer cast shadows and no sunlight glared off the floor.

Scanning the audience, most fans couldn't help but notice the collection of tall teenagers sporting orange and black letter sweaters with a large *L* on the front. LaPorte.

"My dad asked if I was going to the night session and I said, 'No, I'm not sticking my head out of the house,'" Ralph Jones said. "My dad said, 'No, you're wrong. You're going to go. You are going to put on your letter sweater and you are going to call your buddies and you all are going to go.'" Following his father's instructions, senior Ralph Jones dutifully called two teammates and the boys appeared at the Elston auditorium that night. "My dad made us go to the Sectional because it was the right thing to do and he said that we didn't have anything to be embarrassed about. 'If [you] didn't play your hardest, then you should be embarrassed, but if not, you should go because it is the right thing to do.' My dad was that way." Jones' father was right, of course. It was one of those valuable life lessons fathers teach their sons.

The players caught the eye of Joe Eyler who commented on their attendance in the newspaper the following day, "The Slicer team turned out in a body for the evening games." Scanning the crowded auditorium, another group of fans caught the eye of both Eyler and Bill Redfield. Some LaPorte fans turned out carrying a large banner that read, WE WILL RETURN.

The Michigan City and Westville players also attended Friday night's games and watched who they might play if they made it to the Sectional championship game. In the first game, rival schools—Wanatah and LaCrosse—played. The only thing separating the two towns was an eight-mile stretch of road. Straight down Highway 421.

The Wanatah Midgets had blossomed late in the season—very late—and proved they weren't ready to go home just yet. The team was on a winning streak and advanced to the second round of the Sectional tournament by virtue of its second two-point victory of the season. For the LaCrosse Tigers, their new gymnasium failed to spur a flurry of victories. After starting the season with a string of narrow one and two point losses, LaCrosse recovered to assemble seven wins.

Fans settled into their seats fully expecting LaCrosse to put a quick and decisive end to Wanatah's lucky streak and advance to the Sectional semifinals the following afternoon. At 7 p.m. the two teams tipped off to start the evening session.

Wanatah led at the end of the first quarter but fell behind at halftime, 19 – 16. Then it rallied in the third quarter and retook the lead, 34 – 30. It seemed Wanatah was prepared to treat fans to another close game, and this time it was a barn burner. In the fourth quarter, Arnie Rosenbaum traded baskets with three different LaCrosse players. At the automatic timeout with 2:59 left to play in the game, Wanatah actually clung to a five point lead. The Midgets found themselves in a position they'd never experienced—if they could stall through the restricted period, a win was guaranteed. Usually the boys were way behind by this point and desperately tried to make up ground, so the team had little experience with this kind of game and its efforts to hold the ball were shaky, no doubt about it.

LaCrosse capitalized on Wanatah's unease and chipped away at the lead: 43 – 40, 46 – 42, and then 46 – 46. Expecting a bit of a sleeper, fans couldn't believe their eyes and the game piqued everyone's interest. The crowd hung on to every possession. Were the Wanatah Midgets actually going to pull this thing out? Could this be another upset?

Seconds later, LaCrosse fouled a Wanatah player in the act of shooting and his second free throw gave Wanatah the lead, 47 – 46. Again, the boys just needed to *hang on to the basketball*—not turn it over—for thirty seconds and victory was theirs. Oh, but that was too much to ask of the hapless Midgets. Bill Redfield observed, "Coach John Dunk's team had a little trouble trying to stall out the 47 – 46 edge over LaCrosse as the Midgets hadn't had to play a possession game very much during the season." Indeed, Wanatah not only turned over the ball to LaCrosse, but then fouled Ralph Meiss with two seconds on the clock! They fouled him! *Ralph Meiss.* One of the finest free throw shooters in the county who shot well under pressure. In the county tourney, he knocked down twenty-eight of thirty-six free throws, including a last-second game winner against Clinton Township.

The familiar scene—the game on the line, a few seconds left, a player at the free throw line—had the crowd worked into a tizzy. With everyone in attendance standing, Ralph stepped up to the free throw line, took the ball from the referee, lined up his game-tying free throw and—

missed it! He missed his free throw! In the final two seconds, LaCrosse couldn't manage a basket and Wanatah outlasted its rival for a one-point victory.

For those keeping track, Wanatah had just won twice as many games in *one day* than it had in the entire four-month-long season. Advancing to the Sectional semifinals, the Midgets were two more wins away from a Sectional championship. "Some of John [Dunk]'s friends claim he learned some tricks playing against the Globetrotters which have made his Midgets potent," Redfield wrote. Whether Dunk's experience against the Globetrotters inspired his team or not was anybody's guess, but everyone was shocked over his team's sudden success.

"When Wanatah won the first one they thought, well okay, but when they won the second one, they said, 'What?!? How'd they do this?' They couldn't beat nobody all year," said Elston's Joe Tanski.

"I couldn't get over that myself," noted Goog Dunfee.

Could the Wanatah Midgets have more surprises in store? At this point in the tournament anything seemed possible, but Goog and his fellow Vikings had more important business at hand. They waited patiently in a nearby hallway, prepared to play their second game of the day.

Third Time's a Charm

Accustomed to playing in cramped quarters before capacity crowds of five-hundred fans, the Elston gymnasium was a whole different experience for many county school players. "Any time that we played a game in the Civic in LaPorte it was a big deal because of the hugeness of it," Goog Dunfee said. "Michigan City was bigger. I mean just huge. A Mill Creek player was asked over the radio what he thought about the Michigan City High School gymnasium. He said it was intimidating for us because the county schools had such small gymnasiums. It was intimidating!"

It was widely held that the small schools would get lost in the bigger gyms with full-sized playing floors, high ceilings, and capacity crowds in the thousands. One week earlier, Stillwell and Hamlet had played in the LaPorte Civic Auditorium and eight-hundred fans turned out—nearly double what Stillwell's own gym could hold. Friday night of the Sectional tourney, over 3,200 fans eagerly awaited the Stillwell Vikings' triumphant return to center court and when the boys rushed out onto the floor for warm-ups, the crowd greeted them with enthusiasm.

"When Stillwell played in the Friday night game against Union Mills, we were the darlings of the tournament. When we took the floor Friday night, a huge cheer went up for us," Bill Singleton said. "The only people rooting for Union Mills were from Union Mills."

Stillwell was the Cinderella and everybody wanted them to make it to the ball the following night. Everybody, that is, except Union Mills, which had its own intentions of attending the last dance: the Sectional championship game.

As the two teams warmed up, fans contemplated the situation about to unfold. Stillwell and Union Mills were good. *Very* good. The two teams had a combined 33-9 record and had met twice already that season. Union Mills won both games—the first one by six points and the second one, a two-point nail-biter. Beating a good team was one thing. Beating a good team twice was no easy task. But beating a *very* good team *three* times? That was something entirely different. It was nearly impossible.

Stillwell was riding a major high, having handed LaPorte its first loss to a county team ever. On the opposing bench, Coach Sanders understood the rigorous physical demands of the Sectional tournament and had rested his squad when they rolled Rolling Prairie in its first game earlier that day. The question was—would the Vikings build on their adrenaline rush and continue their winning ways, or would the rested Millers prevail? At 8:15 p.m. the time for guesswork ended as the final event of the night got underway.

The two teams played an even game that night. Union Mills took sixty-seven shots; Stillwell took sixty-three. Union Mills shot eighteen free throws; Stillwell tossed twenty. Union Mills relied on its steady one-two punch of Hadella and Rosenbaum who combined for thirty points. Stillwell center Gael Swing put forth a Herculean effort scoring twenty-seven of his team's forty-nine total points, but no other Viking was able to score double-digits. The lead hovered between three and five points throughout the game with the Millers holding the upper hand. In Stillwell's defeat of the LaPorte Slicers, Goog Dunfee led the fourth quarter charge, scoring twelve of his twenty-two points; however, he managed just eight points against Union Mills.

Many people felt the Stillwell team had exhausted so much energy in its game against LaPorte that there was nothing left in the tank when it faced Union Mills. Others believed Stillwell was suffering a hangover of its huge morning game and it was virtually impossible for them to compete again in the same day. It was the second tough game Stillwell played in one day, that was true, but the Vikings remained within striking distance of the Millers from start to finish. Perhaps there was something else that led to the Millers' command of the game. Maybe somebody had kept a secret to the team's success for all these years.

Watching Stillwell's miraculous win over LaPorte, Park Sanders was as ecstatic as anybody in the building. He was happy for his good friend Hobart Martin, and it was great to see a fellow county school upset a big city school, but Sanders knew his team could have been the next victim of the Vikings onslaught. He knew how hard it was to repeat against a quality team. His team had beaten Westville only to fall to them two months later. Sanders needed an edge. And then, he noticed something during Stillwell's fourth quarter surge and it was Eben Fisher's responsibility to carry out the strategy.

"If Dunfee could click his heels together when taking his two-hand shot, you might as well go back to the other end of the floor because he'd make it. So, I'd put my foot between his legs so he couldn't click his heels together. When I put my feet between his, he knew dang well he couldn't click those heels and I affected him," Eben said, pointing to his head. "Park Sanders was the one who picked that up and he said, 'Don't let him click those heels together.' That's what we did to old Goog Dunfee. That was one way we beat Stillwell because they were a really good ball club. They had talent and they could really shoot the ball. That's how we beat Stillwell."[19]

---

[19] Sixty-two years after that night, I asked Goog about his two-hand set shot and he explained that clicking his heels together was key to his success. When told about Eben Fisher's defensive strategy, Goog grew angry and then wailed with laughter. "I played golf with Eben for years and that SOB never said a thing about that! Their strategy sure worked, I'll tell you that much."

Union Mills led from early in the first quarter until the very end, beating Stillwell for the third time that season, 53 – 49. Six points, four points, and two points separated the two teams in each of the three games they played head to head. When the two coaches met outside the locker rooms, Hobart Martin said, "Sanders, let's play one more time and I'm gonna beat ya!"

It had been a long day of intense basketball action. Close matches included a pair of one-point games, a two-point contest, and a four-pointer. During Friday's games, fans watched as teams scored 723 points, committed 332 fouls, and shot 403 free throws. There had been eight winners and eight losers. There was one major upset and one big surprise. Fans were exhausted and elated.

That night, the Union Mills team headed north up Franklin Street just blocks from Lake Michigan and enjoyed dinner at Chicken in the Rough, which specialized in fried chicken and French fries, before returning home for the night. The boys hoped to play another two games the following day.

22

Sectional Saturday

Early Saturday morning, the temperature bottomed out at five below zero. As the Michigan City Red Devils slept soundly in their beds, farm boys who played for Westville, Wanatah, and six members of the Union Mills team woke up before daybreak and walked out the door. The frozen air stung their faces as they trudged through the snow to the barn. The boys went through the morning chores—feeding, cleaning, and milking the cows. Basketball was important, but nothing—*nothing*—came before farming.

Between the four semifinal schools, none of the boys seemed to be particularly nervous before Saturday's big games and thoughts of *what if we win?* didn't dance in the minds of the county school boys. Play your best and let the chips fall where they may and the players all expected the chips to fall in Michigan City Elston's favor when it was all said and done.

There were no film reviews or special practice sessions that morning. Nobody walked through any new plays because nobody had drawn any up. As Bill Hannon recalled, "We didn't have any special practice. We didn't have any special strategy session. We showed up in Michigan City on Saturday and played the game." It was as simple as that.

In the top half of the tournament bracket, the few minor surprises took place in the first round when St. Mary's and Mill Creek both won. In the second round, the planets realigned and everything went down as expected. Michigan City and Westville found their way to the semifinals and were slated to face off Saturday afternoon. Although Westville had no trouble with Mill Creek in the second round, a chink in Westville's armor may have been exposed in the first round against Springfield that could prove troublesome against the likes of Michigan City, if uncorrected. Joe Eyler observed that, "The Blackhawk guards either don't shift on defense or are very slow to do so and Springfield's guards were driving around easily." Although Westville bounced back and made quick work of Mill Creek in round two, Michigan City was no Mill Creek.

"We were aware of Westville in particular—that they were a really good team," Gene Gielow said. The boys from Elston knew all about center Bill Hannon too. It was hard not to notice him. He was among the tallest players in the county and his named repeatedly appeared in the newspapers throughout the season. Hannon beat out Tony Hadella of Union Mills to lead the county in scoring and the boys had an opportunity to witness his nifty hand and foot work firsthand when he dominated Mill Creek the previous afternoon.

The Elston team wasn't intimidated though. They had already faced some of the best teams and the best players in the state of Indiana, including future Hall of Famer Entee Shine of South Bend Central.[20] The Red Devils had a tall front line of its own with Gene Eggers (6'2"), Bernie Hoogenboom (6'2"), Gene Gielow (6'3"), and Chuck Trottier (6'0"), as well as a strong backcourt in Joe Taski and Lawrence Witek that would prove a significant challenge to the Blackhawks' resolve to show—much like Stillwell had—that the county schools could compete on the big floor with the city schools.

As predictable as the top half of the bracket turned out, the bottom half of the bracket busted. Everyone expected the LaPorte Slicers to be in the semifinals and *nobody* expected Wanatah to still be playing on Saturday.

---

[20] Entee Shine is a member of the Indiana High School Basketball Hall of Fame. As a junior, he helped South Bend Central reach the Final Four. As a senior, he led his team to a 26-2 record and a Semi-State appearance. Shine went on to play for Notre Dame University and was drafted by the L.A. Rams NFL football team.

At 12:45 p.m. the Elston Red Devils and Westville Blackhawks ran
through their warm-up drills. The officials stood on the floor, the radio
announcers sat at their microphones, Joe Eyler and Bill Redfield were
perched in the crow's nest that hung from the auditorium rafters, the
yell leaders led their fans in cheers, and there wasn't a vacant seat in the
house. With such an improbable tournament unfolding, any fan with a
ticket wasn't going to miss one of the last three games.

Including fans, players, administrators, and the press, 3,400 people
officially were in attendance. The IHSAA kept tight control of tickets
and the available number of seats was capped, but no doubt more than
one fan found an alternative way into the gymnasium to catch the action firsthand. Legend has it a handful of men once walked up to the
gate of the Sectional tournament carrying large pails of ice and indicated the concession stand had run out. Shortly afterward, fans visiting
the men's room wondered aloud, *Who filled the sinks plumb full of ice?* The
deliverymen disappeared into the crowd.

Fans chanted in unison and the cadence of hands clapping beat out
a rhythm that announced basketball action was about to resume. All
eyes focused on center court and the noise and energy inside the gymnasium insulated fans from the bitter temperature outside. Again, light
shone brightly through the windows of the crowded auditorium and
Westville's shiny new orange uniforms appeared pink in the glowing
sun. At 1 p.m. Bill Hannon and Gene Eggers stepped into the center
circle. The referee blew his whistle, bounced the ball off the floor, and
then tossed it into the air between the two big men.

Westville scored first and maintained a three-point lead at the end
of the first quarter. The crowd was optimistic, but cautious. They had
seen this all before. Many a county school opponent came out strong
and led at the end of one or even two quarters only to be blown away
in the second half. Westville opened the lead, 18 – 11, in the second
quarter and the county school fans cheered the game's developments;
however, the boys from Elston gave its fans a reason of their own to
stand and scream as they closed the gap to one point at halftime.

To start the second half, Lawrence Witek sank two free throws to
give Elston the lead. Don Layton scored for Westville and Witek again

converted from the free throw line. Tie ball game. Layton nailed a deep shot from the corner and Eggers countered for Michigan City with a free throw. The two teams seemed evenly matched and the Blackhawks were not intimidated by Elston's size or its schedule strength. Then, disaster struck. What Joe Eyler later described as "a melee under the basket," Bill Hannon took an elbow to the face that resulted in a deep gash under his eye. The bleeding refused to stop, forcing the county school scoring leader out of the game. Layton managed to grow the lead to three points, but Elston slowly battled back and took the lead at the end of the third quarter, 31 – 30.

Most fans wondered, hoped, prayed that Westville's big man would return to the game. The Union Mills team was in the audience as well. They felt they could beat the Blackhawks again if given the chance and were thrilled by the possibility of an all-county school Sectional final, something that had never happened before. The boys were pulling for their fellow county school. That is, all of the boys but one. Tony Hadella, the quick little forward, was rooting for Michigan City. But why?

Tony saw it this way: Wanatah wasn't going to be a problem and Union Mills had already proved they could beat Westville. If they were going to win the whole tournament—the school's first Sectional championship ever—they *had* to play the biggest dog in the fight: Michigan City Elston. The other boys were unsure of his logic, but they all agreed their chance to play in the Sectional championship game was pretty good.

As the Union Mills team made their way to the locker room to get dressed for their game, the fourth quarter between the Blackhawks and Red Devils resumed. Westville asserted itself as a worthy opponent and gave Michigan City everything it could handle and more. For the next five minutes the two teams traded baskets. At the automatic timeout with three minutes to play, Michigan City hung onto a one point lead and Bill Hannon returned to the game. The bleeding finally stopped enough to get some butterfly bandages on his wound to hold it shut. Michigan City's Joe Tanski wasn't surprised to see Hannon back in the game, "Of course Bill wouldn't quit playing because it was a big game for both of us."

The crowd was engrossed in the game yet again and the noise level rose. With 1:10 remaining, Hannon's shot gave Westville the lead, 38 – 37. The entire auditorium was on its feet cheering and screaming. The pressure was hot on the floor, but the players remained focused on the game. With fifty-five seconds to play, Joe Tanski took a shot from the top of the free throw circle that gave the advantage back to the city team. Down 39 – 38, the game was now in Westville's hands. Score a basket and advance to the championship game. Don't score and they would be watching the final game from the bleachers. While some fans held their breath, others screamed and yelled, and it seemed like everyone wanted another basket to fall for the Blackhawks.

But, the ball never again fell through the bottom of the net. Not for the Westville boys anyway. Unable to score, the ball wound up back in Elston's hands and after a free throw, the city boys held on to win 40 – 38.

Gene Gielow and Gene Eggers combined for twenty-two of Michigan City's points and played a major role in holding Bill Hannon to six points that night, not to mention the cut below Hannon's eye that would require five stitches to close it up. Everybody knew just how close the game had been. It could have gone either way and as luck had it, it went Elston's way that afternoon. As Elston fan Jerry Jones said, "If Hannon hadn't left the game vs. Michigan City—Westville might very well have won the Sectional that year."

In the next game, everybody wondered, could the Midget Miracle continue? Union Mills guard Eben Fisher wasn't concerned. "Wanatah had Arnie Rosenbaum and I'm telling you, he was one tough cookie. He was quick—quick moves—and Rosenbaum had to guard him. Him and Uridel. If we have to play Wanatah, we'll play Wanatah, but we knew we could handle them. They had one guy. Let him have all the points he wanted and we'd get the rest of them out."

On a three-game win streak, Wanatah must have been feeling pretty good about their odds of winning at that point, and midway through the first quarter they were behind by a single basket. The two teams took turns stringing together points, with Union Mills holding the upper hand. At halftime the score settled at 31 − 21, Union Mills. But Wanatah wouldn't go away. Perhaps the Millers, already looking forward to the championship game, had been a little too confident. Perhaps they overlooked a team they shouldn't have, which was always a dangerous thing to do in sports. Perhaps Wanatah was for real after all.

In the second half, Union Mills regained its focus and went on a tear. The boys outscored the Midgets 18 − 3, and held a commanding twenty-five-point lead at the end of the third quarter. With his eye on the championship game, Coach Sanders sent in the reserve players for the fourth quarter. This gave Dean Werner, Harold "Bub" Clindaniel, and Warren Malstaff a chance to play in the Sectional tournament. With the starters resting, Union Mills' bench players added twelve more points of their own and the Midget miracle run had ended. And just like that, the Union Mills Millers became the Cinderella headed to the ball that would start in less than five hours.

The boys from Union Mills returned to the Spaulding Hotel after the game. In a matter of hours, they would play for the Sectional championship against the largest school in the county and the tournament. Coach Sanders hoped the team would get some rest, but that wasn't realistic. They were typical teenage boys and mostly goofed off. However, two members disappeared: manager Gene Goad and senior Warren Malstaff. When they returned to the gym for the final game Saturday night, teammates asked, "Goad, where were you at?" The two had been doing what most spectators and fans did during Sectional week: shopping along Franklin Street, walking around, and catching a movie. Somehow, they had no idea the rest of the team was at the Spaulding. "Yeah, those guys were supposed to rest, but I guess they partied the whole time," Gene said. At least he and Warren caught the second half of a movie.

For the Westville boys, the loss to Elston had been a bitter pill to swallow. None of them had grand expectations of a Sectional championship, but reality started to set in. They had missed the chance of an upset by the narrowest of margins. It *was* a possibility. It *could* have happened. With their season over, the boys watched Union Mills defeat Wanatah. The eight Westville seniors would never play together or put on a Blackhawks uniform again. Despite this sad reality, the boys bounced back quickly and focused on more important things in life: girls. The boys learned the Union Mills cheerleaders had a room at the Spaulding Hotel too, so they paid them a visit and flirted with the girls. The clever young men also picked up some valuable information during their visit: there was going to be a party at the house of cheerleader Pinki (Haspel) Bowman after the championship game.

Westville made another visit at the Spaulding Hotel and this time they had business in mind. Basketball business. "We went up to the hotel where Union Mills was staying and talked to guys and told them they could beat Michigan City and gave them a big pep talk," Bob Spencer said. Bitter rivals during the season, county schools stuck together and Westville served as Union Mills' personal scouts, sharing everything they'd learned about Michigan City Elston in their afternoon game.

The sky grew pitch black and sidewalks and businesses along Franklin Street were quiet as fans returned to the gymnasium once again. Every seat was taken inside the auditorium and fans could hardly wait for the championship game to start. Union Mills had played brilliantly in its first three games of the Sectional and, yes, Westville had come close to beating Michigan City Elston, but facts were facts. The city school played a much more difficult schedule and its front line (6'3", 6'2", 6'2") outsized that of Union Mills (6'1", 6'0", and 5'7").

Although Westville scared Elston in the afternoon game, it didn't detract from the fact that the real threat—LaPorte—was out of the tourney. Gene Gielow pointed out that "the big guy was out of the way, so it should be reasonably easy to get to the Regionals now and especially after knocking off Westville. If Westville could give us trouble, Union Mills could do it too. We just felt that we should win these two." Joe Tanski was thinking the same thing: "When we beat Westville, we thought we had it."

Nobody would have disagreed with the Michigan City boys either. The last two times county schools made it to the Sectional championship game, a city school crushed them. Just the year before, LaPorte beat Mill Creek by twenty points in the championship game. Three years earlier, Elston defeated Clinton 40 – 17 in the championship game. No, things usually didn't end well for the county schools and fans kept their expectations in check. Union Mills cheerleader Pinki (Haspel) Bowman admitted, "I really didn't think we were going to win the Sectional."

Before the game, the mood in the Millers' locker room was lighthearted. "No, we didn't have any expectations that we were going to win the Sectional, none whatsoever that I can remember," Gene Goad said. "In fact, two or three of us when we were down in the shower room getting dressed to go out to play Michigan City—nobody ever beat Michigan City on their floor—we were kinda joking about one thing and another, not derogatory, but not positive either."

Union Mills took the floor one time before tip-off. Park Sanders never led his team back into the locker room for a final word with his players or made a second dramatic entrance onto the court. When the Millers left the locker room to warm up, that was it. If Coach Sanders had something to say behind closed doors, it was said before the team left the locker room the first time. As he'd done before every other game, Sanders lit a cigarette and took several deep drags while his boys goofed off, much like they had done all afternoon. He put out his cigarette butt and said, "Huddle up." The team quickly shifted from horsing around to focusing on their coach. Sitting at attention, the boys quietly waited for Sanders' final instructions and words of encouragement.

Instead, they got nothing. Not a word.

The clock on the wall ticked off the time and it felt like a small eternity. In the background, the boys could hear the noise of fans getting excited in the crowded auditorium as the buzz intensified. Still, Coach Sanders stood quiet. Motionless. The boys hadn't seen their coach do this before.

Finally, Sanders turned around, faced his team and asked, "Is there anybody in here who doesn't think we can beat them guys?" He stared at the boys and silence pierced the room. "Then let's get the hell out there and let's beat them!"

With that, the boys ran up the stairwell from the locker room and stormed out onto the floor and the crowd greeted them with a roar. The audience was a mix of players, cheerleaders, parents, students, and good old Hoosier basketball fans. The two radio stations sat courtside, describing the events and making their predictions. Joe Eyler and Bill Redfield squeezed into the crow's nest high above the floor, jotting down notes and trading their opinions. Union Mills had eighty seats for its fans while Michigan City maintained 1,011 seats. Despite that fact and that the tournament took place in Michigan City, the people cheering for the Millers actually outnumbered that of the Red Devils.

Union Mills starting guard Eben Fisher vividly remembered the experience when he hit the court. "All them Red Devils down at the end of the gym and you knew when you got down there and you were shooting, they'd really be on ya. '*Farm boy*,' they'd call us and that stuff. But the best part was the crowd. You know you had the Michigan City fans and then the rest of the stadium was with Union Mills. The atmosphere was really something and we had the whole county rooting against Michigan City."

It was a rare occurrence for Michigan City fans to be outnumbered inside their own gymnasium. The county school fans all rooted for one of its own to beat the city school and the LaPorte fans who turned out had no sympathy for them either. They badly wanted to see their rival get beat to help heal the wound of their own upsetting loss. It was payback time, as far as they were concerned.

At 8:15 p.m. on February 25, 1950, Hoosiers crowded into gymnasiums in sixty-four cities and towns throughout Indiana and watched 128 teams tip off Sectional championship games. It was then that Ray Rosenbaum of Union Mills and Gene Eggers of Michigan City stepped into the center circle to start the final basketball game of the LaPorte County basketball season.

The two teams immediately traded baskets. Back and forth they went. There were five ties and three lead changes in the first five minutes of play. Near the end of the first quarter, Coach Dee Kohlmeier gave his starters a rest and the Millers used that opportunity to finish the period with a run to take the lead, 16 – 10.

It was a tight, tight game. Perhaps the biggest game in Union Mills basketball history. And that's when forward Loren "Uke" Uridel launched a wild, no look, behind-the-head shot. "Ray [Rosenbaum] told me, 'Keep practicing that, Uke, and one of these days you're going to make that basket in a game that's gonna really count,'" Loren recalled. "I kept practicing and practicing and in the Sectional game, Eben [Fisher] passed me the ball and I didn't even bounce the ball one time and I took it straight from him and went straight up over my head with it. It went right in! I looked at the coach at the other end and he pulled his hat down over his eyes!"

Coach Sanders maintained a disciplined basketball team and more than one person was surprised that a Sanders-coached player would take such a shot, especially at a time like that. "Later on, Coach said, 'I couldn't believe you did that. . . it's a good thing it went in. If you would have missed that, I would have killed you! Who do you think you are, a Globetrotter? Where did you learn that?'" Loren's answer: Playing basketball in the barn, of course.

But it wasn't the bizarre no-look shot that frustrated the Red Devils the most. It was an undersized five-foot-seven-inch forward. "There was a player named Tony Hadella who ran all over the floor all the time, moving around," guard Joe Tanski said. "We called him 'get-on-your-nerves Tony' because he was here, he was there, he was everywhere."

Lawrence Witek felt the same way. "I didn't like him. Until this day I don't like him. That's because he was a thorn in your side the whole game." Lawrence's comment wasn't mean-spirited. Not at all. It was a testament to the players' competitive spirits. They all wanted to win and get-on-your-nerves Tony was making things difficult.

In the second quarter, Michigan City battled back and tied the game at eighteen points before Rosenbaum's free throw and Hadella's push shot gave Union Mills a three-point advantage at the break. A three-point ball game and the county school was winning. Huh, who would have thought? The crowd was getting everything they'd hoped to see. "There was a lot of feeling that you have these twelve county schools with maybe sixty or seventy students in each one and then you have the two big behemoths with hundreds of students and all of those resources to pick from, so people always rooted for the underdog," Bill Hannon said.

Yes, the underdog! Everybody loved him and not only was the underdog staying with the Elston Red Devils, but it had the lead! Of course, Union Mills wouldn't have been the first county team to lead a city school at halftime, only to lose in the end. In 1941 Clinton had a star center and a three-point lead over Elston, only to lose by eleven points at the end of the game. Fans knew their history and as a result, they were cautiously optimistic.

The two teams returned to the court and the third quarter opened with a bang. Michigan City struck first and the game was soon tied at twenty-two points apiece. The two teams were evenly matched and neither group of boys gave so much as an inch to its opponent. They continued to battle back and forth:

24 – 22, Union Mills.
25 – 24, Michigan City.
26 – 25, Union Mills.
26 – 26, tie game.
28 – 27, Michigan City.
30 – 27, Michigan City.

With the clock ticking off the final seconds of the third quarter, Union Mills' reserve player Woody Jacobs cut across the lane for a shot and got fouled. The basket fell and Jacobs made his free throw.

30-30, tie game.

The third quarter came to a close and the crowd yelled and screamed with approval. If the boys didn't believe it before, they believed it now: Union Mills *could* win this game. The Millers *could* become Sectional champions. With the game dead-even, eight minutes separated one team from the Sectional championship and the other team from defeat. The fans began to sense the same thing the players realized: it was anybody's basketball game.

The energy level rose with wild speculation and hope. Charlie Stevens attended the game, but didn't remember anything about the action on the playing floor—after all, he was only a first grader at the time—but he remembered one detail without question. It. Was. *Loud.* Union Mills cheerleader Pinki (Haspel) Bowman described the crowd that night: "It was so exciting and the crowd was screaming and screaming. I mean—what a roar! You would try to get them to cheer with you and they couldn't hear you because of the screaming!"

In twenty-four minutes of play, the score had been tied nine times. Unable to contain its excitement, the crowd rose to its feet and as the fourth quarter opened, points poured in. Hadella dropped four free throws to give his team the advantage. Tanski hit a shot for the Red Devils, but Hadella quickly responded with a long-range set shot. Fritz Sperling hit a jump shot for the city team; Uridel countered with a layup for the Millers before Eggers dropped in a one-pointer from the free throw line.

38 – 35, Union Mills.

"We may not be the best team, but we'll be the best conditioned team." Coach Park Sanders drilled this into his players time and time again. Every one of his boys recalled these words as if Sanders had just uttered them. Practices were brutal as the boys went through the same rigors Sanders implemented as a physical trainer to condition young GIs preparing for combat during World War II. His teams were short on extravagant strategies and only had a couple of plays in their playbook. With only thirty boys in the whole high school, talent was limited, so Sanders did what he knew best to try to win games: he conditioned them.

Sanders' advice for the championship game: Run them to death. "They couldn't press us because we wouldn't give them a chance," Eben Fisher said. "Once we got the ball, we'd get it in and throw it right down the court."

The Millers picked up the tempo. The boys snapped the ball around the floor and continued their attack against the Michigan City Red Devils.

The crowd went wild with the rapid pace of the game. After Uridel scored on a pivot shot, it was Rosenbaum's turn to take over and he dropped in two hook shots of his own.

40 – 35, Union Mills.

42 – 35, Union Mills.

44 – 35, Union Mills.

Eggers scored for Michigan City and Hadella quickly fired back with a layup.

46 – 37, Union Mills.

Fans turned to face Ray Rosenbaum's father, Bud, with wild looks of disbelief as one basket after another dropped in for the Millers. Ray scored on a put-back.

48 – 37, Union Mills.

Wide-eyed fans turned and smiled. Bud Rosenbaum smiled back. Something special was happening.

With one minute remaining in the game, the Millers' lead grew to twelve points, 51 – 39, a moment Eben Fisher never forgot. "I remember looking up with about a minute left and we had a lead and I was thinking, *We got these birds!* We knew it!"

The Millers rang up twenty-four points in the fourth quarter—more than they'd scored in the entire first half—while the Red Devils only managed fourteen. Jerry Jones took great pleasure in LaPorte's upset loss the previous day, but he wasn't quite as enthused about this game's outcome: "We thought it wasn't going to happen—a county school beating one of the city schools. All of the county schools played in very small gyms where the floors were narrow and we believed they played a tough inside defense and when they hit the big floor, they couldn't handle it, but they did! When Union Mills beat Michigan City, I just thought, Oh my goodness sake."

For the second time in two days, a city school had been defeated by a county school. A bunch of farm boys and hay fielders. Never before had the two city schools been beaten by two county schools in the same year and it would never happen again.

Overjoyed, the crowd erupted when the game clock stopped moving. Wrapped up in the excitement, the Union Mills boys jumped up and down and raced out of the gym.

"I think we were so happy, we ran off the floor and we didn't care what was going on out in the gym," Eben said. "We were so happy to get off that floor! We didn't care!"

As the boys celebrated, jumped up and down, and hugged one another in the locker room in the basement, fans celebrated in the crowded auditorium above.

Bill Redfield loved his Red Devils, sure, but the small county schools held a special place in his heart. First and foremost, Redfield loved sports and, frankly, he knew a good story when he saw one. He and a photographer ran down the stairs after the team.

Hey fellas, we gotta get your picture! The boys jumped together right there in the locker room and the flash bulb popped. Look carefully at that photograph—the same one that hangs on my wall. It captured the shock and joy those boys experienced at that moment.

Courtesy of Gene Goad

The locker room soon filled with visitors. Among the first to arrive were the Westville Blackhawks to congratulate their county school friends. Joe Eyler pointed out the Blackhawks "seemed just as happy as if they'd won." Coach Park Sanders did what great coaches and leaders do—he heaped praise on his boys and gave them credit for the win. Not once did he take credit for the game.

Throughout the tournament, Sanders had kept his cool, calm demeanor. He never raised his voice and rarely got agitated. Eyler took notice and wrote that "Coach Park Sanders seemed to be the calmest man in the auditorium during and following the game. He stood seemingly unruffled among his jubilant cagers in the dressing room. . . After some of the noise had died down he said to us: 'Say, what was the final score anyway?'"

Union Mills – 54, Michigan City – 44.

Back in the gymnasium, a janitor carried a ladder and a pair of scissors out onto the gym floor and set it underneath one of the baskets for the ceremonial cutting of the nets. But since the boys raced off to the locker room, there was no team on the court to climb that ladder or to use those scissors. The janitor waited patiently but nobody showed up. As the crowd trickled out the doors, the janitor shrugged his shoulders, folded up the ladder, and put it back in the closet.

After such an exciting game, the crowd found itself a bit hung over. The court emptied of players so quickly that they didn't know what to expect. Some fans headed out into the crisp night air to get a bite to eat and to revel in the unexpected outcome. A group from Stillwell, including Goog Dunfee, headed to the 8th Street Café that overflowed with joyous fans reliving all of the tournament's excitement.

A handful of people waited in the auditorium and another call went in to the Union Mills locker room, "Hey fellas, get out here. Your fans are waitin' for ya!"

Fans? What fans? The boys were unaware they had an adoring audience waiting to see them again, or that they had a responsibility to cut down the nets. None of them had ever done it before.

Already showered, the boys quickly changed into their street clothes and resurfaced from the locker room. The remaining audience greeted them with cheers and applause. Intent on cutting down the nets, the boys now faced a daunting challenge: there was no ladder. Or scissors. Ahh, but farm boys, as a general rule, have always been a resourceful bunch. Someone produced a pocket knife. Ray Rosenbaum and Dean Werner hoisted Gene Goad onto their shoulders and handed him the knife. Hovering above the team, Gene opened the pocket knife and promptly sliced his finger open and bled all over himself.

Undeterred, he finally put the knife to good work on the net and freed the cords from the bright orange basketball goal. And everybody was smiling. Well, everybody was smiling except for the Michigan City Red Devils.

"Everyone wondered how this could happen," said Joe Tanski. "This one was supposed to be, and it was written in the stars . . . LaPorte and Michigan City. *These* were supposed to be the dominating two. No one else was supposed to win it. How did they get in there?"

The Red Devils locker room was quiet after the game. Coach Kohlmeier talked to his boys, but there were no harsh words. He knew his boys were disappointed and the loss stung.

"He sympathized with us," Gene Gielow recalled. "We all felt bad. We took the game serious. We wanted to go to the Regional."

The season was over and if the boys from Michigan City wanted to attend the Regional, it would have to be as spectators. The boys didn't know what to say or do. Stunned by the loss, they made the usual "see you in school" good-byes and went home. Joe said, "That was the end of it right there. Since it doesn't happen very often, you're kind of in shock over what took place. But it proves that one time or another, it can happen."

All of the boys took the loss hard, especially Lawrence Witek. "It was almost an embarrassment for Michigan City to be beat by a county school in the Sectional."

Although the season was over, Coach Kohlmeier's work wasn't finished yet. He knew there was more coaching to be done when classes resumed Monday morning.

23

The Party and a Bittersweet Loss

After the Millers won the Sectional championship Saturday night, the *Herald-Argus* newspaper dispatched a reporter to the town of Union Mills to observe the celebration; however, when he got there, there was nothing to report. "Union Mills was a quiet town Saturday night. . . What celebration there was amounted to a gathering of rabid fans at the Union Mills tavern and a small bonfire in the town's main street." Men crowded into Novak's tavern and among them were five members of the 1930 Union Mills team. The Sectional victory served as sweet redemption for the men who'd been robbed of victory against LaPorte twenty years earlier.

That night, Park Sanders was exhausted. He had kept tabs on his boys for two full days, coached four games in thirty-one hours, and had an infant daughter at home. "I was too tired to celebrate," Sanders reported. "My wife and I went home and we had a few callers; that was all." Again he gave credit to his boys and added, "They're the ones who deserve to do the celebrating."

And celebrate they did. The *Herald-Argus* reported that "The team spent a quiet evening visiting friends and receiving congratulations." The reporter couldn't have been more wrong. The town was quiet largely because most of the high school students were at an old farmhouse outside of town where cheerleader Pinki (Haspel) Bowman lived.

Pinki's parents, Michael and Elizabeth Haspel, emigrated from Austria to the United States in 1927. Michael took a job as a carpenter while Elizabeth primarily stayed home and looked after the children. Whereas Michael took night classes to learn English, Elizabeth relied on her children to share their English lessons from school to improve her language skills. Due to her thick Austrian accent Elizabeth tended to shy away from big social events, but she was comfortable around people and loved to entertain in her home. When her kids brought over friends from school, she was always glad to see them and was an amazing host. The Haspels were kind, friendly, and best of all they fed their guests well—all important considerations to teenagers. Graham cracker cream pie and freshly brewed coffee were standard fare at the Haspel house, making it a popular place for kids to visit when they had the chance.

When the post-Sectional celebration unfolded, the Haspels were true to their Austrian roots and rolled out a heavy dose of old world hospitality. They freely shared all the food, beverage, and good cheer they had available.

The party was well attended and the house overflowed with kids. The Union Mills basketball team was there. Many students were there too, including Etta Mae Malstaff, whose older brother played on the team. Ever since the boys from Westville learned about the party that afternoon, they had every intention of showing up. When they crashed the party that night, they were welcomed with open arms. After all, it was a county school victory just as much as a Union Mills victory.

Nobody liked to lose, especially Bill Hannon. He wished he could find a way to score one more basket. Grab one more rebound. He wished he'd seen that flying elbow swing toward his face and gotten out of the way. That didn't happen and Michigan City won, but it turned out to be a bittersweet loss for him.

"Did Bill tell you I sat on his lap at the party?" Etta Mae asked.

"Yep, right there in front of God and everybody," Bill added with a laugh. "That was the benefit from Union Mills winning the Sectional."

The following week at Union Mills High School, the principal called Etta Mae to his office. She had a phone call. She picked up the receiver. Hello? "Hi, Etta Mae," a familiar voice said. During lunch, Bill had walked to the principal's office at Westville High School, asked to use the telephone, and then dialed Union Mills High School. Bill asked Etta Mae what school dance she would be attending that weekend and then met her there. "You had to meet the girls there—couldn't afford to pick them up with a car and spend fifty cents for their ticket into the dance," Bill laughed.

In the following weeks, Bill traipsed down to the principal's office, dialed the number to Union Mills High School, and asked to speak to Miss Etta Mae Malstaff. "I'm not sure why [Principal] McComas put up with that, but he did." For a while anyway. Once the two principals caught on, the phone calls came to an end, but the groundwork had been established.

In June 2014 Bill and Etta Mae celebrated their sixtieth wedding anniversary. Over the years, conversation occasionally shifted to which team was better that season: Union Mills or Westville. Of course, Etta Mae brought up Union Mills' Sectional championship.

"She reminds me every day—it's like a sword dangling over my head!"

Etta Mae smiled, shook her head, and walked out of the room.

Victory.

The Agony of Defeat, the Thrill of Victory

The City Schools

Senior Ralph Jones walked down Lincolnway Avenue in LaPorte, but nobody booed. When classes resumed Monday morning, the halls of LaPorte High School were quiet as students remained in a state of shock over their team's loss. A solemn cloud hung over the student body as the traditional end-of-season assembly honored the basketball team. Nobody heckled the players or begrudged the loss. In fact, nobody ever said a word about the first loss LaPorte had suffered to a county school. Nobody liked it, but everyone accepted that Stillwell had won, fair and square.

Of course Jones wanted to win, but looking back after sixty years, he harbored no bitterness. "That is what makes sports great. How things can turn around." Despite the loss, Jones' feelings about the Sectional tournament that year were all positive. "I wouldn't trade it even though we got beat. It was a wonderful four or five days—sixteen teams from all around here and the crowds—they all came then. It was a big, big thing."

Meanwhile in Michigan City, some fans felt a little bitter about the tournament results. Sophomore Roger Bixler recalled his reaction,

"Devastating. Totally devastating to get beat by a county school. We were disappointed. I'd give them guys [on the team] crap about that— 'how could you let that happen?' Then, who was I? Baseball student manager."

All of the players took the loss hard and getting beat in the Sectional was the low spot of Gene Gielow's basketball life. The reaction of some of his classmates didn't help. "They would ask, 'What did you guys do out there?' I didn't need that. You wanted to say, 'Hey, at least I made the team and if you could have done better, where were ya?' But you just listened. Take it and forget it."

"You always wonder what if you'd done this and what if you'd done that—would you have won?" said Joe Tanski. "If is a big word."

"That was unusual for county teams to have, you know?" Joe said. "Maybe one good team would come out of there, but you had two [Westville and Union Mills] there that season. And you had other different teams that could pull upsets during the season like Stillwell. They came out of nowhere. When Wanatah won the first one they thought well, okay, but when they won the second one, they said, 'What?!! How'd they do this?' They couldn't beat nobody all year! It was the year of the upsets."

Lawrence Witek felt the loss was a "tragic disappointment" and Coach Dee Kohlmeier was concerned with the young man's demeanor after the game, sensing that Lawrence had taken the loss too hard. The coach needed to talk to him and help him get through this. "Coach called me while I was in class. He called me into his office and he sat me down and he talked to me about that and he said, 'You forget it. Don't you ever forget that happened—just don't carry it with you.'"

It was a moment Witek would never forget and he took the lesson to heart. "I think you just learned to let it go. You're not going to take that with you. There are bigger things in life than that basketball game even though when you think about it, there was nothing bigger at the time. And yet, just let it wash off. It's like saying, 'Do you remember beating so and so in an upset game?' No, I don't remember winning that game, so why should I keep the Union Mills loss in my mind? We learn things out of it."

Coaching is about much more than conditioning and training, wins and losses, X's and O's. It's about people: those young players and the relationships that can be formed and the life lessons that can be taught. Dee Kohlmeier knew it. Great coaches still do.

Westville

Going in to the Sectional tournament, Bob Spencer had no real expectation of winning it, but contemplating just how close Westville had come to upsetting Michigan City Elston, he couldn't help but think, "We could beat them. But we were leading and some big guy of theirs takes his elbow and split Bill Hannon's eye open."

"You never go in to a game or tournament without thinking you are going to win and hoping you are going to win," Bill Hannon said. "That was the case for us that year. We hoped we would win, but it didn't turn out to be." His mind took him elsewhere as he paused for a moment, caught up in thought. He considered the idea of lacing back up again, cracked a smile and said, "I wish we could do it over again."

Stillwell

When asked what he remembered about the championship game between Michigan City and Union Mills, Stillwell Coach Hobart Martin was quick and to the point, "The thing I remember is not being able to go on!" His team had lost. That was it.

Make no mistake: everybody from the small towns and schools scattered throughout the county were happy Union Mills had won, but there was a bit of jealousy. Every town and every player wished it was *them* who had won the Sectional title. They wanted to travel to Hammond for the Regional in Union Mills' place. And why not? Not only were the teams competitive, but every one of them had just as good a chance of winning it as Union Mills had.

"I felt downhearted about it all," Goog Dunfee said, "thinking maybe we should have put in more effort to win our game [against Union Mills]. How are we going to go down to the Butler fieldhouse? You know what I mean? Little bitty group." His voice trailed off. His mind took him elsewhere for a moment and then returned. "We could have been there [the Regional] playing just as much as Union Mills."

To be that good of a team, to be that close-knit and to share those experiences with your best friends and teammates, to come that close again and again, but fall short again and again. It was heart-wrenching. Yes, the Stillwell boys had the distinction of delivering LaPorte its first loss at the hands of a county school, but would anybody remember? Did it even matter?

As downhearted as the boys felt, Bill Redfield took great satisfaction in Stillwell's win over LaPorte. He knew the boys were disappointed when they lost to Union Mills, but he held the Vikings' accomplishment in high regard. He wanted to show his appreciation of their accomplishment and ensure Stillwell's victory would be remembered for years to come. He wanted to create some lasting vestige of the team's victory. Redfield thought about it and then an idea struck him. It was a good one, he believed, and he began making arrangements immediately.

LaCrosse

Monday morning after the Sectional tournament, LaCrosse cancelled classes. It wasn't because they were sore losers, or that snow blocked the roads. LaCrosse didn't have enough coal on hand to heat its school building that day. In all of the basketball excitement, many forgot that a coal crisis dragged on.

Union Mills

Monday morning, school buses pulled into the parking lot at Union Mills School as usual, but the energy that enveloped the red brick building was anything but routine. The hallways buzzed with loud, uncontrollable chatter and uncontainable excitement.

Can you believe it?

That was so exciting!

What if our boys win the Regional? How great that would be!

After the teachers took attendance, they threw their lesson plans out the window. The parking lot and street outside the school soon filled with fat bumpers and shiny chrome grills as cars streamed into town. The whole community showed up that day. At 9 a.m. everybody packed into the tiny gymnasium to celebrate together. All of the seats quickly filled and the audience overflowed out onto the gym floor and standing in the outgoing doors and hallways. The cheerleaders fired up the audience.

> Hurray for Union,
> Hurray for Union,
> Someone's in the cellar yellin',
> Hurray for Union!
> One-two-three-four,
> Who ya gonna yell for?
> Union—that's us.
> Rah, rah, rah!

A frustrating pattern against overwhelming odds had finally been broken. More than one speaker commented, "They said it could never be done, but we did it." The town physician, Doc Moosey, served as emcee and opened the assembly on a proper note: "It's certainly wonderful to see such a marvelous crowd out here this morning. We got a right to cheer, so let's have it." The crowd roared in response.

WLOI LaPorte radio newsman Cy Parker kicked off a long series of speakers, "I just wanted to come down here this morning from LaPorte and tell you how tickled we are that you won that tournament." Skeptical applause and mumbles greeted his words. Fans suspected insincerity and started to snicker. Parker realized he was losing his audience and sensed he needed to do something fast. "Really and truly," he said. "After that little inspired and determined band of Stillwell Vikings put us out of the tournament, you brought us out of the doghouse Saturday night." The crowd responded with laughter and cheers, but Parker had more important business on his mind. "I'm glad to be here this morning because here it is twenty years after. . ."

Uh-oh. He intended to talk about LaPorte's alleged game-ending shot that beat the Millers by a single point. What was this man thinking? Union Mills fans wholeheartedly believed that team was cheated out of victory. One slip-up here and he'd be thrown out on his ear.

The room fell silent. Parker felt the temperature in the room change and proceeded cautiously, "I'm thinking of that afternoon back in LaPorte in 1930 when a Union Mills team should have won that ball game. Really and truly." He recognized some of the players from that team by name, and finished by saying, "That was a great Union Mills team and now we have, twenty years after that, another wonderful Union Mills team." The crowd replied to Cy Parker's acknowledgement with appreciative applause.

Next, "the best coach in LaPorte County," Charles Park Sanders, was greeted by an extensive ovation when he stepped to the microphone. Soft-spoken as usual, Sanders kept his speech brief. "There isn't much to say now because we're still in this ball game," he said. "I don't want to congratulate the boys too much. Let's just wait till it's all over. I know they did a wonderful job and I couldn't ask for any more from anyone.

"I hope that we see a lot of you folks over to Hammond next Saturday. I know we're gonna be in there pitching. They're a good team. We've got a good team. The best team we've ever had. The best team in LaPorte County." The audience erupted in raucous cheers and whistles.

Principal Walter Richards arrived late in a dizzied state of confusion. His phone had been ringing all morning with newspaper reporters and radio stations asking about Union Mills' improbable win. He assured fans that everyone who wanted a ticket to the Regional would get one. Another source of phone calls came from the other schools competing in the Regional. Figuring Union Mills couldn't *possibly* use all their tickets, they asked the school to hand over tickets for *their* fans too.

Bill Redfield endeared himself to the town when he spoke, which actually wasn't that hard. He was friends with the local tavern owner, Paul Novak, and liked Doc Moosey so much he drove all the way from Michigan City every time he got sick.

"In Michigan City, they're rather unhappy that they lost," Redfield said, "but you can't expect much else, and they said if they had to lose to a county team, no better team to lose to than Union Mills, which appeared to me to be the best team in the Sectional this year. And without a doubt they could pull a few surprises at Hammond, and they might win at Hammond, and go on to Lafayette, and Park has promised me a couple tickets to State."

More wild cheers filled the cramped gymnasium.

Joe Eyler presented the team with a trophy for being co-champions of the County Conference, but nobody had forgotten Eyler's words about the near-impossible odds a small school stood to win the Sectional, and they weren't about to let him forget it either. When he stepped to the microphone, the audience laughed at him, but Eyler took it in stride and played up on his errant predictions. After a bit of stammering, Eyler smiled and said, "It's sometimes very delightful to be embarrassed. And this is certainly one occasion where I am more than happy to eat all the crow you can serve up to me." This time the crowd was laughing with him and cheered his words of support for their boys.

Players and students took turns at the microphone. One of Union Mills' first basketball coaches said a few words. A county commissioner, the township trustee, a representative from the American Legion, and someone from the PTA spoke as well. One man represented local businessmen and another spoke on behalf of area farmers.

When the assembly finally ended two hours later, nearly every person in town had been paraded in front of the microphone or acknowledged for one thing or another. Finally, the principal dismissed all classes for the rest of the day and it was announced that students would receive a free hot lunch the following afternoon. As everyone made their way out of the tiny gymnasium, students had to wonder: if the team managed to win the State championship, would classes be cancelled for the remainder of the semester? Now *that* was something truly to cheer for.

Later. . .

When Stillwell held its awards banquet to honor the basketball team, Bill Redfield made sure he attended. Ohh, how he loved those potluck dinners and he wouldn't miss one for the world, but he'd also been working on his big idea and couldn't wait to reveal it. The only thing left was to make a presentation to the team and hope everyone liked it.

When the time arrived, Redfield stepped in front of the small Stillwell crowd and unveiled a twelve-inch heart-shaped statuette. Inscribed on the heart was the name of all ten LaPorte basketball players. Redfield presented the trophy to the team and declared, "This is the heart that Stillwell took out of LaPorte."

Everybody loved it.

That heart was prominently displayed in the Stillwell trophy case and remained there until the school closed its doors for good. When Stillwell succumbed to the waves of consolidation, its kids went to LaPorte High School. The trophy, not surprisingly, was left behind.

25

Regional Week

February quietly slipped away and March cut in. Seven-hundred-sixty-six teams had been whittled down to sixty-four survivors, including Union Mills, to compete in the sixteen Regionals.

In LaPorte County, the final tally for the Sectional receipts had been completed, totaling in at $7,705.80. First, each school was reimbursed for its expenses such as meals ($1,320), travel ($272), and lodging ($288). Then, each school received an equal share of $102.49. The rest of the tournament money distribution was based on enrollment and ticket sales. The numbers revealed a striking story.

Michigan City Elston	$670.37
LaPorte	$589.42
St. Mary's	$226.09
Rolling Prairie	$185.07
Springfield Twp.	$154.70
Mill Creek	$146.18
Westville	$140.25
Union Mills	$137.12
Union Twp	$136.59
LaCrosse	$132.86
Stillwell	$131.26
Jackson Twp.	$130.73
Wanatah	$128.59
Hanna	$127.76
Kingsbury	$125.93
Clinton Twp.	$117.41

That's right. Although Union Mills had won the Sectional, it received less than one-fourth the amount of LaPorte, which hadn't won a single game. With regard to the divisional share, the two biggest city schools averaged fifteen times the amount of money as the average county school ($527 vs. $35) and nearly five times as much money in the final take ($630 vs. $138).

Revenue increased thirty-two percent over the previous year's tournament, which had been held in LaPorte, and guess who flouted that fact in the press? "The report on the financial end of the 1950 sectional basketball tourney here provides more ammunition for those desiring to make it a permanent Michigan City fixture," wrote Bill Redfield.

In the Regional tournament, the afternoon session pitted two "people's choices" against two behemoths. Union Mills (now with a 20-4 record) was scheduled to play one of the largest schools in the state: the Hammond High School Wildcats, backed by 1,464 students. The fourteenth ranked Wildcats (21-4) were aiming for their third straight Regional championship. Union Mills now had sixty-five kids and had just won its only Sectional title.

The other half of the bracket was a battle of devils and the only question was, red or blue? The Wheatfield Red Devils (21-4), the second people's choice with 152 students, faced the Gary Froebel Blue Devils (23-2), which had total enrollment of 620 students. Froebel also finished the season ranked fourth in the state.

The four teams had racked up an impressive number of wins and each one had its own strengths to exploit. Hammond was quick, had great rebounding ability, and a deep bench that scored twenty-five percent of the team's points. Union Mills had great shooters, hitting .364 from the field in the Sectional.[21] The other two teams both had superior height: Wheatfield had two boys who stood six-feet-three-inches tall

---

[21] .364 field goal shooting in 1950 was incredibly good. Joe Eyler wrote that, "Any team which can consistently hit above the .300 mark is going to cause plenty of trouble."

and Froebel was the tallest team in the tourney with John Moore and Vladimir Gastevich at six-feet-five-inches apiece.

But where did all the teams stand in relation to one another? Bill Redfield looked at head-to-head matchups and found the connection that gave Union Mills hope. "Hammond bumped Froebel, 38 – 36, and topped Michigan City, local sectional finalist, 49 – 47, in a December overtime clash. And Wheatfield lost by five points to Westville which lost to Union, 48 – 43, and beat the Millers, 43 – 42. Just where does that put the Millers? Well, they breezed over Michigan City, 54 – 44. The Wildcats of Hammond had an uphill battle all of the way."

Hammond and Gary Froebel were bitter conference opponents in neighboring cities. Local fans eagerly awaited a rematch of the two top-ranked teams in the Regional final; however, Hammond Head Coach Bob King was more cautious. He knew the scores and didn't get a solid scouting report on the Union Mills squad. Trusted insiders from LaPorte County made it clear that the Millers could not be overlooked. The *Hammond Times* sports editor, John Whitaker, called the LaPorte and Michigan City sports desks hoping to dig up some information on the team. After Whitaker had insulted LaPorte earlier in the season, Joe Eyler had no interest in helping. Bill Redfield was long on praise of the Union Mills boys. Whitaker reported that Redfield "had predicted Union Mills would beat out the perennials, LaPorte and Michigan City, for the sectional crown."

Perhaps it was bad reporting, or maybe Bill Redfield had taken several creative liberties when he spoke to Whitaker on the phone. When Whitaker covered the Union Mills team, he wrote that Tony Hadella was five-feet-ten inches tall (he was three inches shorter), Ray Rosenbaum was six-feet-two-inches (he was an inch shorter), the Millers used man-to-man defense (they always played zone), and that Union Mills' field goal average in the Sectional was forty-two percent (it was thirty-six percent). When the Red Devils fell to the Millers in the Sectional championship game, Michigan City rallied to the aid of its country cousins and supported them every way they could, including a bit of embellishment, if they thought it might help.

When Joe Eyler read about Redfield's miraculous prediction that Union Mills would win the Sectional, he could hardly control himself. Eyler had taken a heavy dose of ribbing from area fans for his disastrous predictions and he fully owned up to his failings. The following day he grumbled in his column that "Modest William must be hiding his light under a bushel basket because no one around here can remember reading anything like that in the News-Dispatch."

Another fact revealed itself that made Hammond fans second-guess their seemingly clear path to the Regional final: the Millers' inside track. Carl Sanders, former Union Mills basketball coach and older brother of Coach Park Sanders, coached the Griffith High School Panthers. At the exact same moment Park's boys beat Wanatah in the Sectional semifinal in Michigan City, Carl's boys were giving Hammond High everything they could handle and then some. Carl's team led Hammond at halftime but couldn't keep up in the fourth quarter. And since Carl married a girl from Union Mills, there was no question where his allegiance went and he shared all of his knowledge about the Hammond team with his younger brother.

The Hammond Wildcats didn't want to be the second upset victim of the tiny bunch from Union Mills and Coach Bob King kept his team focused on Union Mills before thoughts of the team from Gary Froebel High School danced in his players' heads.

All things considered, speculators started to feel that the "people's choice" teams of Union Mills and Wheatfield would give the Hammond and Gary teams trouble, but it was also noted that above all else, the two little schools needed to avoid stage fright when they took to the floor in the Hammond Civic Center. Redfield again pitched in to help Union Mills. He knew everybody was caught up in basketball fever—especially the boys in Union Mills—and read the sports page every day. He wrote that although Hammond sat two-thousand more people than the Michigan City gym, crowds over three-thousand all just looked the same.

One needn't wonder why Indiana erected mammoth high school gymnasiums in the '50s and '60s. Tickets were an ongoing problem in the state basketball tournament and the 1950 Regional in Hammond was no exception. The Hammond Civic Center comfortably sat over 5,300 people and the participating schools received the following number of seats:

1,919 tickets went to Hammond High School,

1,131 to Gary Froebel,

685 to Wheatfield, and

605 seats for Union Mills.[22]

Hammond Times Sports Writer Jim Skufakiss believed tickets for the Hammond regional probably wouldn't be as difficult to obtain this year. "Because Union Mills and Wheatfield have small student enrollments, they may be unable to dispose of their big allotments. . . There is a strong possibility that the Union Mills and Wheatfield principals will deem it best to accept only a portion of their ticket allotment, thus giving Hammond High and Froebel a bigger slice of the supply."

What was he thinking? Skufakiss must have lived in a bubble! He apparently had never left the cities of Hammond and Gary in his life. He clearly underestimated the excitement fans had for the game of basketball. Furthermore, considering a portion of the school's payout for the Regional was based on ticket sales—and after seeing the revenue distribution Union Mills received after the Sectional—there was no way the school would turn back tickets.

On the other hand, the town of Union Mills only had 505 people in town and only sixty-five high school students. Was it possible that every man, woman, and child in the tiny community would drive to Hammond to watch a basketball game?

Joe Eyler wrote that "Principal Walter W. Richards of Union Mills has become the most harassed man in LaPorte county this week." Richards' phone rang off the hook and his office saw a steady flow of fans not only from Union Mills, but as far away as Gary and Hammond, trying to buy tickets. It was reported that a man with a Ham-

---

[22] This doesn't add up to 5,300 tickets. First, distribution went to media and various officials. Then, twelve tickets went to each school that participated in the four Sectionals feeding the Regional, and those tickets were intended for the basketball team. At least sixty teams played in the four area Sectionals.

mond license plate stopped along a curb in Michigan City and asked a passerby if this was Union Mills. Somewhat amused, the pedestrian responded that yes, this was Union Mills, but there were no Regional tickets here—they were sold out. The motorist thanked him and sped off.

Reporters from Hammond showed little respect for the small-town folks in the upcoming tournament. They were surprised when Union Mills took its full ticket allotment and when the little school reported all of its tickets were gone. Sold out. The *Hammond Times* reported that Union Mills ran out of tickets because it had given many of them to LaPorte and Michigan City fans. The absurdity of that statement struck Bill Redfield to write, "That's going to be news around here. Michigan City received something like a dozen tickets and that's all." Joe Eyler also fired back and pointed out that LaPorte received exactly twelve tickets and they were going to the basketball team. No, Union Mills had sold 605 tickets and *all of them* went to people living *in and around Union Mills*.

At the pep rally Monday morning, Principal Richards indicated there were plenty of tickets and everybody who wanted one would get one. Three days later, he remarked that he could have sold six-thousand tickets. His supply disappeared in just two days.

Union Mills used every trick it could think of to prepare for the Regional. Hobart Martin told Park Sanders how he had removed the bleachers for his Sectional preparation, so Sanders' team practiced in Stillwell's gym on Tuesday. Wednesday morning, the city of LaPorte threw open the doors to the Civic Auditorium for the boys to practice in a bigger facility. Thursday, the team headed to the Hammond Civic Center for their official Regional workout. The boys piled into three cars and drove forty-one miles to Hammond. Park's older brother Carl met them there and the two brothers watched the boys go through drills. Halfway through practice, Carl turned to his younger brother and said, "Better start shooting baskets." The team from Gary had arrived and there were so many doors to the Civic, there was no way to prevent someone from scouting their work-out.

The practice agenda switched and Coach Sanders called his student manager over, "Goad, you better go down to the shower room." The teams shared the same locker room and the boys from Union Mills left their belongings, including their wallets, lying out in the open. Gene Goad—all four-feet-nine-inches of him—went down to the locker room to protect the team's belongings.

When Gene arrived, there was the Gary Froebel basketball team. John Moore[23] and Vlad Gastevich each stood a full twenty inches taller than Gene. Seeing Vlad's feet, Gene recalled, "By God, his foot was longer than my body! And I walked in there scared to death with these trees." Then one of the trees called out to Gene.

"Hey, Shorty! What are you doing in here?" John Moore asked.

"I am the student manager of Union Mills," Gene replied.

John asked if he was in high school and how old he was.

He said, yes, and that he was sixteen years old.

John Moore turned to his towering teammate, Vladimir and said, "Hey, Gastevich! This little guy is older than you!"

Gene flashed a smile and the two boys laughed. Hammond was about as far as he'd ever traveled from his family's farm and he had never experienced the diversity reflected in its people or those from Gary. In fact, John Moore was the first black person Gene had ever met in his life. John had no way of knowing that, but he quickly demonstrated that the only difference between him and the boys from Union Mills was the color of their skin. Basketball can teach all kinds of unexpected lessons.

After practice, the three cars pulled up in front of a stainless steel railroad car diner. Fathers of two of the players—Ben Werner and Bud Rosenbaum—helped drive the team to practice and together they bought hamburgers, French fries, and malts for the boys. Then, they got back on the road and headed home. After dropping off the boys at

---

[23] John Moore graduated from Gary Froebel in 1951, was a member of the Indiana High School All Star team, and went on to play basketball at UCLA for Coach John Wooden. At UCLA Moore was a four-year starting forward, the first Bruin to score 1,000 points in a career, and a Consensus All-American his senior year.

the school, the two fathers drove their sons, Dean and Ray, home to do the afternoon milking.

Union Mills started buzzing as soon as it won the Sectional and it hadn't stopped for a full week. Nobody could help but get caught up in the excitement, including Gene Goad's parents, who had never attended a Union Mills basketball game. Gene always caught the fan bus to get a ride to away games and Coach Sanders always picked him up to attend practice and home games. But the idea of the little team from Union Mills playing in Hammond piqued everyone's interest. When Gene finished chores Friday night, his dad shocked him with the news that he would take Gene to the Regional game in Hammond the following day. "You are?" Gene asked. Yeah, his dad answered. His younger brother would handle all the milking chores and they would ride with neighbors to the game. The following day, Gene piled into the neighbors' car with his parents and the five of them headed off for Hammond.

Having sold 605 tickets in a town of 505 people, Union Mills had two problems. First, it had no police force and a burglar could have cleaned out the whole town without being bothered. Worse yet, if a red-hot coal ember found its way outside a stove or furnace, the whole town could have burned to the ground with nobody to notice and no bodies left to extinguish the flames.

Michigan City's mayor saw the potential for a real problem—and some good publicity. The day of the big game, Michigan City firemen manned the volunteer fire department equipment in Union Mills and when the last cars honked their horns and sped out of town, two Michigan City Police officers wished them good luck and waved good-bye.

**Captain Lloyd Storey and Officer Lawrence
Sobecki guard the town of Union Mills during
the Regional.**

26

What's the Matter with These Farmers?

The Union Mills Millers were scheduled to play at 1 p.m. and arrived in Hammond early. Whereas the boys were loose and unworried for the Sectional championship, their feelings shifted dramatically when they entered the Hammond Civic Center with all the seats pulled out and signs up.

The Civic Center was an impressive structure. Constructed by the Public Works Administration during the Great Depression, area residents used it for badminton, swimming, dances, volleyball, handball, wrestling matches, boxing matches, tennis, theater events, and swimming. In the main auditorium where basketball was played, the balcony sat 3,100 people—about as many people as Elston gym could hold in its entirety—and made a full circle around the playing floor. On the floor were another 2,200 seats.

Junior guard Dick Tillinghast captured the teams' feelings when they arrived in Hammond. "You walked into that Hammond Civic Center and—Christ, we thought we were in the Coliseum in Rome as big as that place was! Boy, I tell you. A country boy from Union Mills, fourteen kids in your class, and walk in and look at that place—and that place was packed!"

In the movie *Hoosiers*, the Huskers were awestruck by the humongous Butler Fieldhouse. To combat their fears, fictitious coach Norman

Dale pulled out a tape measure to show that the dimensions were the same as their gym back home in Hickory. Their worries melted away as they smiled. That exercise would have been wasted on the Union Mills Millers. In their cigar box of a gymnasium the ceiling was low, the walls marked out of bounds, it was narrow, and it was way too short. A tape measure would have exacerbated the team's fears.

"My God, this was like a palace! What were we getting into?" senior Warren Malstaff said. "We were just little guys from this little gym of ours in this big place. We were nervous. We never saw anything like this. We may have watched a game, but we never had to *play* in this place. You know, they had boxes where people announced everything."

Eighty fans in Elston's gym was one thing, but 605 people had abandoned town and drove to Hammond to watch them play. All of the boys grew nervous. All but one, that is. When the team reached the locker room, fiery forward Tony Hadella dropped his gear, laid down on a bench, and fell fast asleep.

All across Indiana 85,000 rabid basketball fans filed into sixteen gymnasiums to watch Regional basketball action. Among those in the audience at the Hammond Civic Center were Bob Spencer and the rest of the boys from Westville. Coach Hobart Martin and his wife Dee took the Stillwell boys to the game. Joe Tanski and the guys from Michigan City went to the game, but Gene Gielow wasn't with them. "I was still sore," he said. "I didn't even want to look at a basketball for a couple weeks." He stayed behind and like most county residents, he listened to the game on the radio. Far from a spoilsport though, Gene rooted for the Millers and couldn't wait for them to upset the Hammond Wildcats.

Fans packed into the crowded auditorium and filled the room with noise. Cheers rose to the rafters and the applause pounded off the walls and floor as the teams stormed out onto the court. "The auditorium was enormous and all these people were screaming and hollering and then this little tiny team from Union Mills comes out on the floor,"

Pinki (Haspel) Bowman said. "Every time they got a score, everybody would really, really cheer for them."

More than 3,200 people supported the people's choice—Union Mills—leaving the Hammond Wildcat fans outnumbered in their own town, but that didn't deter them. Hammond jumped to a 7 – 0 lead before Union Mills gained its composure and battled back with six unanswered points of its own. The first quarter closed with Hammond leading, 16 – 10. In the second quarter, the two teams went back and forth trading baskets and the point difference stayed the same.

The Millers had held their own. The little team was for real and every time Union Mills scored, fans screamed for the troupe of farm boys to take down the city slickers. The noise was deafening and the players couldn't hear a thing. The energy thrummed and people could sense the Millers weren't about to go away. They were going to stay with this team and possibly upset another big city favorite.

It would be nice to say the Millers closed that six-point gap. That they won by a last-second shot. Or lost by a last-second shot. Or lost by a couple points even. But that's not how things went down on the afternoon of March 4, 1950. To finish the second quarter, the Hammond Wildcats poured in fourteen points while Union Mills managed one free throw. Coach Sanders pulled Loren Uridel out of the game.

"Uke, what the hell's the matter?" he asked.

"I don't know, Coach. I can't make a basket," Loren replied.

"Well, get out there and make a basket," Sanders said and put him back in.

Sanders' frustration was as obvious as the hat on his head. The *Hammond Times* noted that "Charles Sanders, the Union Mills coach, either believes in informality or else he planned a quick dash home after his team's appearance in the regional . . . Sanders showed up in a gray felt hat that he either wore, or as things became darker for the Millers, clutched firmly in his fist."

In the second half, Hammond continued its onslaught, but nobody expected a break. "Because we'd upset Michigan City, those people over there were after our ass because they didn't want to get beat by us," Dick Tillinghast said, "and they didn't!"

The Hammond Wildcats came prepared for the Union Mills Millers and held nothing back. Points rained in for Hammond while the drought continued for Union Mills. With fifteen seconds remaining in the third quarter, Union Mills finally scored another field goal.

All twenty players from both teams played in the game. Whereas all ten Hammond players scored at least one point, only five Union Mills boys made it into the scorer's column.

If the two teams played ten times, Hammond might have won seven, eight, or nine of those games, but not a soul could be found who believed Hammond High was anywhere near thirty points better than Union Mills, as the final score reflected. No, lack of talent wasn't their downfall. *Hammond Times* Sports Editor John Whitaker observed that "Ray Rosenbaum could make any varsity in the Calumet," and that, "No better little man has trod the Civic Center hardwood than Hadella." He seemed to attribute the Millers' lackluster performance to stage fright, and the box score agreed with him. Tony Hadella, who slept in the locker room before the game, led all Regional players with twenty points that day.

Joe Eyler had his own theory and wrote that "One great lesson was learned in the Union Mills defeat—either build a new gym, or preferably, consolidate. Under present conditions the Millers will never have a chance during the regular season to meet competition the likes of Hammond Saturday. The Hammond defense kept the Millers from working the ball in close and when your gym doesn't allow practice on long shots what are you going to do for an outside attack?"

Bill Redfield pointed out that the Millers consistently shot well over .300 from the field in January and February, but it was as if someone had put a lid on the basket. The Millers managed to hit only twelve out of fifty-four shots. As far as Redfield was concerned, Loren Uridel summed it up best: "The ball just got away from us."

In the end, Hammond played magnificently and Union Mills played poorly that Saturday afternoon. It was as simple as that.

Like the rest of the teams from LaPorte County, the Union Mills Millers ended its season in defeat. It was a terrible loss and everyone was disappointed, but it had been a great journey. The dances after the games, playing in the county tourney, sharing the County Conference championship, the screaming fans at the Sectional, becoming the best team in the whole county, the pep rally on Monday morning in that cramped—oh, so cramped—gymnasium filled with people. The cheer that went up when everybody let loose and expressed how much that victory meant to them.

The radio broadcast, the busy telephones, the crazy tickets, the outpouring of support. The people reliving the games in diners and taverns. The optimism of what might happen next. The attention in the press. The chucks on the shoulder, the tousling of hair, the pats on the back. The endless *atta' boys* and *way-to-go's*. The smiles—yes, the smiles! They were everywhere! The huge roar that went up at the Regional.

My uncle, Dean Werner, scored only eight points that season, but he was a part of it all. The mad excitement of that season swirled all around him and contributed to his restless spirit. It led him to brag about his coach and team to his army buddies half a world away. It was that kind of experience that takes men back to another place and another time, and wish—just for a moment—that they could lace up the sneakers one more time. Drain every last drop of sweat against a tough opponent one more time. Make one more shot. Grab one more rebound. Try to win one more time. After all, when in life do we get the opportunity to pour so much energy and emotion into something that means so much to so many people and be recognized for it?

Look into the eyes of any former Indiana basketball player, cheerleader, student manager, coach, or fan—it's still there. They know what that experience meant. What it was all for. That was *their* team. That was *their* boys. It was *their* school. It was *their* tournament. It was *their* game. It belonged to them. All of them. Together.

Hoosiers from nineteen to ninety can sit down and share stories about basketball. They laugh, smile, and nod with understanding. They share stories of big wins, terrible losses, tough practices, crazy crowds, and inspiring coaches—funny stories about the game and everything that went on around them. Fans share their stories of triumph and heartache. If you still can't grasp it—if you still think basketball is just a game or it only meant something to the biggest winner on the biggest stage, consider the following obituary:

> Richard Lee Tillinghast, 79 of La Porte, Ind., died Wednesday, August 15, 2012 at the University of Chicago Hospital, Chicago, Ill, following a brief illness.
> He was born July 3, 1933, in La Porte, son of Lee Ross and Ruth Hartman Tillinghast. Most often called Dick throughout his life, he was a 1951 graduate of Union Mills High School and *was on the 1950 Union Mills Sectional Championship Basketball Team* which defeated Michigan City. He was a proud U.S. Army Veteran serving in the Korean War. On September 24, 1960 in La Porte, he married Iris West and was married for almost 52 years.

Basketball—right up there with being born, serving your country, and spending fifty-two years with your sweetheart. The winners *and* the losers, big cities *and* small towns—they all participated in Indiana basketball and all contributed to the mystique known as *Hoosier hysteria*. If somebody tries to say otherwise, then they just don't understand.

Back in the Hammond Civic Center, the boys from Union Mills licked their wounds after that terrible loss, but there was more basketball to play. In the second Regional game, the Gary Froebel Blue Devils sprinted past the Wheatfield Red Devils and never looked back. The boys in blue doubled up the boys in red, 28 – 14 at halftime, and won by nineteen points. Whereas the Wheatfield team gave every boy a chance to play in defeat, Froebel played only five boys in the game and that victory sealed a rematch between two state powerhouses for the Regional championship game that would start at 8:15 p.m. When Hammond and Froebel played three weeks earlier, Froebel lost only its second game of the season in a two-point decision. Both teams finished the regular season ranked in the top twenty and everybody expected a real torcher.

While some people from the losing teams thought about going home—perhaps to do the afternoon chores—the majority stuck around to watch the championship game. Since tickets were so hard to come by, none of them had ever attended a Regional basketball tournament before. Besides, they earned the right to be there just as much as the remaining two teams. They were as much a part of it as anybody else. This was their tournament too and they wanted to watch two of the state's finest basketball teams play head to head.

During the break, men and women crowded downtown businesses and restaurants. Scalpers scoured the crowd hoping to buy tickets to the Regional championship from fans of the losing teams. But some of those city school fans found themselves slack-jawed. In one attempted negotiation, a pair of city school fans offered Union Mills and Wheatfield people the tidy sum of ten dollars for their tickets[24] to the night's game, but their offer was declined. Stunned, one of them said to the other, "What's the matter with these farmers? They won't go home after they are licked."

I'd like to think those farmers smiled from ear to ear at those city slickers who just didn't understand.

---

[24] $10 in 1950 was $99 in 2014 dollars.

Epilogue

1950

Hammond High School beat Gary Froebel, 45 – 42, to win the Regional championship, but lost the following week in the Semi-state to a similar-sized school, Lafayette Jefferson. In the State championship game in Indianapolis, Lafayette Jeff was beaten by a school a fraction of its size: the Madison High School Cubs backed by 270 students.

The day after the Regional tournament, John L. Lewis and the mine operators signed a two-year contract that put the United Mine Workers of America back to work. The labor agreement virtually gave Lewis everything he demanded and it led to several years of peace between the miners and operators.

The week after the Regional tournament, LaPorte County coaches met again for the junior high basketball tournament. All twelve county school teams participated and four middle schools that fed into LaPorte and Michigan City joined as well. Just like the Sectional, the tournament featured a field of sixteen teams and just like the Sectional, a Park Sanders-coached Union Mills team came out on top.

Springfield Township graduated the largest class in school history: twenty-two students. It turned out to be the last graduation commencement exercise for Springfield High School. The remnants of the burned-out building were demolished and the following year, students attended Michigan City Elston High School, but it wasn't the same. "At Springfield, if you were having problems at school, the teachers would be there and you could go after school for help," Jim Strakowski said. "When you got to Elston, forget about all that. You had to make it on your own."

1951-52

With Springfield High School gone, the teachers had to find new jobs. Coach Bill Yates replaced George Bock as the basketball coach at Union Township. Yates quickly discovered a problem. The team wasn't very good and there was a disagreement over which boys should be playing. Yates wanted to play the younger boys—including a talented freshman who happened to be black[25]—while the townspeople preferred to see the upperclassmen play. In his first year as head coach of a losing program, Yates was in a tight spot. Do what he thought was right and risk losing his job, or do what the community wanted. Then he got an idea.

Coach Harlan Clark and his Rolling Prairie Bulldogs had talent, height, and size few teams could match. As a result they had won fifteen of their eighteen games when they played Union Township near the end of the season. Yates approached Clark before the game.

"I'd like to ask you a favor," Yates said. "When you go up a bunch of points—and you will beat us by a bunch of points—I want you to keep your first string in for a while until I give you a signal."

Yates explained his situation and Clark agreed. The Bulldogs' lead grew to ten points.

Then, twenty points. Then thirty, then forty points.

---

[25] Lemmie Bynum was one of the first black students to play varsity basketball in LaPorte County and the first to play in the county schools.

Clark grew a little concerned. He believed in good sportsmanship and watched Yates closely, waiting for that signal. Finally, Yates gave Clark the nod.

"I started switching my players and he put in the boys he wanted to play and it made them look good in the fourth quarter," Clark said.

It was the only time in Clark's coaching career that another coach thanked him for beating his team.

In 1951, the county schools scored another shocking victory. Michigan City Elston beat LaPorte in the semifinals of the Sectional tournament, but then Coach Harlan Clark and the Rolling Prairie Bulldogs, who already had won twenty-one games, knocked off Elston to win the Sectional championship, 43 – 38. The city of LaPorte volunteered its police and fire departments to patrol the town of Rolling Prairie while the townspeople attended the Regional tournament in Hammond. Thinking back to the aid Michigan City provided for Union Mills the previous year, LaPorte upped the ante and found volunteers to milk cows for farmers as well.

Much to Bill Redfield's satisfaction, 1951 was the last Sectional held in the LaPorte Civic Auditorium. The tournament moved permanently to Michigan City the following year.

Everyone believed the county schools' back to back Sectional championships were evidence of a new era of Indiana high school basketball. No doubt the small schools would put up stiff competition year-in, year-out and win Sectional titles on a regular basis, everyone thought.

In 1952, Michigan City Elston won the Sectional in Coach Kohlmeier's third year as head coach. That victory marked the first of twenty-four straight Sectional championships Elston would win. When Michigan City's string of Sectional titles was broken, LaPorte cut down the nets. Neither a county school nor a school created by their consolidation won another Sectional basketball championship in LaPorte County.

The Sportswriters

Bill Redfield stopped riding the rails and made Michigan City his permanent home. He edited the sports page of the News-Dispatch for twenty-eight years and those who remember his work or have had the opportunity to read his writing hold him in the highest regard. After battling Parkinson's, he passed away at age sixty-one.

Jonathan "Joe" Eyler moved to Muskegon, Michigan, in 1953. He worked as sports writer, sports editor, and staff writer and columnist at the *Muskegon Chronicle* until he retired. His years in Indiana stuck with him and he frequently mentioned Hoosier hysteria and his experiences in LaPorte in his writing.

The Players and Student Manager

Gene Gielow graduated from Michigan City Elston High School. He worked at Allis-Chalmers in LaPorte for a year and a half before settling into the family business, Gielow's Sales & Service. He and his brother sold televisions and radios and installed antennas for fifty years.

Bernie Hoogenboom earned a Ph.D. in chemistry from Iowa University. He moved his family to St. Peter, Minnesota, and taught at Gustavus Adolphus College until retirement.

Joe Tanski earned a full football scholarship to the University of South Carolina. He wasn't prepared for the racial disparity he witnessed and as a result stayed only two years. When he returned to Michigan City, he worked for the South Shore Railroad and then got a job working in the mills at Bethlehem Steel where he met Union Mills graduate Warren Malstaff. There, the two men had their "jive sessions" and rehashed that fateful game in 1950. "We rehashed this game more than you realize!" Joe said.

And how did that turn out?

"Well, the same thing: Union Mills won and we lost. We always got back to the same thing," he said with a laugh.

Making a friend with a member of that small school made a difference. Warren told him how Union Mills really whooped it up after the team won the Sectional. Sure, Joe suffered the agony of defeat, but he realized how another group of boys experienced the thrill of victory.

"Talking to Warren took the sting off," Joe said. "Warren told me, 'Don't feel bad. When we walked into Hammond, we were petrified. It wasn't LaPorte County anymore.'"

Ray Rosenbaum played baseball at Purdue University where he struck out 108 batters in twenty-eight appearances over three years. While serving in the army, Ray pitched for his camp's team and was named the top baseball player in Europe. As his reward, the army flew him to New York City to attend the World Series accompanied by Joe DiMaggio, who then escorted him back to Paris, France. He named his son Park after his old high school coach. Ray unexpectedly died in an automobile accident.

Gene Goad graduated from Union Mills High School in 1952. Gene kept the scorebook for Park Sanders and after he left, continued to do it at Union Mills and then South Central High School for thirty years. He had a successful insurance career and considered his father and Park Sanders two of the greatest mentors in his life.

Bill Hannon graduated from Westville High School. He had a partial scholarship to play basketball at Notre Dame when his dad got a phone call from Judge Al Smith. The Congressional district's West Point appointee and alternates failed the entrance exams, Smith told Bill. Would he be interested? Before answering, Bill drove to the library—he had no idea where West Point Academy was. When he found out he answered, yes, he was interested. Bill passed his exams and attended West Point Academy instead of Notre Dame and played basketball for the Army Black Knights. In 1952 Hannon led all NCAA players with 355 rebounds—an average of twenty-one per game. Bill Hannon retired as a commander after twenty-six years in the military.

Bill Singleton left Stillwell, Indiana, for good on September 8, 1952. He had no idea where he was going to sleep that night. He only knew one thing: he was going to attend mortuary school. When he arrived, the dean of the school sent him to the south side of Indianapolis where he found a room and a part-time job while he studied. Bill never left and eventually opened Singleton Mortuary, which he still ran at the time of publication.

Gael Swing graduated from Stillwell High School and then attended Franklin College and Indiana University. The last fifteen years of his life, he served as president of North Central College. The college named the prestigious Gael D. Swing Award for Meritorious Service after him. He died of cancer at age fifty-eight.

Everett "Goog" Dunfee graduated from Stillwell High School and accidentally joined the military. A friend who was in the navy asked him to go shoot hoops at the LaPorte Armory. When they got there, young men were standing in two lines. The friend told him one of the lines was for guys who wanted to join the navy and the other line was for guys who didn't want to join. Goog had no interest in the navy, so he got in the proper line and signed a paper. The next morning he got a phone call. Get your butt back here, the naval officer told him, you're going to basic training. There never were different lines.

The Coaches

Bill Yates coached twelve years at Union Township School. Over the course of thirteen seasons as a basketball coach, Yates won 180 games and lost ninety-five. He also recorded four seasons in which his teams won twenty or more games. In 1961 Union Township went 24-0 before losing to Michigan City (21-2) in the Sectional championship game. When Union Township closed its doors for good, it consolidated with LaPorte Schools and Yates worked as the principal at Boston Middle School until he retired.

After winning the 1952 Sectional, Dee Kohlmeier and his family moved to California. An old friend from the navy, J.D. Morgan, was the head tennis coach at UCLA and alerted him about a nearby basketball coaching job. With Morgan's help and a letter of recommendation written by John Wooden, Kohlmeier got the head basketball coaching job at Hoover High School in Glendale and led his 1956 team to the CIF semifinals (the equivalent of the final four). Wooden later offered him the freshman basketball coaching job at UCLA, but he turned it down. He had two young boys and couldn't afford the pay cut the job afforded. Kohlmeier and Wooden remained good friends nonetheless.

After beating Michigan City Elston to win the Sectional in 1951, Harlan Clark coached Rolling Prairie to a victory over the LaPorte Slicers in 1954. For reasons he really couldn't explain, he said, "Beating Michigan City wasn't all that big of a deal. I wasn't satisfied till we beat LaPorte." After beating LaPorte, he and Betty moved to Knightstown High School where he coached in the same gymnasium where Hoosiers was later filmed. In 1956, Clark led Knightstown to its first victory over New Castle, then coached by Marvin Wood.[26] In 1958, Knightstown won its first Sectional championship under Clark's leadership. The following year he coached Salem High School to a Sectional title. That made three Sectional titles at three different schools in nine years. Clark coached one more year, then moved on to be principal at Frankfort High School where he retired.

John Dunk became the principal at Mill Creek High School, then Rolling Prairie, and retired as the first superintendent of South Central School. For years, he attended the retirement parties of every teacher he'd ever hired, but he never forgot those early days at Wanatah. Sixty years later, Dunk ran into an old Wanatah student from that 1950

---

[26] Wood coached Milan High School in 1953 and 1954 when the teams went to the State. They won it all in 1954.

season, Shirley (Scholz) Lewis, and introduced her to his friends as his favorite cheerleader.

Norman J. Hubner retired from coaching in 1952 but continued as the athletic director at LaPorte High School. Today, the LaPorte Slicers Athletic Hall of Fame bears his name.

Steve Pavela left St. Mary's in 1955 and returned to his home state of Wisconsin where he spent twenty-nine years as the executive director for all non-public high school athletics. When he announced his decision to go back to Wisconsin, many LaPorte County coaches sent letters of congratulations and best wishes. The bookends that Bill Yates made for him still sit on Pavela's shelf in his home.

Waldo Sauter, the head coach at Kingsbury High School, earned his doctoral degree and landed at Central Michigan University. There, he served as the assistant coach for the football and basketball programs and the head baseball coach from 1963 – 1970. Sauter was the first coach in CMU history to accumulate two-hundred wins and finished his baseball coaching career with 210 wins against ninety-one losses.

Hobart Martin worked at Stillwell High School two more years and then took a job teaching and coaching at Hamlet in the neighboring county. But Martin didn't stay in education long. Like most teachers he worked every summer and when he looked at his paycheck, he saw that his summer job earned him more money than his teaching job did. In 1956 Martin opened his own business, Farm Fertilizers, Inc., but he remained close friends with his old County Coaches Association buddies. One summer, Martin needed to two large tanks for his business and he needed them fast. The closest ones were 220 miles away and it was getting late in the day. Martin didn't want to drive a truck twelve-plus hours round trip by himself. Not only was it boring, but if he got tired it would be dangerous. But he needed the tanks the next day. He picked up the phone.

"Hello, Bill? You want to make a run to pick up some stuff with me in Peoria, Illinois?"

"When?" Bill Yates asked.

"In another two or three hours," Martin replied.

Count me in, Yates said.

"We had to get over there—a guy was staying over there waiting on us—and we traveled about all night long," Martin said.

Martin ran the business until he sold it in 2004. At the time of publication, Hobart Martin still attended area basketball games.

Park Sanders

Union Mills High School never played another game in its cigar box of a gymnasium. Folklore indicated that the IHSAA condemned the gym for basketball games. Another story claimed that other schools simply refused to play there, but it was unlikely the county coaches would gang up on one of their own like that. Perhaps one night while sitting in the Westpoint Inn, Park Sanders asked his fellow County Coaches Association members to refuse to play there and then used his newfound power as a Sectional championship coach to force the people of Union Mills to build a new gym or he'd never coach another game.

Whatever happened, Union Mills finished construction of its new gymnasium in 1952, but forever dedicated to saving money, the township wouldn't pay the extra money for glass backboards, which had become the standard across Indiana. So, Coach Sanders and his players walked through harvested cornfields, picking up ears of corn that had been dropped, and then sold them back to farmers to raise enough money for glass backboards.[27] In the 1953 Sectional tournament, Sanders coached the Union Mills Millers to victory over LaPorte.

In 1954, eleven students graduated from Union Mills High School and as Park Sanders made his way through the reception line after the commencement exercises, he stared at the ground the whole time. He

---

[27] In the 1950s corn pickers weren't very efficient. It was common for people to walk through cornfields and pick up the ears of corn the machines had missed and farmers paid workers by the bushel.

shook hands with each of the graduates, quickly nodded his head, and moved on. When he freed himself from the reception line, Sanders turned away and broke down in tears.

Coaching had taken up all of Sanders' time. His four-year-old daughter Brenda said she wished she was one of her dad's players because then she'd get to see him more often. That was it. Sanders resigned as teacher and coach at Union Mills and accepted the principal job at Galena Township Elementary School. That job took up a lot of his time and he missed the camaraderie of coaching. As a result, he spent a lot of his time engaging in local politics or hanging out with the guys at his favorite tavern.

But Park Sanders didn't enjoy being a principal. He didn't enjoy the administrative headaches and he missed being in the classroom with students every day. After five years as principal, he headed back to the southern part of the county and took a job at Clinton Township School. That same year, the Indiana legislature passed the School Corporation Reorganization Act of 1959. The legislation effectively dismantled the vast number of township-run schools scattered throughout the state. Whereas there were eleven county schools in 1959 in LaPorte County, only four schools remained outside Michigan City and LaPorte in 1970. The County Conference disappeared and the county tourney had been dissolved.

Clinton, Hanna, and Union Mills consolidated to form South Central High School and Park Sanders continued to teach there. His old coaching buddy from the Wanatah Midgets, John Dunk, became the superintendent. As baby boomers filled schools, enrollments swelled and that growth spurred an addition onto the school building.

One afternoon, men unloaded massive lengths of steel under the watchful eye of the project leaders. As Sanders looked out the window, one of them looked familiar, he thought. Focused on the task at hand, the project superintendent was startled when somebody from behind tapped him on the shoulder. When he turned around, Sanders asked, "What are you doing here?" The project superintendent was Dick Buell—one of Sanders' student from his first class at Springfield Township back in 1939.

"I was surprised to see him," Dick said. "We'd lost track of one another and it was good to hear he was teaching such young kids. We reviewed some of our experiences. He brought up his fingernail that got caught in my teeth (laughing). We had quite a conversation."

It made Sanders happy and proud to see one of his young students doing well. His experience as a teacher had come full circle and two years later, he retired from teaching.

After his retirement, the 1950 Union Mills Millers gathered at Park Sanders' favorite tavern during the last week of February. They held a banquet to honor their coach and commemorate their Sectional championship. Other boys who had played for Sanders showed up as well. The men drank, told stories, and enjoyed the camaraderie—everything Sanders loved in life.

Sanders' health quickly deteriorated, but the boys insisted the annual get-together continue. "A few times when he was getting really bad when he was in the hospital, we'd go get him out," Eben Fisher said. "We'd get a pass for him to get out—to go to the banquet." Now it was his former players who were saying, I don't give a damn, and taking charge. They were going to do what they wanted to do and didn't care what anybody else thought—just like wearing a fedora inside a gymnasium during a game. Sanders loved every minute of it.

Charles Park Sanders passed away at age sixty-five. Even though he hadn't coached high school basketball in twenty-four years, the pallbearers at his funeral included his former players and his old coaching buddies Hobart Martin and Noel King.

Acknowledgements

Glen Rosenbaum made the first few phone calls that got the ball rolling on this project. Gene Goad's memory was amazing and he repeatedly set the record straight and confirmed one fact after another. Eben Fisher, my first interviewee, provided humor, support, and generosity from the beginning. When I was overwhelmed and ready to give up, my fourth grade teacher, Mr. Bruce Johnson, convinced me to press on.

Goog Dunfee was always good for a laugh and served the coldest beer in LaPorte County. I greatly enjoyed my conversations with Hobie Martin and he was always ready to answer any question I could think of. Janet Schwind provided editorial comments and proof-reading that made a big difference.

Thanks to Clarence Walters who loaned me some of his 8mm films of LaPorte County basketball games from the 1950s and thanks to Shannon Miser-Carr who typed up hours and hours of interview transcripts—without her help I would have been lost.

Below is a list of people and organizations who helped along the way.

Arnie Rosenbaum

Bernie & Louise Hoogenboom

Bill Allen

Bill & Etta Mae (Malstaff) Hannon

Bill Homan

Bill Singleton

Bill Swedenberg

Bill Wampler

Bob Spencer
Bob Wellinski
Bob & Becky Werner
Brenda Sanders-Warnke
Bruce Johnson
Carrie Kane
Clarence Walters
Clinton Alumni Association
Dale Ciciora
Dennie & Judith (Helt) Thomas
Dick & Iris (West) Tillinghast
Dick Howell
Don Bradfield
Don Fisher
Eben Fisher
Ed Bidga
Elsie (Kuszmaul) Burns
Eric Korchnak
etpearl.homestead.com
Everett 'Goog' Dunfee
Fern Eddy-Schultz
Fran (Shippee) Bolles
Fred Pizarek
Gene Gielow
Gene Goad
Gene Rice
Gene Shurte
George Bock
George Thompson
Gerald Woodrick
Glen & Shirley (Liggett) Rosenbaum
Harlan & Betty Clark
Harold & Ruby Olson
Hobart Martin

James & Lila (Ames) Hagenow
James Robertson
James Strakowski
Jane (Shippee) Lindborg
Janet Schwind (editor)
Janice (Schoof) Hadella
Jeanne Howell
Jerry Jones
Jill Redfield
Jim Howell
Jim Smoker
Joe Tanski
Ken Schreiber
Kirt Kohlmeier
La Porte County Historical Society
Laverne 'Pinki' (Haspel) Bowman
Lawrence 'Benny' Witek
Loren Uridel
Lou Perschke
Marilyn (Marquart) Buerger
Mark Yates
Melissa Mullins Mischke
Mike & Sharon Kegebein
Myrtle (Allmon) Skinner
Paul Snyder
Ralph Jones
Richard Buell
Roger Bixler
Ron Chapman
Ron Clindaniel
Rose Haite
Ross Graham
Shannon Miser-Carr
Shirley (Scholz) Lewis
Springfield Alumni Association

Stan Nedza
Judge Steven King
Steve Pavela
Susan Eyler-Engweiler
Susan (Redfield) Jones

Ted & Irma Jean (Hayter) Daube
Tom Eyler
Vern Snyder
Wes Heironimus
whatsnewlaporte.com

*If a name was omitted on accident, it was an honest mistake.

Notes & Information

This section includes interesting notes (in my opinion anyway), comments, additional information, and identification of people in the photographs where there wasn't enough information to name everyone. They are organized by section/chapter and the page number.

Book Cover

Front—1950 Sectional champion Union Mills Millers. Photograph is the author's personal picture from his Uncle Dean. Left to right: Harold Clindaniel, Sherm Lute, Tony Hadella, Dean Werner, Woody Jacobs, Coach Park Sanders, Gene Goad (holding the ball), Dick Tillinghast, Loren Uridel, Warren Malstaff, Eben Fisher, and Ray Rosenbaum.

Back—Photograph is from the Union Mills vs. Michigan City Elston Sectional game. UM: Tony Hadella (13), Loren Uridel (12), Ray Rosenbaum (8), Eben Fisher (7). MC: Gene Eggers (22, holding his leg), and Bernie Hoogenboom (12). Official: Don Polizotto. Photo provided by the LaPorte County Historical Society.

Chapter 1 – Hoosier Hysteria

Page 10—The reported number of seats in New Castle Fieldhouse varies slightly. It typically is listed as holding 9,325 or 9,314 people, depending on the source. For special events, the fieldhouse has accommodated 10,000 or more spectators.

10—To say that ninety percent of schools never advanced to the State Finals from 1936 to 1997 is a conservative estimate. Ninety-seven different teams advanced to the final four of the state basketball tournament in that time frame. The number of tournament entrants peaked in 1938 at 787 schools. According to a database of school consolidations, at least 209 new schools were created as a result of consolidation. That means the total number of schools that participated in the state tournament between 1936 and 1997 was at least 996 schools (787+209). 996 divided by 97=9.7%, leaving 90.3% of schools never advancing to State. But these numbers do not consider private schools and all-black high schools that were barred from participating in the state basketball tournament before 1942, schools that might have been renamed, or newly created schools that were not a result of consolidation. The actual percentage of schools that never advanced to State probably is somewhere between 91% and 92%.

Chapter 2 – Charles Park Sanders

12—Contrary to popular belief, Crawfordsville, Indiana, was not the location of the first basketball game played outside Massachusetts, nor the first place where basketball was known to have been taught or played in Indiana. February 6, 2008, Bill Pickett wrote to the Basketball Heritage Committee and cited evidence that showed that basketball was played in Indianapolis and Evansville prior to the now-famous game played at the Crawfordsville YMCA. In fact, a November 20, 1894, article in the *Crawfordsville Star* stated that, "Basketball was introduced into the state by the Indianapolis association [of the YMCA] through its physical director." However, the first known game to be scheduled between teams from two different towns and the resulting score was the one held in the Crawfordsville YMCA on March 16, 1894.

Chapter 3 – The Door! LaPorte County, Indiana

25—In the picture of Lila Ames, notice her left shoe. The big toe was cut out to make room for her growing feet.

Chapter 4 – From the Front Line to the Side Line

36—The article that mentioned the Wanatah Midget Five appeared in the *LaPorte Herald-Argus* on December 9, 1929, but the author was not identified. The "Midgets" team name wasn't original. An independent basketball team in LaPorte in 1929 was already known as the Midgets. 37—Bill Allen was the former reporter who commented on John Dunk's calm demeanor.

Chapter 6 – Autumn Meant Baseball

52—The Soviet Union's firsts atomic bomb detonated on August 29, 1949. The U.S. government learned about it on September 3, but President Truman didn't announce it to the American public until September 23.

Chapter 7 – The Sports Writers

62—Bill Allen was the former employee who fought with Bill Redfield and Redfield offered to share his prescription nonetheless.

Chapter 8 – Predictions and Final Preparations

74—Milan, Indiana, resident Dean Voss was the one who believed Dee Kohlmeier was the greatest athlete to ever come out of Ripley County. 76—Enrollment at the fifteen LaPorte County high schools was as follows: Michigan City Elston (freshmen not included), 801; LaPorte, 955; St. Mary's, 227; Rolling Prairie, 159; Springfield, 102; Mill Creek, 83; Union Mills, 65; Union Township, 65; Westville, 63; LaCrosse, 54; Stillwell, 54; Wanatah, 51; Hanna, 49; Kingsbury, 46; Clinton, 29. 79—Robert Misick was the local businessman who donated the letters and numbers for Stillwell High School's scoreboard.

Chapter 9 – Cage Season Commences

84—LaCrosse High School still uses the gym it built in November 1949. It is believed to be the oldest actively used gymnasium by a high school varsity basketball team in Indiana.

Chapter 11 – Park Sanders Returns to Springfield

115—Former Stillwell head basketball coach, Austin Dentin, wrote the article that covered the Union Mills vs. Springfield Twp. game.

Chapter 13 – Fire

120—The two Springfield Township students who were quoted after the school burned were Delores Benford (16) and Donna Schaffer (15).

Chapter 13 – Life Goes On

135—The old farmer who was glad to leave the good old days behind him was Clinton Township resident Dwight Smoker—Jim Smoker's dad.

Chapter 14 – Basketball Heats Up

139—The official at the Union Mills vs. Stillwell game was Ward Singleton.

Photographs

166—Wanatah vs. LaCrosse action shot: Arnie Rosenbaum (4) jumping against Wayne Pfledderer (LC); and then L to R is Ralph Meiss (LC), Carl Lippelt (LC), Howard Hunsley (W), Willie Meiss (LC), Dick Goodwin (W).

166—Hanna vs. Rolling Prairie action shot: Gerald Masterson (10), Walt Zolman is behind Gerald, Jim Reese (16).

167—Union Mills vs. Springfield action shot. Union Mills: Ray Rosenbaum (8), Dick Tillinghast (6), Loren Uridel (12), Eben Fisher (jumping in white). Springfield: Marion Waldo (2), Al Gloy (behind Fisher), Gerald Woodrick (13).

171—St. Mary's basketball team. Knealing L to R: Coach Pavela, Bill Bishop, Larry Gondeck, Don Miller, George Sobecki, Lloyd Timm. Standing L to R: Jerry Knoll, George Bartels, Dan Levendoski, Tom Wozniak, Gene Heuck, Fran Mark.

171—Rolling Prairie team. Kneeling L to R: Elwood Mangold, Howard Brown, Coach Harlan Clark, Joe Bozek, Student Mgr. Sammy Zolman. Standing L to R: Bob Peterson, Gene Mrozinski, Walt Zolman, Jim Reese, Bill Rehlander, Joe Hunt, Bob Kirkham.

173—Stillwell vs. Kingsbury action shot. Kingsbury Kings: Herman Jonushaitis (9), Dave Bealor (6). Stillwell Vikings: Allen Dickson (54), Gael Swing (43), and Dean Robison (55).

173—Sectional action shot. Union Mills in white: Tony Hadella (13), Loren Uridel (12), Ray Rosenbaum (8), Eben Fisher (7). Elston in dark: Gene Eggers (22, holding his leg), and Bernie Hoogenboom (12). Official: Don Polizotto.

Chapter 18 – Luck of the Draw

176—In 1953 Milan High School's principal resigned under pressure after townspeople felt he didn't distribute tickets properly when their basketball team made the first of two historic runs to the State Finals in Indianapolis.

177—Although 766 basketball tournament invitations were sent to Indiana schools, there were 767 member schools. Jeffersonville High School was barred from participating in the tournament in 1950 because head coach Ed Denton got caught recruiting players from another school. Jeffersonville returned most of its players from a team that went 20-5 the previous year and was expected to make a run for the state championship.

184—Jack Werner went on to become the all-time scoring leader at Hanna High School with 1,078 points.

Chapter 20 – Friday Morning Blizzard

199—LaPorte vs. Still action photo. Ralph Jones has the ball. Stillwell (in white) L to R: Don Bradfield, Dean Robison (55), and Gael Swing (43). Bill Singleton is behind Swing.

204—Legend held for years that Allen Dickson made two free throws to win the game, but two separate news reports show Dickson made one. However, while he was alive, Allen always let other people tell the story that it was two. In fact, Allen himself never mentioned that basket to anyone—he always let other people tell the story and simply smiled and agreed with whatever rendition the story-teller offered. No doubt, Allen enjoyed hearing other peoples' interpretation and smiled as the story grow over the years.

204—The happy octogenarian was quoted by reporter Howard Cartwright.

Chapter 21 – Friday Afternoon Action

211—Despite having some great teams over the years, a St. Mary's/Marquette basketball team has never beaten a Michigan City High School team (Elston, Rogers, or Michigan City), except in the case of a forfeiture. As Joe Tanski pointed out, "It's funny how you can hold something over somebody and they can't get to you."

Chapter 22 – Sectional Saturday

228—In 1950 the entire state of Indiana was actually on the same time zone. Indiana has a long history of battles over time zones and time changes. In 1949 the Indiana legislature passed a hotly contested law that kept the entire state on Central time and outlawed observance of Daylight Savings time. The legislation did not include any enforcement and many communities simply observed whatever time they wanted.

230—Indiana Basketball Hall of Famer Howard Sharpe coached the Clinton team and Jim Howell scored 27 of Clinton's 45 points in that game on nine of eighteen shooting and nine free throws. Elston later played a nail-biter against LaPorte in the semifinals of the Sectional, only to be beaten by Rolling Prairie in the championship game. The only county school Sectional championship prior to 1950.

233—How big of an upset was Union Mills' victory, really? *The Indianapolis News* sponsored an annual Sectional guessing contest. Every one of the sixty-four Sectional winners was selected by at least one entrant in the contest, but no team was chosen less often than Union Mills. In fact, Carl B. Thomas of Castleton was the only entrant of 575 contestants to correctly pick Union Mills to win the Michigan City Sectional.

233—The photo of the 1950 Sectional champion Union Mills Millers from left to right: Harold Clindaniel, Sherm Lute, Tony Hadella, Dean Werner, Woody Jacobs, Coach Park Sanders, Gene Goad, Dick Tillinghast, Loren Uridel, Warren Malstaff, Eben Fisher, and Ray Rosenbaum. Also, notice that Park Sanders signed the basketball "Chas Sanders 1950."

Chapter 23 – The Party and a Bittersweet Loss

236—Names of the men who congregated in Novak's Tavern the night Union Mills won the Sectional were actually published in the newspaper. Members of the 1930 basketball team at the tavern that night included Elmer Schoof, John Young, LeRoy Werner, Gordon Hicks, and Hubert Brose. Other former players at the bar were Jerry McCarty, Johnny Clements, Cleo Eaton, Ed Gajda, Gerald Sanderson, Charles Howell, Morris Ryan, and Don Wakefield.

Chapter 24 – The Agony of Defeat, the Thrill of Victory

243—WLOI radio recorded the pep rally, edited it, and played it on the airwaves later that day. It was recorded on a double-sided broadcast disk and that recording managed to survive all of these years in a closet. You can listen to the whole recording on youtube.com. Search for the title, "Union Mills Sectional Championship pep rally 1950." Or type the following link in your web browser:
http://www.youtube.com/watch?v=iioUi8Rq1Wg

Chapter 26 – What's the Matter with These Farmers?

257—Joe Tanski recounted his conversation with Warren Malstaff and attributed the quote to Warren. Warren passed away eight years before this project began.
261—Dick Tillinghast's obituary was reprinted with permission from the author, Iris Tillinghast—Dick's wife.
262—The quote "What's the matter with these farmers. . ." was reported by Joe Eyler, who overheard it and got such a kick out of it he had to mention it in his column.

Epilogue

263—Ron Grimes, archivist Jefferson County Historical Society, conducted a headcount of the 1950 Madison High School yearbook.
263—For more information on the bizarre situation that surrounded the coal mine operators settlement with the United Mine Workers, look up George H. Love, John L. Lewis, and Secretary of Labor James

Mitchell; United Mine Workers v. Pennington; and the Noerr-Pennington Doctrine.

272—The 12,000 square foot addition built onto South Central School that Dick Buell worked on was named after Park Sanders and another teacher, Stanley Fair.

Matthew A. Werner grew up in Union Mills on the same farm as his dad and his Uncle Dean. Like many Indiana farm boys, Matt loved the game of basketball, shot hoops in the barn, and played for his local high school team. For the past seven years, Matt has been teaching management and leadership.

Dean Werner 1950

Matt Werner 1992

18088750R00180

Made in the USA
Middletown, DE
21 February 2015